GWR | GOODS TRAIN WORKING

From Control Offices to Exceptional Loads

Volume Two

TONY ATKINS

Dedicated to the late Declan Barraclough

First published in 2017 by Crécy Publishing

A CIP record for this book is available from the British Library

Design: Mark Nelson

Printed in Malta by Melita Press

ISBN 978 1 90932 854 9

Noodle Books is an imprint of Crécy Publishing Limited
1a Ringway Trading Estate,
Shadowmoss Road, Manchester M22 5LH

www.crecy.co.uk

Note: Illustrations are credited where known. If no annotation is shown this is because there was nothing quoted on the rear of the print. We apologise to any photographer should this result in a missing or incorrect interpretation.

Publisher's note: chapters 1 to 11 are included in Volume One.

Cover captions:

Front cover top: A train of Morris cars for the November 1938 Glasgow Motor Show. The train of G26/G32 Asmo vehicles from Cowley is headed by 4-4-0 No 3832 *County of Wilts* (built in 1904; No 3475 before the nominal date of renumbering of 1 January 1913). It has been pointed out that the train in this posed picture seems to be facing in the wrong direction for Glasgow. *GWR/D J Hyde collection*

Front cover bottom: An '87XX' on goods passes through Kensington. Departing South Lambeth at 2pm, the train was a feeder at Acton for the 8.5pm Paddington to Bristol E-headcode that left Acton at 8.59pm. The headcode of three lamps all along the buffer beam is special for the West London line. The name of the station was Kensington (Addison Road) from first opening in the 1860s but changed to Kensington (Olympia) on 19/12/1946. *W Beard*

Back cover main: Tavistock Jct yard, looking towards Plymouth Laira, on 28 August 1943 during track alterations. *GWR/ D J Hyde collection*

Back cover bottom from left to right: An Austin Six car in an Asmo at Longbridge, Birmingham. *GWR/D J Hyde collection*
An ex-Vale of Rheidol engine, GW No 1212, is pictured loaded on a C10 Crocodile at Swindon yard in December 1932. *S Carpenter*
Carboys are a forgotten type of container for corrosive liquids. Here they are packed closely together in an un-diagrammed three-plan open wagon. *GWR/D J Hyde collection*

Title page: The 'Grocer': the 11.40pm Southall-Crewe, C-headcode partially-fitted express goods. The first two iron mink ventilated vans are vac-fitted and have axlebox tiebars to take the strain of more powerful braking than that of loose-coupled trains. Only 11 iron minks had this equipment following their conversion in 1915 to cordite paste vans (see *GWR Goods Wagons*). Returned to ordinary traffic in March 1919, they were allocated in 1927 to Lyons tea traffic and branded 'Return to Greenford', hence their appearance in this train. Curiously the 'Grocer' did not have a train number in the STT. *Moore postcard*

CONTENTS VOLUME TWO

CHAPTER TWELVE

CONTROL OFFICES

ONCE telephones became common at the turn of the 19th/20th centuries, railways set up Control Offices to supervise the efficient running of trains in districts where density of traffic was very high (particularly, at first, for coal traffic). Improvements resulted in the efficiency of disposal of loaded and empty wagons, locomotive usage, enginemen and guards' duties, the minimisation of freight train engine-hours and so on, that previously had been difficult to manage owing to a lack of instant 'on-the-ground' communication. The concept of such control had been introduced on the Caledonian Railway in 1890 and the District Railway in 1905, but it first came into use on a large scale on the MR near Rotherham in 1907, and on the L&Y.

The Great Western opened its first Control Office in 1909 at Newport to supervise coal and industrial traffic from the Monmouthshire Valleys. (E S Hadley, later to become Editor of the GW Magazine, was chief clerk to the assistant divisional superintendent at Newport at the time and was involved in the setting up of the scheme.) All the various stations, yard inspectors' offices, engine sheds and signal cabins were connected by telephone to the Control Office, as were the many collieries and works. At frequent intervals, information came through as to the overall 'state of play' of traffic, the number of loaded wagons waiting to be cleared at collieries and their destinations, the number of empties on hand, expected requirements later in the day etc, from which the controller would modify train services by stopping or altering booked trains, ordering specials, and rearranging duties. Were there a derailment, the controller imposed alternative routes to keep traffic flowing; this was especially important in mining districts as, without a constant disposal of their output, collieries could not continue working (there was no flat land for wagon storage sidings).

The Train Control Office, Swansea Divisional Area of GWR, in the late 1920s. There was a separate Control Office for movements within the Swansea Docks area that came under the jurisdiction of the Docks Manager.

GREAT WESTERN RAILWAY.

Daily Statement in Regard to Wagons at all Bristol Depots (excluding Avonmouth).

This return to be sent by the District Goods Manager to the General Manager, the Chief Goods Manager, and the Superintendent of the Line by UP Mail each night.

THURS day of SEPTEMBER 30th 1920. (5481)

DEPOT	Number of wagons applied for yesterday for to-day's loading	Number of empty wagons available for to-day's loading				Number of wagons loaded away by close of day's work†	Position at close of day's work†		Number of wagons under load with inwards shed traffic on hand at close of day's work†			Number of Mileage traffic wagons under load at close of day's work†			Number of wagons under load (included in column 14)	Wagons under load on one day's forwarding (Add demurrage 7, 11 and 14 to-day's total and divide total by to-day's col 6)
		On hand (col (7) from yesterday's return)	Received*	Made available*	Total for day		Number of empty wagons left over	Number of equivalent wagons OR wagons left over for lack of empties	In position for unloading	Out of position	Total	In position for unloading	Out of position	Total		
	(1)	(2)	(3)	(4)	(5)	(6)	(7)	(8)	(9)	(10)	(11)	(12)	(13)	(14)	(15)	(16) Days
Temple Meads	200	20	134	272	426	426	-	2	40	22	62	2	-	2	-	.4
Canons Marsh :—																
(a) Shed	50	59	30	42	131	121	10	-	-	8	8	-	-	-	-	.7
(b) Dockside and Mileage Yard	20	13	32	71	116	97	19	-	-	-	-	88	-	88	6	1.4
Pylle Hill	-	-	-	43	43	43	-	-	45	34	79	49	43	92	1	3.4
Wapping Wharf	80	-	73	43	116	108	8	-	-	-	-	76	3	79	5	1.2
Redcliff	-	12	-	26	38	32	6	-	-	-	-	38	30	68	1	2.2
Kingsland Road	-	3	-	20	23	19	4	-	-	-	-	37	12	49	6	2.8
St. Philip's Marsh	-	16	-	30	46	31	15	-	-	-	-	62	60	122	-	4.1
Portishead Docks	134	38	50	9	97	41	50	-	-	-	-	21	-	21	-	2.6
TOTALS	484	161	319	556	1036	918	118	2	85	64	149	373	148	521	21	2.0

* Between the following times — Temple Meads, Canons Marsh (a) Shed 8.0 p.m. yesterday and 8 p.m. to-day; (b) Docks & Yard 2.40 p.m. yesterday and 2.30 p.m. to-day. All other places.

† Close of day's work — Temple Meads, Canons Marsh 10.0 p.m.; All other places 5.0 p.m.

‡ Indicates Wagons arriving too late for to-day's use

SPECIAL NOTES.

A second Control Office in the South Wales coal area was opened in 1911 at Tondu. The independent Barry, Rhymney and Taff Vale railways opened Control Offices in 1913 and 1917, which were absorbed at the Grouping. There were five on the GW by the end of World War 1, and eventually they were to be found throughout the whole system covering all traffic (not just mineral and goods). They were based on Traffic Divisions and included Acton, Birmingham, Bristol, Cardiff, Exeter, Gloucester, Newport, Reading, Swansea, Swindon and Westbury. After 1923 Control Offices gradually became the focus of the GWR daily merchandise wagon census at depots in the four categories used by the Traffic and Goods organisations, namely:

(i) Inwards Loaded Wagons on hand 8 o'clock;
(ii) Empty Wagons on hand at the same time;
(iii) the number of wagons unloaded each day;
(iv) the number loaded out.

All this information was relevant to the statistics gathered at Paddington to determine how well the railway was doing its job. By the 1930s, the *GWR Magazine* ran articles on the GWR 'Operating Efficiency Index' involving, for example, average wagon loads, average train loads, wagon-miles per engine-hour, goods train-miles per train-hour, and so on.

A major part of the work of the controller between the wars was the provision of relief staff. Formerly, this had been rather haphazard, though it became important as the hours of duty came down to the eight-hour shift, with additional payment for any overtime. The particulars of every train running in the control area were entered on cards. Such information related to the origin and destination of the train, its loading, the class of locomotive and the duty rosters of the locomen and guard. In this way, the stations at which relief crews had to be provided could be identified. Nock explains how 'double-home' working (lodging away from home after the first shift, taking their own rations to be cooked by the landlady, often a railwayman's wife) had been a way of life for most established railwaymen, where driver, fireman and guard would go out as a team to see the whole job through, working back the following day (or night) with a similar train and their own engine. This all came to an end in World War 2, owing to shortage of accommodation following bombing, evacuation, military billeting etc Subsequently, both enginemen and guard had to be returned to their own shed in a single day's or night's work. Arrangements had to made for re-manning trains at places from where a return working to the enginemen's and guard's home depot was possible. For example the C-headcode express goods train nicknamed the 'Northern Flash', previously non-stop between Greenford and Shrewsbury, had to have a stop at Banbury to change crews. Even if a fresh crew were waiting, the changeover took time and added to the duration of the journey. Furthermore, freight train running during and after the war was often subject to delay, and Control still had to get men back to their home shed. Lack of wagon maintenance led to many 'stop and examine' orders from signalmen to look for failed wagons, and the time taken to examine the disabled train ate into the crew's shift time. Controllers had to improvise duties, and even send men back 'on the cushions'.

Perhaps surprisingly, most coal in South Wales was cleared from the mines by services that were *not* timetabled as such in the STT, but by what were known as 'Control Engines'. Such locomotives and brake vans became available at scheduled times each day (and were listed in the STT), but the points between which they worked on any particular day were regulated by the controller on the basis of known traffic requirements. For instance, on 25 September 1946, the 4.10pm control engine from Aberdare

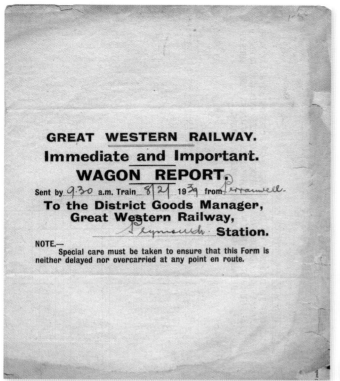

GREAT WESTERN RAILWAY.
Immediate and Important.
WAGON REPORT.

Sent by 9.30 a.m. Train 8/2/ 19 39 from Perranwell.

To the District Goods Manager,
Great Western Railway,
Plymouth. **Station.**

NOTE.— Special care must be taken to ensure that this Form is neither delayed nor overcarried at any point en route.

GREAT WESTERN RAILWAY. (5781)

Station No. 52

THIS RETURN MUST BE WRITTEN IN INK.

DAILY REPORT TO DISTRICT GOODS MANAGER OF POSITION AT 8 A.M. FOR RAILWAY COMPANIES' GOODS ROLLING STOCK, SHEETS AND G.W. ROPES; ALSO TOTAL NUMBER OF RAILWAY COMPANIES' WAGONS AND SHEETS DETAINED UNDER LOAD OVER 48 HOURS.

At Perranwell Station. Date Feb. 8th. 1939.

DESCRIPTION (code)	INWARDS LOADED 1	2	3	EMPTY 4	5	6	7	8
†† Opens						2		
" A								
" B								
(1) Total						2		
One Plank Opens								
Conflats								
Serpents								
Match Trucks								
(2) Total								
(3) Opens C								
Minks	1							
Vac. Minks								
(4) Total								
Fruits A								
Micas								
A & B						3	2	
Cones								
Motor Car Vans								
(5) Total						3	2	
Macaws								
Macaws A								
" B								
" C								
" D								
" E								
" F								
" G								
" H								
† Mites								
(6) Total								
Mex					1			
" B								
(7) Total					1			
Loriots								
Corals								
Crocodiles								
Roll Wagons								
(8) Total								
(9) Sheets								
(10) Ropes (G.W.)								

Total

NOTE.—Col. 6. Must not include empty wagons awaiting repair, which must be shewn in Col. 8.
Col. 7. Must not include partly loaded wagons which must be shewn in Col. 8.
Col. 8. Must include loaded wagons held back, partly loaded wagons and empty wagons awaiting repair.
* Insert Types.
† Twin Timber trucks to be counted as one.
†† Excluding types shewn below.

Signature

Station Masters and Goods Agents will be held personally responsible for satisfying themselves that the statement is accurately prepared.

This return must be completed as soon as possible after 8.0 a.m. daily, and despatched to the District Goods Manager by the first available train.

6,000 pads, 100 lvs.—B.M.N.2 1938-9 (2) S.

Wagon report for 8 February 1939 from Perranwell (first station out of Truro on the Falmouth branch) to be returned to the District Goods Manager's Office (Plymouth in this case).

took coal from the Aberdare Valley to Barry; on the following day it worked to Treforest; and on the next day to Newport. Again, the 4.10pm engine from Barry went to Aberdare and back; to Rhymney and back on the second day; and to Bridgend and back on the third. In 1938 in Monmouthshire there were 63 control trains booked up the Western Valley, and 17 for the Eastern Valley. The total number of control trains on the GW was over 300 per day.

Control engines carried circular target plates with a letter and number as dictated by the STT which were placed on one of the headlamp brackets. The letter indicated the locomotive shed, and the figure to the turn of duty. Thus, 'B6' was the locomotive from Barry at 7am, whilst 'A12' left Aberdare at 3.35pm. Other letters applied as follows: C — Cardiff Cathays; D — Cardiff East Dock; F — Ferndale; H — Cardiff Canton; J — Abercynon; K — Dowlais (Caeharris); M — Merthyr; PR — Pontypool Road; R — Rhymney; T — Treherbert; X — Coke Ovens; Y — Radyr. Controllers knew typical outputs and conditions at different collieries, and they aimed to avoid any interruption to production at the pits by ensuring the arrival, at the right times, of sufficient empty wagons. When there were no immediate orders for shipment coal, the mines would send loaded wagons to the docks for storage, having obtained a 'release' to do so from the GWR Docks Department, who wanted to be ready to load ships immediately upon arrival. On occasions there might be 20,000 such wagons standing, representing perhaps 400 different brands of coal. According to the 1933 STT, loaded shipment coal wagons destined for Penarth Tidal Harbour were to be forwarded immediately once they were labelled as they were not subject to a release order being held; the amount of shipment traffic at Penarth was in rapid decline at

that time and to try and keep business up, wagons were forwarded without delay. The engine power required in South Wales was considerable: there were 400 freight engines allocated to the Newport Division alone.

Sometimes, scheduled trains were listed in STTs to start their timetabled journey and run as normal goods trains until some station was reached, after which they would be ordered what to do by Control. For example, the 7am local trip ex-Bordesley arrived at Handsworth at 7.19 'thence as ordered by Control'. Again, the K-goods leaving Merthyr at 5.15am (**MX**) proceeded down the Taff valley by way of B&M Lower Jct (5.18-5.35); Pentrebach (5.40-5.50); Quakers Yard Low Level (6.11-6.35); pinned down brakes at the top of the incline before Abercynon (6.47-6.50) and unpin before arriving at Stormsdown Jct at 5.55am. The STT then said 'thence as ordered by control'. An E-goods departed Neath General at 7pm, passing Briton Ferry West at 7.6 and Port Talbot General at 7.12 and then stopped at Margam Middle box after which it ran as ordered by control. Control might also order trains to go beyond their timetabled destination. In the 1933 STT, a K-goods left Waterhall Jct at 2.50pm and eventually passed on to the South Wales main line to call at Port Talbot, Briton Ferry West, Neath General, Skewen Middle, Skewen Valley Jct, and Landore Steel Works to terminate at Landore at 7.25pm. But it could be 'extended as ordered by Control'. Other arrangements were far more local: trips along the Burry Port and Cwmcapel Colliery siding branch were arranged as necessary by the Pembrey station master.

In 1939, all PO coal wagons were requisitioned by the Government into a wagon 'Pool'. Responsibility for keeping pits supplied with empties lay now with the railways, and was performed by the controllers (in World War 2 GWR Control had a 'Wagon Pool' section), who aimed to give a fair distribution among different coal fields, and to save empty train miles by working wagons to the nearest convenient colliery rather than to the original owner's premises. As far as possible, the 7,000 'Pole' 20-ton mineral wagons were kept in the same streams of traffic as pre-war, any surplus being sent to those collieries having sufficient headroom under the screens to use them. There was a national control of pool wagons at Amersham that continued in existence after the war. In 1946, there were about 5,000 to 6,000 empty coal wagons per day in South Wales, of which 1,000 had returned from England. The numbers of empty wagons originating in South Wales from the 350 or so works, stations, mileage yards, private sidings, repair shops etc. were fairly predictable, but those from the docks fluctuated considerably (between 650 per day and 2,000 per day in autumn 1946). Empties were worked to the nearest local traffic yard, such as the ex-TVR yard at Radyr, north of Cardiff, for concentration and subsequent conveyance to the pits.

GREAT WESTERN RAILWAY. DAILY FREIGHT ROLLING STOCK RETURNS. (blank form 6471, Est. 659, 7-41)

CHAPTER THIRTEEN

SHUNTING & MARSHALLING YARDS

THE rapid increase in goods traffic in late Victorian times meant that, at large depots, nearly all the sidings were being used either for loading and unloading traffic, or for storing empty and loaded wagons needed for traffic through the goods shed. Eventually, separate marshalling yards ('sorting sidings' or 'concentration yards') – independent of the town goods yards – had to be provided at a convenient point to receive incoming trains and make up or re-form departing trains. Marshalling yards were also needed to intercept and return empty wagons from foreign lines and from other parts of the GWR. Full trainloads were made up for different lines radiating from that particular yard.

In 1938, the full list of marshalling yards listed by the company was (by Traffic Departments):

London
Old Oak Common
Acton
Southall
Reading
Didcot
Oxford

Bristol
Swindon
Westbury
Weymouth
Bristol:
  Stoke Gifford
  East depot
  West depot

Exeter
Taunton
Exeter
Newton Abbot

Plymouth
Plymouth:
  Tavistock Jct
  Laira
  Truro

Newport
Severn Tunnel Jct
Newport:
  Alexandra Dock Jct
  East Usk Jct
Rogerstone
Pontypool Road
Aberdare

Cardiff
Cardiff
Tondu

Swansea
Neath
Felin Fran
Landore
Llandilo Jct/Llanelly
Carmarthen Jct
Fishguard

Gloucester
Gloucester
Hereford

Worcester
Honeybourne
Worcester

Birmingham
Banbury
Leamington
Birmingham:

Bordesley
Hockley
Handsworth
Langley Green
Dudley LMSR
Wednesbury
Wolverhampton, Oxley sidings
Stourbridge Jct

Chester
Hollinswood
Shrewsbury:
  Coton Hill
  Coleham
Wrexham, Croes Newydd
Chester:
  Saltney yard
  LMSR yard
Birkenhead LMSR yard

Even though the work of marshalling yards was totally concerned with goods trains, their management came under the Traffic Department, not the Goods. Every yard was administered by a Yardmaster, who was also sometimes the local Station Master (as at Banbury and at Severn Tunnel Jct). Shunters working within goods depots were under the supervision of the local Goods Agent but motive power for shunting was provided by the Traffic Department (Superintendent of the Line). Particulars of work performed by shunting and pilot engines at different locations were listed under 'Banking and Shunting Engines' in STTs. Strings of loaded wagons formed up by the Goods Department were placed on particular sidings at the depot to be accepted by the Traffic Department that either took the wagons to nearby marshalling yards by pilot trips for regrouping,

A '57XX' near Bedminster *en route* for Malago carriage sidings Bristol with a K-headcode transfer freight. No Toad but a red tail lamp will have been hung from the coupling hook of the last wagon. The Down 'Bristolian' is in the background. *G H Soole*

Tavistock Jct yard, looking towards Plymouth Laira, on 28 August 1943 during track alterations. *GWR/ D J Hyde collection*

or ran through trains to their destinations directly from the depot. The point-to-point timings of goods trains was the responsibility of the Traffic Department, but the departure and arrival times were fixed by arrangement with the Goods Department to fit in with depot working hours and busy periods. The procedures were reversed for an arriving goods train.

Marshalling yards varied in size and type according to the traffic handled, and the geography of the district. At busy centres, a number of small yards scattered over an area of five or six miles was often found — not only because of the cost of purchasing a single piece of land for one large central yard, but also because it was simply not possible to concentrate all the marshalling at one point when branch lines might intersect towns and docks, and where various main lines ran in different directions. This meant a great deal of transfer work and sub-division of traffic between different local yards. Around Bristol, for example, there was a chain

of marshalling yards, owing to the crossing of trunk routes from London (via Bath or Badminton), from the North (via STJ), from the Midlands (via Cheltenham and Gloucester), from South Wales, and from the West Country. There were large marshalling yards at Bristol West depot (near Portishead Jct, on the line to Exeter), Stoke Gifford (on the Badminton line), and Bristol East depot (near St Anne's Park, on the London line).

Most marshalling yards were laid out on nominally flat ground (or better on a slightly falling gradient, to avoid the risk of wagons running out of the sidings and fouling the shunt road), whilst shunting necks (spurs) were laid preferably on an easy rising gradient to help the locomotive when pushing off a string of wagons. The sorting of wagons in flat yards was done by locomotives drawing out and propelling wagons from one siding to others. In large yards, shunting was carried out mainly by dedicated tank engines, as opposed to train engines utilising time

Gloucester South yard with two panniers at work, both having a shunting truck attached. On the right-hand side a load of steel plate is loaded on the slant on to a Macaw B to keep it within gauge. The photograph was taken from corrugated iron roof of the goods shed. *GWR/D J Hyde collection*

Vehicles standing at Lords Hill bridge outside Paddington Goods depot, including a rake of goods brake vans, with a cattle truck and shunter's truck at the head, and various large capacity Mink vans at the left. *D J Hyde collection*

between legs or turns. Taken to its extreme, shunting on adequately falling gradients could be performed without locomotives at all, where wagons were secured by hand brake on sloping reception sidings, and then one by one, or in groups, were uncoupled and allowed to run down into appropriate sidings (the LNWR had opened such a 'gravitation' yard at Edge Hill, Liverpool, in 1881). There were no gravitation yards as such on the GWR, though Down goods trains terminating at Oxley sidings (Wolverhampton) were disposed of by gravitation from Oxley South.

In the absence of helpful downhill geography, and yet to replace the back-and-forth shunting of flat yards, an alternative arrangement was to bank up the ground artificially into a 'hump' over which wagons were run down into the yard on a gradient of something like 1 in 30 for about 200ft followed by progressively shallower grades (1 in 300, say) before reaching the sidings. Hump yards were particularly appropriate at places where there was a continuous flow of terminating incoming trains, and where traffic previously sorted at outlying stations could be concentrated into through trains. The shunting (hump) engine needed to cover busy periods only, and five or six trains could be allowed to arrive before shunting started, particularly when dealing with mineral traffic. This greatly reduced shunting power and staff. Hump shunting was more efficient than at flat yards as yard staff were

'Vertical shunting' at Moor Street Birmingham in 1916. The wagon lift gave access to the wholesale fruit and vegetable market below (see volume 2B *GWR Goods Services*). Note the small end ventilator bonnets on the three-year old V14 Mink. When the X-bracing was later removed, a redesign permitted larger vents to be used. A Brunel-designed wagon hoist connected the high-level coal yard to the main goods yard at Paddington before redevelopment in the 1920s.
D J Hyde collection

required siding. The hump locomotive also fetched out wagons shunted into the wrong siding. Starting just before World War 1, and ending in the early 1930s, the GWR converted a number of flat yards at important junctions into hump yards, but most GW yards remained flat.

In large yards, a resident Inspector was responsible for dealing with goods trains, and working under him was a number of shunting gangs consisting of a foreman, a head shunter and under-shunters. The head shunter controlled the work and directed the movements of the engine, and the under-shunters were positioned to operate points, receive the wagons and attend to brakes and couplings; a good deal depended on teamwork and common sense, and the efficient working of a yard had a far-reaching effect on the working of trains. Correct anticipation of the head shunter's hand, or lamp, signals was essential. Were one wagon to slip unnoticed into the wrong siding, traffic piled up, and difficult and time-consuming problems of sorting out would follow. Work in the yards was demanding and dangerous especially in the early days – poor yard lighting, oil (later carbide, and later still perhaps electric) hand lamps gave indifferent illumination, while manual coupling/uncoupling was often carried out in terrible weather. Danger of accidents was reduced when wagons had 'either-side' brakes (see Chapter 8).

In the 1931 edition of the GW's *General Directions to Agents*, rule 195 states that 'Before shunting is commenced, it must be seen that the doors of wagons are secured, and chains or other appliances with which the wagons may be fitted made perfectly secure and safe'.

Shunting operations were often intricate: strings of wagons varied in their composition, yard layouts and capacity differed from one place to another, and the nature of traffic changed from place to place. Curiously, there seems to have been little formal instruction or training of the staff in the important work of marshalling and shunting, and learner shunters acquired the basic knowledge on the job alongside experienced staff.

According to Grant's *Reminiscences*, shunters at Westbury in 1865 worked 12-hour shifts (6 to 6) and received 20 shillings/week, with a new overcoat every two years. Day and night and in all weathers, they stooped under the buffers of wagons to deal with the heavy links and chains, with a danger of getting clothes caught under wheels. Their work involved running from one end of the yard to the other, across sidings, over rough ballast, through pools of water (in winter, water stood between the rails of the longitudinal baulk road). The only lighting was the shunter's hand lamp. Furthermore some wagons had no brakes in those days, and scotches (wedges under the wheels) and sprags (sticks through wheel spokes) had to be used to keep them in place.

Owing to the number of fatal accidents that occurred when coupling was done by hand, use of the shunting pole was made compulsory in the 1880s. According to the GWR *Temperance Union Record*, the 'champion coupling contest' was held at Swindon in April 1889, following preliminary rounds across the system. There were 10 finalists. Twenty trucks were placed together and each competitor was required to couple with the shunting pole on his upwards journey and immediatly uncouple on the return. The wooden poles were 6ft long made of 2in diameter ash. At that time there were three patterns of hook (of pigtail shape), and any could be used. The winner was F Winter from Swindon who took

unhampered by engine movements round and about, and the risk of accidents to shunters crossing and re-crossing tracks was diminished. A steady movement of the hump engine at about 2mph propelled wagons to the summit of the hump where a wagon, or group of wagons, was uncoupled and allowed to gravitate into sidings at about 10mph. Each cut of wagons was indicated by chalk marks on the ends of the vehicles, or by 'cut cards'. Depending on how full the receiving siding was, and how free-running were the wagons (grease-box wagons were slower than oil-box vehicles, particularly in cold weather), the brakes of wagons coming down the hump were put on as necessary by 'wagon chasers' running alongside. Chasers were usually below 30 years of age. Slipper-type wagon skids were sometimes used as well as the wagon brakes themselves to slow wagons and avoid rough shunting. Not more than six wagons coupled together were allowed at any one time to gravitate over a hump, while boiler wagons, wagons with defective brakes - or wagons of live-stock - were not allowed to run free down the hump at all and were placed in the appropriate siding by loco. The shunting engine could proceed over the hump into the sidings to close up wagons, or to deal with wagons that had not run freely enough to enter the

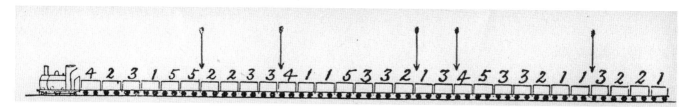

Saving of engine power by uncoupling between particular wagons during shunting.

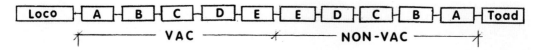

Groups of wagons for the same destinations marshalled in particular order so as to minimise shunting at intermediate stations.

one minute 46 seconds to do the job; the slowest two minutes 24 seconds. Finalists came from Basingstoke, Bordesley, Gloucester, Pontypool, Reading, Redbrook, Stourbridge, Shrewsbury and Swindon.

Problems in shunting and how to solve them was a topic discussed by P Glover in the 1908 session of the *GWR (London) Lecture and Debating Society*, and the same material was later used in competitions in the 1920 *GWR Magazine*. For example, consider the case of a train shown in the figure with a thoroughly mixed load of wagons and destinations arriving at a yard to be sorted. There are 30 wagons to be shunted into five sidings, as indicated by the numbers above the trucks. One method is to draw all the wagons clear of the points, uncouple the end wagon, and shunt it into siding No 1; then draw ahead over the points again, uncouple the next two wagons, and shunt these into siding No 2; and so on. By this method the wagons near to the engine are conveyed to and fro a great number of times before their turn comes to be shunted off. This not only wasted engine power but also was undesirable for goods that might move within wagons and possibly break after a succession of bumps and jerks. Mr Glover showed that by the application of a simple rule, superfluous conveying of wagons to and fro in this way could be avoided:

'Counting from the end where the engine is attached, we uncouple immediately in front of the first wagon that is for the same siding as any previous wagon or batch of wagons. Here we have 4, 2, 3, 1, two 5's, and then another 2. This wagon for 2 is what we shall call the first repetition. We uncouple immediately in front of it, as indicated by an arrow. Then shunt the two 5's into their proper siding, then the 1, afterwards the 3, and then, instead of shunting into No. 2 siding with the next wagon, set the engine back against the train and couple up. This brings the three trucks for siding No. 2 together. We then repeat the process of dividing the wagons immediately short of the first repetition. The trucks on the engine will be 4, three 2's, two 3's, and then 4, which is a repetition of the first wagon. Accordingly we detach in front of the 4, where the arrow is, shunt off the two 3's and three 2's and then bring the No.4 back against the No. 4 on the train, couple up, and continue as before.'

Calculations showed that 22 shunts would break down the train by both methods, but by the first method 342 'wagon-equivalents' were moved, whereas by the second method there were only 118, a reduction of over 65%. Furthermore, a short

shunt (that is, one with only a few wagons) occupied less time than a long one. Where a number of short shunts could be made in place of an equal number of long ones, the saving in time was considerable. Mr Glover had measured the average time taken to shunt different numbers of loaded and empty 10-ton wagons. One loaded wagon took 37 seconds, and one unloaded wagon took 34 seconds; five wagons took 44 and 41 seconds; 10 took 55 and 53 seconds; 20 took 83 and 76 seconds; 30 took 126 and 83 seconds. He demonstrated that by the first method of shunting the 30 wagons would take 27 minutes four seconds, but the second method took only 16 minutes 29 seconds. The rest of the 1908 article contains some fascinating information and other problems (with solutions) for the amateur shunter.

In a related theme, a 1903 *Railway Magazine* article (pages 17-19) has a problem and solution of how successfully to cross two trains approaching each other on a single line at a place where there is one dead-end siding not long enough to hold either.

Sorting wagons into groups for different destinations and different trains was one thing, but nothing was gained if a train serving many stations *en route* set off with all these groups of wagons jumbled up, since a great deal of time would then have to be spent at stopping places in shunting out the wagons to be put off at that point. A train putting off or taking on wagons at a wayside station in an inefficient manner very often held up following trains, and sometimes blocked trains in both Up and Down directions on the main line. The solution was not only that the wagons for each destination should obviously be grouped together, but that the groups should be marshalled in a particular order when the train started its journey. For loose-coupled trains, traffic for the first stop was on the engine and that for the journey's end on the brake van so that the number of wagons moved around during calls at wayside stations was kept to the minimum. That's simple, but what happens when picking up wagons *en route*? Wagons had to be lined up at the intermediate points in 'reverse order', the further-distance wagons being at the front. When these wagons were added to the train, traffic for the next stop came together in the centre of the train, and those wagons came off at one shunt at the next stop. Picking up new wagons in reverse order as before, traffic for the second station came together, and so on, until eventually at the final destination the wagons originally on the engine had worked back to those on the brake van. (An exception to this sort of thing was when a train conveyed wagons of dangerous materials or carried unusual loads when such wagons, whatever their destination, were placed at the rear of the train so that the guard could keep an eye on them.) Another exception was wagons loaded with explosives which were marshalled in the middle of the train.

On partially-fitted vacuum trains, the same principle applied, but now with the wagons in *two* sets. All vacuum vehicles on the engine were marshalled in reverse station order from the front, and the unfitted wagons behind them were in proper station order; this brought the vacuum and non-vacuum wagons for the first station all together in the centre of the train. Thus, at the start of a journey to London, Paddington vacuum-fitted wagons would be formed next to the engine and the Paddington non-fitted wagons on the Toad, with wagons for intermediate calling points in between. Sometimes for local reasons there were exceptions to these rules, as discussed in Chapter 17.

Marshalling had also to take account of destinations on all the other railway companies. For example, in 1911, the 9.55pm Reading to Oxley sidings (45 wagons, or 65 to Hockley if two engines) was marshalled as follows: vac-fitted vehicles for Crewe Goods Shed, Manchester, Birkenhead, Salop,

Market Drayton and Crewe, and Birmingham; then non-vac for Birmingham, Manchester, Scottish, Crewe Exchange, Crewe Goods Shed, LYR, GCR, destinations in Yorkshire, NER, and finally odd wagons and brake van (all non-vacuum). GC wagons came off at Didcot for the 9.30pm ex-Swindon, to be dropped at Banbury.

In the 1936 edition of the *Appendix to the Rule Book*, definitions of two particular sorts of shunting technique were given: *Double Shunt* — propelling two lots of wagons uncoupled from each other, and from the locomotive, into two separate sidings; and, *Fly Shunt* — the locomotive pulls wagons towards a set of facing points and the wagons run on to one line, the locomotive on to the other. This latter definition is different from what many people think is 'fly shunting'.

PARTICULAR YARDS

Acton
Acton was typical of large, flat GWR marshalling yards. The original yard (including the goods shed lines) accommodated 1,260 wagons, and dealt with 139 freight trains daily. In the early 1900s

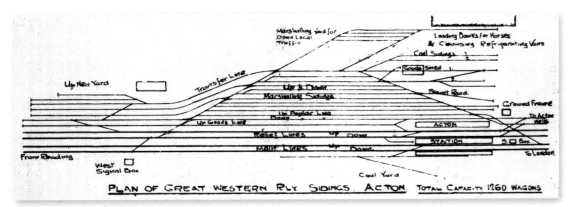

The layout at Acton before World War 1. *Railway & Travel Monthly*

The west end of Acton marshalling yard looking east towards Paddington in 1912. An 'Aberdare' 2-6-0 is at the head of an K-headcode 'ordinary goods train stopping at intermediate stations' that, in the 1903-18 code of headlamps, consisted of three lamps, one at the chimney, one at the centre of the buffer beam and one over the right buffer when facing the loco. A saddle tank shunts in the sidings behind. *Railway & Travel Monthly*

The east end of Acton yard, looking west in 1912. The cattle loading bank is on the right.
Railway & Travel Monthly

A publicity photograph of one of a number of trial runs to demonstrate the hauling power of the Churchward '28XX'. In this case it is March 1913 and No 2834 has arrived at Acton from Banbury with a train of 97 GW and three private-owner mixed merchandise and coal wagons. In April 1906, No 2808 brought 109 grease-axlebox loaded coal wagons from Swindon to London. The three-lamp headcode (H) of one lamp at the chimney, one at the centre of the buffer beam and one to the left (when facing the loco) was the 1903-18 code for 'through goods or mineral trains with full loads for destination'.
GWR

more than 1,000 wagons were received every 24 hours from all directions, and about the same number was forwarded to the North London Line, Smithfield, Paddington, South Lambeth etc.

Locomotives with the Westinghouse brake – such as 1900-built 'Atbara' No 3392 (No 4138 after 1912) *White* and 1904-built Bulldog No 3456 (No 3394 after 1912) *Albany* – were used for interchanging with traffic coming into Acton from the GER, such as trains of horseboxes from Newmarket to racecourses on GW territory. Before World War 1, the staff at Acton consisted of five inspectors, 30 shunters, 11 goods guards and five number takers

(who recorded the running numbers of all vehicles, those of foreign wagons being sent to the Railway Clearing House to work out inter-company payments). Shunting was covered by a locomotive at the east end and another at the west end continuously for 24 hours; one engine at the east end for 12 hours at night; and one engine serving the goods shed and coal yard for six hours, giving a total requirement of 66 engine-hours per day. The approximate annual costs of working the yard (independent of train engines and trainmen's time while in the yard) was about £3,300 for staff and £5,000 for shunting power (in 1914 figures).

No. 17

FREIGHT TRAIN SERVICES FROM AND TO NORTH LONDON LINE Via Acton Wells Junction.

(UNLESS OTHERWISE SHEWN THE TRAINS RUN EACH WEEK DAY).

Target No.	INWARDS Depart.	FROM.	Due Acton.	OUTWARDS Depart Acton.	TO.
GE	‡11.10 p.m.	Temple Mills (RR)	12.30 a.m. (MX)	1.35 a.m.	Temple Mills (RR) (Tues. to Suns.)
GN	11.20 p.m.	East Goods	12.45 a.m.	*1.55 a.m.	Clarence Yard (Tues. to Suns.).
1	12†27 a.m.	Devons Road (MO)	1†16 a.m. (MO)	1.45 a.m.	Plaistow (MO).
3	1†25 a.m.	Devons Road (MO)	2†16 a.m. (MO)	2.35 a.m.	Temple Mills (MO).
29	1.30 a.m.	Channelsea (MX)	2.28 a.m. (MX)	4.30 a.m.	Victoria Docks (MX).
14	1.30 a.m.	Channelsea (MO)	2.33 a.m. (MO)	5.15 a.m.	Temple Mills (MO).
3	1†55 a.m.	Devons Road (MX)	2†46 a.m. (MX)	4. 0 a.m.	Temple Mills (MX).
22	2. 0 a.m.	Temple Mills (MX)	3. 5 a.m. (MX)	6. 0 a.m.	Temple Mills (MX).
33	2†52 a.m.	Devons Road (MO)	3.45 a.m. (MO)	4.30 a.m.	Victoria Docks (MO).
22	4†25 a.m.	Devons Road (MO)	5.17 a.m. (MO)	5.48 a.m.	Temple Mills (MO).
30	4.47 a.m.	Kingsland (4.18 a.m. East Goods)	5.28 a.m.	7.50 a.m.	Willesden Junction.
29MO	3.10 a.m MO	Temple Mills	5.45 a.m.	6.30 a.m.	Poplar
14MX	3.15 a.m MX				
17	6†38 a.m.	Devons Road (MX)	7†30 a.m. (MX)	8.30 a.m.	Temple Mills (MX).
9	7.95 a.m.	Willesden Junction	7.46 a.m.	10.50 a.m.	Temple Mills.
30	8†35 a.m.	Willesden Junction	8†48 a.m.	10. 5 a.m.	Victoria Docks.
46	8.20 a.m.	Temple Mills	9.29 a.m. (SX)	11.20 a.m.	Temple Mills (SX)
46	8.20 a.m.	Temple Mills	9.29 a.m. (SO)	11.35 a.m.	Temple Mills (SO).
45	8.30 a.m.	Temple Mills (SX)	9.50 a.m. (SX)	11.50 a.m.	Plaistow (SX).
45	8.30 a.m.	Temple Mills (SO)	9.50 a.m. (SO)	1.30 p.m.	Fairfield Road (SO).
Mid.	9.15 a.m.	Brent	9.57 a.m.	10.55 a.m.	Brent.
GN	9. 0 a.m.	Ferme Park (SX)	10.25 a.m. (SX)	12. 7 p.m.	Ferme Park (SX).
GN	9. 0 a.m.	Ferme Park (SO)	10.25 a.m. (SO)	12.45 p.m.	Ferme Park (SO).
31	§10. 5 a.m.	Temple Mills (SX)	11.10 a.m. (SX)	12.42 p.m.	Victoria Docks (SX).
31	§10. 5 a.m.	Temple Mills (SO)	11.10 a.m. (SO)	1.55 p.m.	Victoria Docks (SO).
37	10. 0 a.m.	Victoria Docks (RR) (SX)	11.10 a.m. (RR)	12.42 p.m.	Victoria Docks (RR) (SX).
37	10. 0 a.m.	Victoria Docks (RR) (SO)	11.10 a.m. (RR)	1.55 p.m.	Victoria Docks (RR) (SO).
GN	10.35 a.m.	East Goods (SX)	11.41 a.m. (SX)	*1.15 p.m.	Clarence Yard (SX).
GN	10.35 a.m.	East Goods (SO)	11.41 a.m. (SO)	*2.15 p.m.	Clarence Yard (SO).
36	11.15 a.m.	Chanelsea (SX)	12.26 p.m. (SX)	1.50 p.m.	Temple Mills (SX).
Mid.	12. 0 noon	Brent	12.42 p.m.	1.40 p.m.	Brent.
32	12† 0 noon	Devons Road (SO)	1. 0 p.m. (SO)	2.25 p.m.	Victoria Docks (SO).
36	11.10 a.m.	Channelsea (SO)	1.30 p.m. (SO)	3.50 p.m.	Temple Mills (SO).
12	12.45 p.m.	Poplar (SX)	2.22 p.m. (SX)	3.35 p.m.	Temple Mills (SX).
43	1.25 p.m.	Plaistow (SX)	2.27 p.m. (SX)		Control Orders.
19	2.10 p.m.	Victoria Docks (SX)	3.22 p.m. (SX)	6.10 p.m.	St. Pancras (SX).
1	2. 5 p.m.	Poplar (SO)	3.32 p.m. (SO)	4.20 p.m.	Plaistow (SO).
19	2.10 p.m.	Victoria Docks (SO)	3.37 p.m. (SO)	6.10 p.m.	St. Pancras (SO).
29	2.15 p.m.	Temple Mills	4.12 p.m.	5.50 p.m.	Temple Mills
Mid.	3.45 p.m.	Cricklewood	4.25 p.m.	5.20 p.m.	Brent.
35	4. 0 p.m.	Victoria Docks (SO)	5.18 p.m. (SO)	7.35 p.m.	Temple Mills (SO).
GN	4.30 p.m.	Ferme Park (RR) (SX)	5.58 p.m. (RR)	7.32 p.m.	Ferme Park (SX)
35	6.35 p.m.	Victoria Docks (SX)	8. 3 p.m. (SX)	9.20 p.m.	Temple Mills (RR) (SX).
5	7.20 p.m.	Temple Mills (SX)	8.34 p.m. (SX)	9.35 p.m.	Temple Mills (SX).
5	7.30 p.m.	Temple Mills (SX)	8.34 p.m. (SX)	9.35 p.m.	Temple Mills (SX).
2	8. 0 p.m.	Victoria Docks (SX)	9.26 p.m. (SX)		Control Orders.
2	8. 0 p.m.	Victoria Docks (RR) (SO)	9.34 p.m. (RR)		Control Orders.
GN	8.20 p.m.	Ferme Park	10. 2 p.m.	11.35 p.m.	Ferme Park.
34	9. 0 p.m.	Temple Mills (SO)	10.27 p.m. (SO)	11.45 p.m.	Temple Mills (SO).
6	9.30 p.m.	Plaistow (SX)	10.53 p.m. (SX)	12.25 a.m.	Plaistow (MX).
6	9.30 p.m.	Plaistow (SO)	10.59 p.m. (SO)	12.30 a.m.	Plaistow (Suns. only).
GE	9.40 p.m.	Temple Mills (RR) (SX)	11. 0 p.m. (RR)	1.10 a.m.	Temple Mills (RR) (MX).
25	10.35 p.m.	Plaistow (SO)	11.45 p.m. (SO)		Control Orders.
25	10.35 p.m.	Plaistow (SX)	11.50 p.m. (SX)	1.18 a.m.	Plaistow (MX).

*—To leave Acton with L.N.E. Brake Van each end of train.
†—Will run when 10.5 a.m. Temple Mills is cancelled.
§—Will not run when 10.0 a.m. Victoria Docks runs.

SERVICES WILL RUN ON SUNDAYS AS ARRANGED BETWEEN THE CONTROLS CONCERNED.

HAMMERSMITH COAL TRAINS BETWEEN OLD OAK COMMON AND HAMMERSMITH.

Load: 35 wagons and 2 vans. Must run via Up Goods Line from Old Oak Common East to Ledbroke Grove and cross there to the Up Carriage Line and run to Paddington Yard. Engine to run round train in Yard and depart for Hammersmith via Down Main Line and Crystal Palace Loop. Return Train to work as shewn on page 13.

		a.m.			a.m.	
Old Oak Common	dep.	1 10	Westbourne Park	pass	1 38	
Paddington Yard	arr.	1 25	Latimer Road	pass	1 49	Coal Wagons.
	dep.	1 33	Hammersmith	arr.	1 50	

CLOSED TIME FOR FREIGHT SERVICES BETWEEN OLD OAK COMMON, WILLESDEN JUNCTION AND THREE BRIDGES Via Clapham Junction.

(APPLICABLE AT CLAPHAM JUNCTION.)

A closed time will operate for the above Freight Trains through Clapham Jctn. between 6.50 a.m. and 10.0 a.m. week-days. Should any of the trains mentioned be running late and unlikely to pass Clapham Junction until after 6.50 a.m. they must be impounded at Lillie Bridge to work forward as arranged by S.R. Control at 9.50 a.m. The guard of the train it is intended to impound at Lillie Bridge must ascertain from the Signalman at Lillie Bridge particulars of the Siding into which their train is being stabled, in order that this operation may be carried out before the engine is released. After impounding the Southern Company will arrange forward working.

A general view of Stoke Gifford marshalling yards. *D J Hyde collection*

Newly-built 0-6-0PT No 3731 at work in the Stoke Gifford Up yard (north of the mainline) in 1937. The M1 shunter's truck was built in 1895 and is now allocated to Bristol East depot. *G H Soole*

Below: Stoke Gifford marshalling yard, looking west towards Filton Jct and the Severn Tunnel. Re-ballasted track can be seen on the principal lines through centre of picture. *STEAM Swindon*

The London end of Stoke Gifford yard, with 'Star' No 4028 on an Up express. The locomotive was named *King John* when built in 1909, but renamed *The Roumanian Monarch* in 1927 when the King class appeared, then in the same year changed again to *Roumanian Monarch* (name removed November 1940). The Toad in the Down yard is allocated to Stoke Gifford and there's a tank wagon in the Up sidings behind the pair of Toads at the right. A large water tank is at top left (there was one at each end of the yard). *G H Soole*

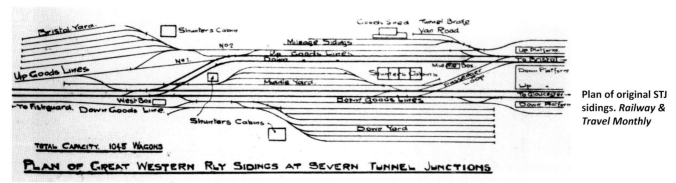

Plan of original STJ sidings. *Railway & Travel Monthly*

In 1932, the western end of Acton Yard was remodelled and extended to become a separate 'Down Yard', the original configuration being renamed as the 'Up Yard'. The new Down yard was, in this instance, on the Up side of the mainline. Shunting at Acton was always flat.

Stoke Gifford and Severn Tunnel Junction (STJ)

The 4¼-mile long Severn Tunnel was opened for regular goods and mineral traffic with a train from Temple Meads yard on 1 September 1886 (an experimental coal train of 14 wagons had run from Aberdare to Southampton on 9 January 1886, so that 'coal which had been raised at the colliery in the morning was delivered at the port in the evening of the same day'; passenger traffic first went through the tunnel on 1 December 1886 after the installation of ventilation fans). Before World War 1, 350 goods trains passed through the tunnel every week, conveying nearly 17,000 wagons; trains were not to exceed 64 normal wagon lengths plus brake van. There were restrictions on what traffic and what vehicles could be taken through the tunnel in order to avoid problems in case of an accident. No crippled or green card wagons

were permitted; no wooden solebar wagons when coupled with steel solebar wagons; no explosives; nor tank wagons or other wagons with inflammable loads (including GWR travelling gas tank wagons, coded Cordon). Perhaps surprisingly, loaded cattle wagons were allowed through, but they would normally have travelled at fitted or partially-fitted speeds.

Once the Severn Tunnel had opened, marshalling yards at each end were established. At the English end, Stoke Gifford yard was located on the South Wales Direct line, opened in 1903. It formed the eastern corner of the triangular junction between the old and the new lines, Patchway and Filton stations on the old line (via Bristol) to the tunnel being the west and south corners respectively. The original flat yard comprised five stopblocked sidings on the Up side and five on the Down, with total accommodation for 500 wagons, and a goods loop line on each side between them and the running lines, which permitted all shunting to be performed clear of the new main line. In 1918, the Stoke Gifford yards were enlarged to 10 longer sidings on each side, with a total capacity of 1,473, and three cripple sidings on the outer edge of the Up side holding 87 wagons. Shunting spurs

The west end of Severn Tunnel Jct marshalling yard, looking east, before World War 1. The photograph was taken from the West signalbox. *Railway & Travel Monthly*

The Up ('Bristol') marshalling yard at Severn Tunnel Jct circa 1911. The photograph was taken from the West signalbox. *Railway & Travel Monthly*

The east end of Severn Tunnel Jct marshalling yard, looking west, before World War 1. *Railway & Travel Monthly*

were also added on both exit sides, as was a refuge loop on the Down side. The 1929 *Railway Magazine* mentions that a train consisting of one coach and five engines that had all finished for the day regularly worked on Sundays from Stoke Gifford to Filton. In one case, the five engines were 4-6-0 No 4068 *Llanthony Abbey*, 0-6-0PTs Nos 1841 and 1230, 2-4-0T No 739 and 2-6-0 No 6373.

At the Welsh end the old route via Gloucester and the new route through the tunnel met. There were originally two flat yards to the west of the passenger station at Severn Tunnel Jct (STJ), one Up and one Down, together with relief, avoiding, and loop lines that could hold 1,045 wagons. The number of wagons exchanged every 24 hours was nearly 3,000 with 150 trains being dealt with daily. All goods traffic to and from South Wales from the west and south of England, Bristol, Swindon, London, Gloucester, Banbury (and a large proportion of the traffic from the Birmingham and Worcester areas) passed through STJ as did goods traffic on the North-to-West route. Trains started from the depot for London, Gloucester, Llanelly, Monmouth, Lydney and the Eastern Valleys. In 1914, the yard and train staff at STJ (under the supervision of the station master) consisted of three senior yard inspectors, two sub-inspectors, 23 shunters, one lampman and 36 goods guards, with a special staff of train examiners who were chiefly employed on trains entering and leaving the tunnel; this consisted of one chargeman, six examiners, three greasers and two wagon repairers.

The extent of the staff and locomotive power at STJ reflected the fact that many goods trains through the tunnel and up to Patchway required banking/pilot assistance (see Chapter 10). In Edwardian days there were nine tunnel banking engines working

540 hours a week (each of staggered 10-hour shifts); of these, two large 2-6-2T engines and one small 0-6-0 tender engine were employed 324 hours weekly. The shifts were largely overnight, with six engines working simultaneously at the early morning peak, and just two during the afternoons. The annual cost in ordinary shunting power and shunting staff to cover the shunting was (in 1914 prices): £4,000 (engine power) and £2,000 (staff).

STJ banking engines in 1929 were:

Target	Hours of duty	Men change at
1	12 midnight to 4pm	8am
2	1am to 5pm	
3	2am to 6pm	10am
4	4am to 12 noon	(MO)
5	9am to 5pm	
6	12 noon to 4am	8pm
7	3.20pm to 7.20am	11.20pm
8	5pm to 9am	1am
9	6.30pm to 10.30am	2.30am
10	7.30pm to 11.30am	3.30am

Before conversion to hump yards in 1931 (see below), STJ dealt with Up traffic from the Cardiff, Newport and Swansea goods districts for the south and west of England and for the London district, but in those days before humps were built, Up traffic from west of Bridgend to London was dealt with at Stoke Gifford owing to lack of capacity at STJ, even though by 1920 the capacity of the STJ flat yards had been increased to 1,552 wagons in 12 stopblocked sidings in the Up yard, and 13 in the Down.

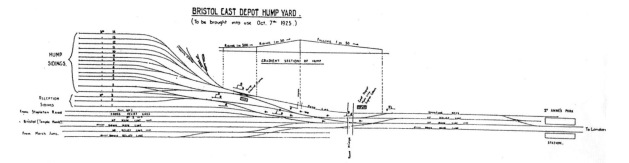

BRISTOL EAST DEPOT HUMP YARD.
(To be brought into use Oct. 7th 1923.)

Plan of Bristol East Hump yard opened in 1923. *GWR/D J Hyde collection*

Wagons being propelled up the gradient to the hump at Bristol East yard about 1926. The locomotive is 0-6-0PT No 1862, built as a '1701' class 0-6-0ST in 1890, and lasting until December 1950. It has an open short cab but with bunker extension. The cliff that constrained the design of this yard is obvious and caused the sidings beyond the hump to be asymmetrical. *GWR/D J Hyde collection*

Below: Bristol East yard in November 1923 showing skewing of sidings to the right, caused by the adjacent cliff. A number of pre-Grouping wagons can be seen including, on far left, Midland Railway, Metropolitan Railway and LNWR. Some former Welsh companies' vehicles have been re-lettered 'GW' — eg on the left, van No 85911 just above the 'Dean Goods' No 2359. *GWR*

HUMP YARDS

The first experimental hump yards on the GWR were at Llandilo Jct (east of Llanelly near one end of the Swansea avoiding lines) and at Briton Ferry Road. The former was converted from the existing flat yard and was opened just before World War 1. The latter was on the north (Up) side of the Vale of Neath double line into Swansea Docks, and was built using spoil from the construction of the Swansea District Lines. In both these hump yards, all points were hand-operated by shunters alongside the track.

The experience of hump shunting gained by operation of these two yards led to one of the flat yards at Bristol East depot being converted in 1922/3. The big improvement over the two earlier hump yards was that all points were connected to a manually-operated ground frame situated at the top of the hump near the 'king' point of the sidings (the first dividing switch). All men in the yard were now free to follow wagons and attend to the brakes, rather than some being permanently stood alongside point levers. Subsequently, using money from the 1929 Government Loan & Development Act (aimed to reduce unemployment), the marshalling yards at Severn Tunnel Jct, Rogerstone, Banbury, the Burrows (Swansea) and Tremorfa (Cardiff Docks) were converted to hump operation in the early 1930s. The ground frame was manually operated at Bristol, but by electro-pneumatic push-buttons at the others.

Bristol East depot had consisted of two flat yards, on either side of the main line between Bristol and Bath. It was the Up yard that was converted to hump operation. There were 17 stopblocked sidings, the first three near the running lines being used either to receive trains waiting to be humped, or to hold marshalled trains waiting to depart. These three sidings together held 131 wagons (No 1, 53 wagons; Nos 2 and 3, 39 each). The remaining 14 dead-end sidings were fed from the hump, and had a total holding capacity of 468 wagons. As was the practice in most yards, the sidings were allocated for particular destinations, as follows: (see table below).

The shunting neck for the Up flat yard opened in 1890 had involved the demolition of a Brunel tunnel and widening of the resulting cutting. Consequently there was a cliff alongside the hump track, and the hump was not on the centreline of the 14 storage sidings, so that wagons for sidings number 12-14 had longer to run

The upper string of wagons are in the Down (non-hump) yard at Bristol East in November 1923, while the lower are in the Up yard, with the mainline running in between. Of the two GW vans at the left upper, one still has the large GW 25in livery whereas the other has the smaller 16in style introduced at the Grouping. There are seven lime-washed cattle trucks coupled to a Toad on the adjacent line. GWR

before clearing the points leading to adjacent sidings. Also problems were sometimes caused when an incoming wagon met the wagon already there on a curve, single buffers engaging rather than two as on a straight section of track.

To enable the shunter to give instructions to the hump engine driver, a Klaxon horn was fixed on the Up side of the line, about 150 yards on the London side of East Depot Main Line signalbox. [Incidentally, the Bristol East Depot box was one of the first to receive track circuiting (in 1909) since after it took over the movements of St Annes Park box that was closed that year, it was found that the Bristol East signalman could not see vehicles at the Bath end of St Anne's Park station.] The following Klaxon code was in operation: one note — go ahead; two notes — come back to hump wagons into sidings; three notes — stop; six notes — obstruction; danger. The Klaxon was used particularly during fog and snow, and the idea was used in the yards converted later to humps. In fact this sort of code, made by horn, whistle, bell or gong was used in other yards by shunters for controlling operations where one note meant go ahead (away from shunter); two notes — set back towards shunter; three notes — stop; four notes —

No of siding	Used for	Wagon Capacity
1	Wagons for transfer to Down yard	37
2	Spare vehicles and wagons for Clifton and Avonmouth Line	36
3	Newbury and beyond	35
4	Melksham, Holt Jct and stations to Newbury (exclusive)	35
5	Reading, Acton, Old Oak Common, and Paddington	37
6	Swindon and stations to Didcot (inclusive)	34
7	Chippenham and Calne	33
8	Stations to Corsham	33
9	Oxford, Banbury, and LNER	33
10	Weymouth, Portland and Easton	32
11	Stations Witham to Dorchester (inclusive)	31
12	Southern Railway, via Salisbury	31
13	Westbury and stations to Salisbury	31
14	Bradford-on-Avon and Trowbridge	30

Plan of hump yard at Severn Tunnel Jct when opened in 1931. *Railway Gazette*

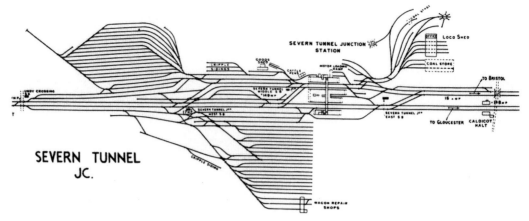

SEVERN TUNNEL JC.

Right: West end of Up-side hump yard at Severn Tunnel Jct in 1943. The line from the bottom of the picture is the dead-end shunting neck, stopblocked behind the photographer. A short siding to the left used for brake vans that is shown in the 1931 diagram of the yard (above), and illustrated on page 343 of the *Railway Magazine* in 1932, has been removed. Note the electric floodlighting; it had previously been gas. *GWR*

Below: Marshalling yard control cabin at Severn Tunnel Junction.

ease couplings; and, six notes — obstruction; danger. A Klaxon was used at Newbury Race Course Sidings. It was worked from the signalbox backing signal to communicate with locomotives on the down mainline between platforms.

After the Bristol Up yard was fully re-opened in October 1923, traffic was dealt with more quickly, the yard kept clearer, and over 100 shunting engine-hours were saved per week. In addition to numerous transfer trips from one yard to the other at East Depot, 41 trains were dealt with daily at the new Up yard and an average of 1,300 wagons were passed per working day over the hump. Lack of land prevented Bristol East from being a doubled-ended yard (ie operated from both ends), but after this time, new yards having dead-end (closed) sidings with stop blocks were rarely laid down by the GW (but see new Down yard at STJ below).

Both the Llandilo and Bristol East hump yards were operated by four men: one uncoupling and chalking wagons where splits were made; two working in the sorting sidings; the fourth man was in the cabin at Bristol, and his equivalent operated the 'king' point at Llandilo in the open air.

At Severn Tunnel Jct both the Up and Down yards on either side of the main line became hump yards, and each dealt with 1,000-1,200 wagons per day. After remodelling in 1930, the total accommodation was increased to 2,652 wagons. Both yards had four reception loops. The Down yard had 22 sorting sidings, and the Up 23, of which four were used to hold already-marshalled trains as required. It proved too costly to install a double-ended yard on the Down side, so both incoming and outgoing trains had to be dealt with from the west end of the sidings which were, however, divided into three groups so that three engines could shunt simultaneously. Up trains terminating at STJ were received into one of the reception lines on the south side of the Up yard, and were then drawn into the shunting neck and dissected into the sorting sidings at the west end. Outgoing trains having to attach or detach wagons were dealt with at the east end of the yard, and operations at both ends proceeded concurrently. After the rebuilding, traffic from the Swansea district formerly dealt with at Stoke Gifford was handled at the enlarged STJ, giving a reduction in the occupation of the tunnel and better use of the gaps between passenger trains through the tunnel for freight

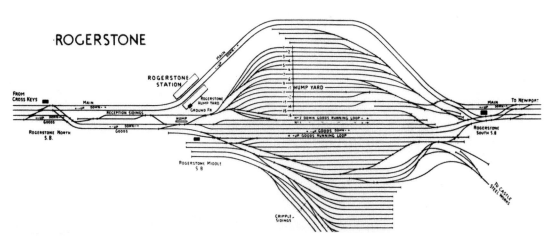

Plan of hump yard at
Rogerstone when
opened in 1931.
Railway Gazette

A photograph taken from Rogerstone Middle signalbox in
1943 looking south towards Newport. The actual hump is
just out of the picture to the left. The track immediately to
the left of the point rodding is a siding, but the same track
approaching it through the double slip in the middle of the
picture is the Up goods running loop (Up here means 'up
the valley', towards the camera). Next over is the Up goods
line, then the Down goods line, then Nos 1 and 2 Down
goods loops, with the hump sidings further to the left.
All the tracks to the right of the rodding form the Up flat
yard. Rogerstone station is out of the picture to the left,
with the passenger lines running all the way round the far
left boundary of the yard to rejoin the freight lines passing
through the middle of the picture. *GWR*

trains. The remodelled yard was provided with gas floodlighting
for night-time work; later electric lighting was installed. There were
21 scheduled goods services every day from STJ to London, Bristol,
Salisbury, the West of England and other places.

The second yard to be remodelled under the 1929 Act was at
Rogerstone where only the yard off the Down line to Newport was
converted. Nine hundred wagons per day from the Western Valleys
were sorted for the docks at Newport, Cardiff and Barry, as well as
inland traffic, including a lot of locomotive coal. The hump yard,
which contained three reception roads and 16 sorting sidings, was

open for only two eight-hour turns of duty a day. Small lots left
over at Rogerstone were sent to STJ to be marshalled into full
trains, or to Pontypool Road from where there were 15 services
daily to the Midlands and the North.

Most north-to-south GWR goods traffic passed through
Banbury, which was also an important interchange point between
the LNER (ex-GCR) and the GWR. The GC branch from Woodford
to Banbury opened in 1899 and improvements to the Banbury-
Cheltenham line in 1906 gave a new north-south route.
A considerable proportion of the traffic dealt with consisted of

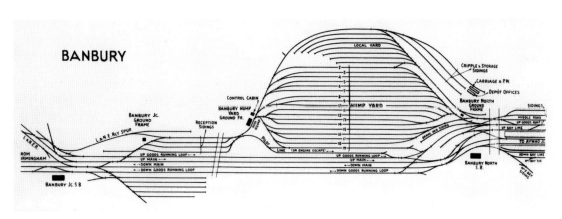

Plan of hump yard at
Banbury when opened
in 1932.
Railway Gazette

coal, iron and steel *en route* from LNER stations. Wagons were mostly worked into Banbury yard on pilot trips from Woodford, although some through trains — from Sheffield, Stairfoot (near Barnsley), Mansfield and Leicester, for example — also ran daily. The LNER had its own marshalling yard at Banbury Junction, with eight sidings situated on the Up (east) side of their line from Woodford, with direct access to the GW reception lines.

The old, flat Up shunting yard at Banbury, with its 11 sorting sidings, could accommodate 424 wagons, but after the 1930/31 rebuilding this figure rose to about 1,600 wagons (1,400 in the new hump yard on the Up side). With four reception sidings accommodating 72 wagons each, and 19 sorting sidings running from the hump, it was the biggest marshalling yard on the GWR. Trains from Leamington, Bordesley and Oxley were worked to Banbury for sorting which, together with all those arriving from LNER, were formed into trainloads for various yards in London, Bristol and the West of England. About 1,900 wagons per day were

humped, of which some 1,000 came off the LNER. Sixty to 70 wagons could be passed over the hump in 10 minutes (shunting that would take about 40 minutes in a flat yard). Just before nationalisation, some 45 trains each day were passed over the hump (one train every 36 minutes, including the time taken for the hump locomotive to dispose of the brake van and to run round to the rear of the next train to be humped).

At the eastern edge of the Banbury yard, alongside the hump, there was a ladder track connecting seven spurs for local and short-distance traffic, holding 236 wagons, with direct access from the south end; access was also given from the London end of Nos 1, 2 and 3 hump sidings. The work at this point consisted chiefly of sorting and marshalling traffic for local services, and dealing with traffic for Banbury proper, and LMS exchange traffic via Banbury. There were also three dead-end sidings (holding capacity 124 wagons) with access off No 1 hump siding, which were used for stabling and repairing cripple wagons, storage of

A view down Banbury hump with the King point at the right. *GWR/D J Hyde collection*

Wagons being pushed up and over the hump at Banbury in May 1931. The full-size cabin is called 'Hump Ground Frame'. Loaded wagon running down the hump is lettered 'E. Foster & Co London'. Numbered 6048 it has a tip end to the left. Wagon arriving at crest of hump belongs to 'Stroud Gas Light & Coke Co. Gas Works. Stroud' and is No 31. Behind that is an LNER six-plank open, followed by another Stroud wagon and a 'Sully & Co' wagon from Bridgwater next to the shunter's truck. The pannier is running bunker first. *GWR/D J Hyde collection*

cattle trucks, etc. Shunting in these small groups of sidings was 'flat', as it was at the Banbury Junction Down yard on the west side of the main line, with its seven stopblocked sidings, to which about 400 wagons were transferred daily for the LNER, and for Midlands and northern parts of the GW.

An outside-framed 0-6-0 on a transfer goods between South Lambeth and Acton passes through Addison Road (Kensington Olympia). The three red-painted headlamps all along the buffer beam appears to be the 1903-18 J-headcode, but in fact is special for the West London line, as shown by a subsequent photograph below. *HMRS*

The operation of Banbury hump yard was similar to the others on the Great Western system, but instead of chalk marks to determine uncoupling and point setting, printed slips or 'cut cards' were used. Cut cards were prepared from the guard's tally of GWR trains, but in the case of LNER trains a shunter had to walk from front to rear of the train to examine all the wagon labels, from which the cut cards were prepared. There were 16 regular GWR freight trains and 19 LNER pilot trips and through trains booked daily to terminate at Banbury in the late 1930s. In addition, eight through GWR freight trains also arrived at Banbury unmarshalled, and were put off in the reception sidings to be humped. At the London end of the hump yard, 13 through trains called, seven trains and pilot trips terminated, and 21 outward trains were dispatched. All this involved detaching an average of 278 wagons and attaching 1,720 wagons. For some local outwards Up trains, the train engine usually picked up a complete load from one siding, but in a few instances, where trains were scheduled to convey traffic for several destinations, it was necessary for the train engine to pick up from two or three sidings and get the wagons into the correct order. Brake vans were stabled in a short dead-end siding built on a ramp at the London end of the yard and after each Up train had drawn ahead on the loop line behind the passenger station, the appropriate brake van was released from the siding to run down on to its train.

Through express freight trains that called to pick up or put off traffic at Banbury ran into the Up Goods loop line, which ran on the level alongside the hump yard, and came to a stand at the London end of the sidings. For example, in the early hours of the morning there were three timetabled Up express freight trains conveying merchandise traffic from the Birmingham and South Staffordshire districts for the various London depots: in 1938, they were the 10.35pm Langley Green to Banbury (nicknamed the 'Queen's Head', due 12.19am), the 11.5pm Hockley to Banbury (the 'Pedlar', due 12.48am) and the 8.10pm Cannock Road to Banbury (the 'Racer', due 1.6am). Each of these trains was dispatched from the Midlands with wagons mixed up for Acton, Old Oak Common and Paddington Goods, so the wagons were re-grouped (together with any London-bound wagons already waiting at Banbury) into three trains, one for each London depot. This was the most intensive period of the night operations at Banbury, the shunting work at the London end of the yard to reshuffle wagons from the three incoming trains being carried out simultaneously

An '87XX' on goods passes through Kensington. Departing South Lambeth at 2pm, the train was a feeder at Acton for the 8.5pm Paddington to Bristol E-headcode that left Acton at 8.59pm. The headcode of three lamps all along the buffer beam is the same as in the photograph above, but the lamps are white painted (so it is after 1936) and codes with three lamps for ordinary trains had ceased in 1918. The name of the station was Kensington (Addison Road) from first opening in the 1860s but changed to Kensington (Olympia) on 19 December 1946. *W Beard*

A pair of 'Bulldogs', Nos 3429 (formerly No 3719 built in 1906 and unnamed) and 3374 *Walter Long* (formerly No 3426 built in 1903), attack the incline out of South Lambeth goods depot on a transfer goods to Acton in 1929. There are two headlamps, one each at the extremities of the buffer beam of No 3429, special for the West London line. Walter Hulme Long, 1st Viscount Long (1854-1924), was a Unionist politician and Director of the GWR. *W Beard*

with the hump operations at the other end. The three London-bound C-headcode trains cleared approximately 200 wagons between them and left Banbury at intervals of 25 minutes as follows: the 'Pedlar' 2.15am direct to Paddington Goods; the 'Queen's Head' 2.40am direct to Acton; and, the 'Racer' 3.5am direct to Park Royal, and thence to Old Oak Common. All ran via Bicester. The engines of the three inbound trains were used for the outbound trains, and allocated according to loads, with 'Halls' taking up to 67 wagons, and '47XXs' up to 70.

The lines of the Rhondda & Swansea Bay Railway (R&SB) into Swansea almost paralleled the GWR lines into Swansea docks, and in the late 1920s R&SB passenger traffic was diverted on to the GWR route, releasing the R&SB lines for mineral traffic only. The Burrows riddling sidings between the R&SB and Vale of Neath lines, near the (then abandoned) Jersey Marine station, were completely remodelled and enlarged, with a hump to deal with sorting incoming coal wagons. The existing Up side hump yard at Briton Ferry Road (to the north of the Vale of Neath line), dating from 1912, which dealt with empties and inwards cargo from the docks, was also enlarged. The old and new hump yards were collectively called the 'Burrows sidings', the total accommodation being increased to 4,800 wagons. Unlike the other hump yards on the GWR that were worked by the Traffic Department, the old R&SB line and the Burrows yards were controlled by the Docks Department (as was the Tremorfa hump at Cardiff), which is why they rarely feature in accounts of GWR hump yards; see *GWR Docks & Marine*.

Sometimes no further shunting was required after vehicles had passed over a hump, such as when they were all for one destination or for another marshalling yard. However, secondary shunting was necessary sometimes either because there was insufficient siding room for the given traffic, or to comply with marshalling instructions for the particular train concerned, such as reverse order/station order for partially-fitted through express freight trains. Secondary shunting was also required for local stopping goods trains calling at several points *en route*. Wagons

for such a train may have been gathered in one or two sidings and they needed to be put into station order. For example, in 1947, vehicles for the 8.5am Severn Tunnel Jct K-pickup goods to Gloucester were humped into one siding and later had to be sorted into 10 sections before the train was complete (Portskewett, Chepstow, Woolaston, Lydney, Awre, Bullo Pill, Newham, Grange Court and Oakle Street), and any vehicles for Gloucester Docks to be dropped off at Over.

Sometimes, sufficient wagons to make up a train for one particular place had been passed over the hump and filled up the relevant siding. Unless those wagons could be dispatched as a train, or moved forward to departure lines, marshalling could be slowed down or stopped.

Many marshalling yards were expanded during World War 2 to deal with the large increase in goods traffic. Banbury had two more reception roads added for the hump traffic, while a bank of eight new sidings (New yard) were added to the Down yard at Banbury Jct. In a few cases, completely new marshalling yards were provided, such as at Hinksey (Oxford) for example, which very largely replaced the work of yards in the city. At Reading, Scours Lane (1941) was used to carry out Down work formerly handled at the West Jct yards, and Moreton Cutting (near Didcot, again 1941) was opened to take Up main line traffic, both also handling Southern Railway transfer traffic.

The working of the yards in wartime conditions was very demanding, with air raid alerts and bombing, anti-aircraft gunfire, and much-reduced yard lighting levels (or none) all adding to the difficulties. During October 1940, marshalling yards in the London area experienced an 'Alert' every night, and of the 382 hours of darkness, shunting had to be carried out in complete blackout for 299 hours. It was said that after bombing, shortages and the much-increased traffic of World War 2, lighting restrictions (the 'black out') was one of the most widespread disabilities from which railways suffered.

Owing to congestion and other difficulties, it became necessary to reroute some freight trains. The important flow of iron ore from Northamptonshire to South Wales, mostly via Leamington, was diverted to run via Yarnton, then Worcester or the Kingham-Cheltenham line. Traffic from the LNE to the Birmingham area, usually run via Banbury, was diverted to the LMS and Bordesley Jct. Yet traffic from the North Eastern and Scottish sections of the LNE to northern parts of the GWR system was now routed via Banbury rather than via Crewe and Oxley. Traffic from the LNE to the SR, taken via Banbury in peacetime, was run via Neasden (LNE/GC) or Ferme Park (LNE/GN).

At marshalling yards in normal times, a single siding would probably suffice for defective (cripple) wagons awaiting acceptance into railway workshops or private-owner wagon repair companies, or for wagons where the load had shifted and needed to be reloaded. But as World War 2 reached its end, thousands of cripple wagons were awaiting repair and clogging railway sidings, even to the extent of hindering traffic operations. Many such sidings were increased during this period - Banbury's three cripple sidings were doubled to six, for example - and cripple wagons had also to be stored in the sidings of Government depots and other sites. In 1948, there were 144,000 cripple wagons nationwide awaiting repair.

EMPTY WAGON MOVEMENTS AND EXCHANGE SIDINGS

EMPTY railway-owned merchandise goods wagons, standing idle, brought no revenue to the GW. In an ideal world, loaded wagons would be unloaded at the destination, and reloaded at the same location (or at least nearby). In reality it was found that stations in industrial centres sent off more loaded wagons than they received, while agricultural areas received more loaded wagons than they forwarded. Circulation of empty railway-owned wagons was therefore inevitable within the GW system. In addition, before World War 1, wagons belonging to other companies that had come on to the GW had to be returned to the parent line within five days, whether loaded or empty, lest fines were imposed by the RCH based on data gathered by their wagon number-takers stationed at junction exchange yards. Return of foreign wagons frequently meant special shunting at marshalling yards and empty haulage to the home junction. This was in addition to the empty haulage of PO wagons. As explained in volume 1 of *GW Goods Services*, there were sometimes 'interception goods platforms' at which merchandise, arriving on

FIG. 131.—GREAT WESTERN RAILWAY
DAILY STATEMENT WITH REGARD TO WAGONS AT BRISTOL FREIGHT DEPOTS

Date.............................. 192..........

Depot.	Number of Wagons Applied for Yesterday for To-day's Loading.	Number of Empty Wagons Available for To-day's Loading.				Number of Wagons Loaded Away by Close of Day's Work.	Position at Close of Day's Work.†		Number of Wagons Under Load with Inwards Shed Traffic on Hand at Close of Day's Work.†			Number of Mileage Traffic Wagons Under Load at Close of Day's Work.†			Number of Wagons Under Demurrage (Included in Col. 14).	Wagon User, Based on To-day's Forwarding. Add'l Yesterday's Cols. 7, 11, and 14 to To-day's Total by To-day's Total by Col. 3 and Divide Col. 6.
		On Hand. (Col. 7 of Yesterday's Return.)	Received.*	Made Available.*	Total for Day.		Number of Empty Wagons Left Over. Or,	No. of Equivalent Wagon Loads Left Over for Lack of Empties.	In Position for Unloading.	Out of Position.	Total.	In Position for Unloading.	Out of Position.	Total.		
	(1)	(2)	(3)	(4)	(5)	(6)	(7)	(8)	(9)	(10)	(11)	(12)	(13)	(14)	(15)	(16)
																Days.
A	200	20	134	272	426	426	..	2	40	22	62	2	..	2	..	0·4
B	50	59	30	42	131	121	10	..	..	8	8	..	..	..	..	0·7
C	20	13	32	71	116	97	19	..	..	..	..	88	..	88	8	1·4
D	..	..	..	43	43	43	..	..	45	34	79	49	43	92	1	3·4
E	80	..	73	43	116	108	8	..	..	..	..	76	3	79	5	1·2
F	..	12	..	26	38	32	6	..	..	..	..	38	30	68	1	2·2
G	..	3	..	20	23	19	4	..	..	..	..	37	12	49	6	2·8
H	..	16	..	30	46	31	15	..	..	..	..	62	60	122	..	4·1
I	134	38	50	9	97	41	50	..	..	..	..	21	..	21	..	2·6
Totals	484	161	319	556	1036	918	118	2	85	64	149	373	148	521	21	Average 2·0

* Between the hours of ...... yesterday and ...... to-day.
† Close of day's work is at ....

RAILWAY AND SEAPORT FREIGHT MOVEMENT

204

Unnamed 'Bulldog' No 3432 (formerly No 3722) seen on coal empties in late 1920s at an unidentified location with an F-headcode. The locomotive looks in excellent condition and may be ex-works. The first wagon is 'Blaina Colliery Co Ltd … Anthracite; the third is 'Crynant'. *LGRP*

Empties returning to South Wales on 7 September 1929. Class 28XX No 2881 of 1919 is taking the train along to Ashley Hill, Filton Jct and ultimately to Severn Tunnel Jct. The Ashley Hill bank out of Bristol was two miles long at 1 in 75. *SLS*

a foreign wagon and consigned to a GW station, was re-loaded into GW wagons for the continuation of the journey.

Some railways got together in World War 1 to form a 'Common User' pool of unfitted open wagons and vans up to 12-tons capacity whereby any company's wagon could be loaded immediately upon discharge by any railway company. The contributions to the pool after the Grouping were approximately: SR 29,000; GW 65,000; LNE 170,000; and, LMS 217,000 — a total of 481,000. The GW vehicles in the pool were 53,000 opens and 12,000 vans. Each railway had its own share in the Common User Pool conserved by means of a twice-weekly balance. The GW was a net receiving company from the LMS and LNER, and empties were daily passed back through exchange

sidings at the appropriate junctions. A penalty of 3s per wagon per day was incurred by a company retaining more 'pool wagons' than its share. Details of the GW's involvement in the pool (including the changing status of GW cattle trucks etc) will be found in *GWR Goods Wagons*. During the period of the 1926 General Strike the GW became a net returning, rather than receiving, company.

None of the GW fitted opens (about 5,000 in number) and fitted vans (also about 5,000) were in the pool, nor any GW high capacity or special wagons. All non-common-user vehicles bore a 'Return to GWR Not Common User' (NCU) inscription. All NCU vehicles were specially traced through RCH records and were to be returned to the GW within six days otherwise penalty charges on a rising scale, were paid by the defaulting railway.

'Aberdare' No 2668 (built in 1902) on a Down goods at Hatton with Bordesley coal empties, showing the 1918-36 H-headcode. Hatton was reached up a bank rising at 1 in 92 from Warwick. *LGRP*

From the data gathered on returns of wagons in three-day periods by RCH wagon number-takers, the assessment of payments between companies for use of NCU wagons, sheets and ropes was evaluated and statistical information generated.

The number of wagons annually forwarded/received at exchange junctions in the 1930s was typically:

Yard	Forwarded by GW	Received by GW
Acton	190,000	230,000
Afon Wen	10,000	8,000
Aylesbury	7,000	6,000
Banbury	280,000	280,000
Basingstoke	83,000	72,000
Bordesley	230,000	230,000
Bristol	79,000	55,000
Cannock Road, (Bushbury)	45,000	51,000
Crewe	148,000	168,000
Dorchester	8,000	12,000
Dudley	60,000	82,000
Exeter	27,000	23,000
Gloucester	70,000	58,000
Leamington	120,000	132,000
Manchester	27,000	37,000
Oxford	12,000	12,000
Patricroft	13,000	8,500
Reading	46,000	47,000
Rhymney	300	400
Salisbury	80,000	83,000
Stratford	800	1,600
Warrington	35,000	55,000
Wednesbury	63,000	74,000
West Cheshire	23,000	44,000
Whitchurch	16,000	13,000
Winchester	1,000	2,000
Worcester	29,000	8,000
Yarnton	31,000	20,000
Yeovil	18,000	15,000

In Section 3 of the 1933 STT, trains that were used to transfer wagons to and from the SR at Basingstoke are listed. These include not only local trains from and to Reading West, but also longer-distance goods trains that brought wagons for the SR via Reading and terminated at Basingstoke SR station. They included the 3.30am from Hollinswood – just south of Wellington (Salop) – (F-headcode, arriving 4.49pm **SX**; on Saturdays terminated at the GW yard at 4.35pm); and the 5.20pm ex-Banbury Jct (H-headcode, arriving at 9pm). Three similar trains ran from the Wolverhampton area: (i) from Victoria Basin on Sundays the 7.10pm (E-headcode, arriving 2.27am); on other days (**MX**) it departed at 7.30pm (C-headcode as far as Reading, then E to Basingstoke arriving at 2.27am); (ii) from Oxley sidings 1.10am (C-headcode, arriving 5.3am **MX** and 5.20am **MO**); and (iii) an Accelerated-E headcode at 2am (**MO**) arr 7.50am, and 2.10am (**MX**), arriving 7.55am.

GREAT WESTERN RAILWAY.
Office of Superintendent of the Line,
Paddington Station, W.2.

24th November, 1940.

MEMORANDUM.

Control and Distribution of Freight Rolling Stock.

Organisation. The supply and movement are vested in two Departments - the Chief Goods Manager and the Superintendent of the Line with their respective District Officers.

In regard to the distribution of empty wagons, the Superintendent of the Line acts as the Agent of the Chief Goods Manager in view of the fact that the Goods Department is responsible to the Trader for the provision of stock and deals with all problems associated therewith direct with the Trader. The Goods Department perform the service of cartage (in direct collaboration with the Road Transport Superintendent); the terminal handling of goods from lorry to wagon and vice versa; the loading and unloading of wagons; the marshalling of the wagons at terminal points (by pre-arrangement with the Superintendent of the Line); and the placing of the trains at the disposal of the Superintendent of the Line at a fixed place at the forwarding terminal points.

The order is reversed at destination terminal points.

The Superintendent of the Line (Traffic Department), accepts the wagons from the Goods Department, orders the engines and runs the trains to their appropriate destinations. The point-to-point timing of the trains is the primary responsibility of the Traffic Department; the departure and arrival times are fixed by arrangement with the Goods Department to fit in with goods terminal working.

Returns. The Goods Department, to carry out their function at terminal points, require to know the position at the start of the day's work, which for general purposes has been selected as at 8.0.am each day. All Stations render a daily report (Form 5781) to the District Goods Manager; this report is in the hands of the District Goods Manager by the early afternoon. The District Goods Manager extracts certain essential details on Summary Form 5825 for the whole district and forwards to the Chief Goods Manager the same night, to reach Paddington the following morning. The Chief Goods Manager and District Goods Manager each in turn take appropriate action with the Stations and District Offices respectively, where necessary.

The Superintendent of the Line moves the stock from point to point as demanded and upon representations, where this is necessary, from the Chief Goods Manager, who is the final arbiter in the matter of stock supply for traffic movement requirements of the Company's Traders. Close contact is maintained between the Chief Goods Manager and the Superintendent of the Line in order that where the circumstances necessitate joint decision and action can be taken. There is similar contact and co-operation between the Divisional Superintendents and District Goods Managers respecting the local movements of stock.

- 2 -

Returns. (Contd) To enable the Traffic Department to carry out their function Stations render Return (Form 5823) to the Divisional Superintendent to reach him not later than 2.0.pm. Where this is impracticable the details are telephoned or telegraphed. The Divisional Superintendent may dispose of wagons to meet needs within the limitations of his Division, subject to the over-riding authority of the Superintendent of the Line.

The Divisional Superintendent prepares from the Station Returns a summary (Form 7550) for his own use, also a daily Divisional Stock Statement (Form 6302) and Special Class Wagon Statement (Form 6992) which are forwarded each night to the Superintendent of the Line by whom the all-line summary (Form 7552) and Special Class Stock Form 7322 are prepared for inter-division distribution and other purposes.

When the Daily Stock Returns have been summarised in the Divisional Office, particulars of empty stock despatched and to spare, together with applications for assistance are advised to Headquarters by telephone or telegram, from whom the Divisional Offices receive disposal instructions.

In addition to routine orders, contact is made between Headquarters and the Divisions during the day and night as to any special or exceptional measures which may have to be taken.

Specimens of forms are enclosed.

Distribution of Requisitioned Wagons. A record is taken twice daily of wagons on hand at stations and marshalling yards which are available for distribution to collieries situated on the Great Western Railway. This information is furnished to the Divisional Control Offices situated in the various Traffic Department Divisions throughout the line. At the same time, information is also obtained of the number of wagons then standing under load which will become available for distribution as empties during the course of the day.

Upon receipt of these particulars they are summarised and the result transmitted to the Central Distribution Control situated in the Office of the Superintendent of the Line, Paddington.

The information from the various Divisions is summarised in the Central Control and the position throughout the line can then be seen both in regard to the requirements of the collieries, balancing records with other Companies and where necessary supply of empties for other than coal class traffic.

So far as the Great Western Railway is concerned the main flow of empties is in the direction of South Wales that being the area where the greater proportion of the coal business is transacted.

In South Wales close collaboration is maintained with the colliery interests. Although there are a large number of pits they are controlled by seven or eight Combines under whose direction the supply of empties to the pits is arranged. This is beneficial for the reason that the Combines are in possession of information regarding the class of coal immediately required and arrange disposition of the available empties with this in mind.

- 3 -

Distribution of Requisitioned Wagons. (Contd) Normally the coal produced in South Wales passes in volume from pit to port and by arrangement with the Combines and co-operation between the Docks and Traffic Departments of the Railways it can be ascertained the number of wagons which will become available during the course of the day from shipment.

There are occasions when it is necessary to allocate privately owned wagons for loading commodities other than coal class and when this arises the Chief Goods Manager indicates his requirements in this respect to the Central Control.

Attached are forms which are in use on the Great Western system and with the exception of one or two designed to meet the requirements of the South Wales shipment trade they are standard throughout the system.

At all the locations listed above, wagons were exchanged between the GWR and one other company, except at Acton, which dealt with both LMS and LNER traffic via the North London route. At Exeter, all goods transfers had to be carried out on the main passenger lines at East box, as there was no connexion between the LSW and GW at the south (west) end of the station.

Wagons might also be exchanged at other places. For example, the 1927 STT talks about the exchange of wagons between the GW and LMS at Shepherds Bush, where wagons (no more than 30 in number) were to be placed in the transferring company's shunting neck to be picked up by the receiving company. It was also noted that care had to be taken when odd wagons from West London line stations were left in the GW shunting neck at Shepherds Bush since a wagon was placed at the stops daily for loading purposes from Messrs T C Jones's yard.

Two additional factors complicated the question of wagon shortages, viz traders (particularly coal merchants) taking longer than they were allowed to unload wagons — fines (demurrage) notwithstanding — and crippled wagons, either the GWR's own or, more particularly after the adoption of the Common User arrangement in World War 1, those belonging to other companies whose condition was often inferior to GW wagons in the pool.

The GW became handicapped by an increasing number of immobile cripple wagons not available for traffic, yet it had to maintain its balance of numbers in the Pool, otherwise the GW became liable for penalty charges. The solution took the form of a daily repayment quota of cripple wagons back to the LNER and LMS. Details of these and other related matters may be found in *GWR Goods Wagons*. Relevant telegraph code words were: 'Frog' - 'Following wagons detained at your station. Get them discharged at once, and send today full written explanation of detention'; and, 'Wagdem' – 'Following wagons under load requiring demurrage'.

Daily stocktaking returns sent from GW goods depots to Goods Districts and then on to Paddington enabled the railway to know the distribution of different sorts of rolling stock. Based on their expected needs for loading, and the number of wagons they had on hand that would be unloaded, depots ordered empty wagons for loading. Before 1922, the Superintendent of the Line's rolling stock inspectors controlled all wagon supply, but subsequently the Chief Goods Manager had final say since the goods side had to deal with customers; the Traffic Department acted as the CGM's agent for wagon movement. There was, perhaps, fuzziness after the change and much discussion on the best way of doing things as illustrated by the letter of 24 November 1940. In the June 1926 edition of *Diagrams of Special Wagons*, it says that application for Crocodile, Macaw C, Pollen and Totem wagons must be made to the District Goods Manager, but applications for all other vehicles in the book must be made to the Divisional Traffic Superintendent!

In the 1920s, the GW Goods Districts normally self-supporting as regards merchandise wagons were Reading, Exeter, Plymouth, Cardiff Valleys, Swansea, Worcester and Central Wales. Those normally requiring supplies of empty wagons were London, Bristol, Gloucester, Cardiff, Birmingham, Shrewsbury and Liverpool. In addition, special allocations of empty stock were required at different times of the year owing to seasonal traffic. For example, loaded wagons arriving in Cornwall in the broccoli season were kept for reloading, but most times in the year they would be sent empty out of the district; similarly for seasonal Channel Islands traffic landed at Weymouth. The pattern for the rest of the year was an upward movement of open wagons and vans to Bristol and Avonmouth Docks from the West of England. Another example related to the movement of empty merchandise wagons from West Wales and the Swansea Docks towards Cardiff, and even as far as Bristol. Between the wars, the Cardiff area required vans to carry flour from Barry and Penarth, and for cement at Aberthaw and Rhoose.

In the mid-1920s, 13 dedicated empty goods stock trains were scheduled to run 'as required' (nominally daily) within the GW system:

Reading Goods District:
12.15am Didcot to Bordesley
7.15am Reading West to Avonmouth, Bordesley or Banbury as required
10.10am Reading West to Banbury
10.40am Reading West to Avonmouth

Bristol District:
1.55am Holt Jct to Stoke Gifford

Exeter District:
5.15pm Taunton to Bristol (West depot)

Plymouth District:
4.15pm Truro to Bristol (West depot)
5.10pm Penzance to Bristol (West depot)

Gloucester District
3.30am Kemble to Gloucester

Swansea District:
12.15am Llandilo to Gloucester or Avonmouth as required
12.50am Carmarthen to Avonmouth
2.10pm Llandilo to Avonmouth
2.15am Llandilo to Avonmouth

Empty wagons were also moved by ordinary goods train, and some hundreds of local services were listed in the STTs as conveying empty stock. Slow coal trains were often used to convey empties, but better use of empty wagons was achieved when faster trains were used. As part of general improvements in services, a new 1.30am Llandilo Junction to Old Oak Common freight train was introduced in 1927 intended to convey wagons loaded with minerals and merchandise traffic and empties formerly taken by coal trains. The telegraph code 'Bovine' meant 'Empties waiting power at undermentioned station. Arrange to clear at once. Special if necessary. Wire what done'.

There was a tremendous amount of traffic in landsale and shipment coal, all of which was conveyed in PO wagons. Railway companies were not permitted to back-load such opens that had to be returned empty to the address on the wagon. Even within a single railway company, this required a great deal of shunting and sorting, and *Marshalling Instructions* directed outward and return routes. For example, empties for the Llanelly district had to be dropped off at Felin Fran, Llandilo Jct, Llanelly and Pembrey depending on where the collieries were situated. When empties were conveyed in slow loose-coupled trains, it was undesirable to have the empty wagons marshalled in front of, say, a string of loaded coal wagons since, on the train being braked, the inertia of the heavy coal trucks could damage the light empty wagons. Guards were instructed wherever possible to get empty vehicles behind heavily-loaded wagons.

The circulation of cattle wagons was greatest between March-June and August-September in connexion with cattle markets and horse fairs. In addition there was a year-round supply of empties to Fishguard for Irish cattle. Unlike those of other foreign railways, GW cattle wagons were not in the Common User Pool.

In the same way as wagons, the supply of containers around the GWR had to be regulated, and this was done by the container control section in the Chief Goods Manager's Development Office at Paddington (see *GWR Goods Wagons*).

CHAPTER FIFTEEN

COAL AND MINERAL TRAFFIC

CLASS 1 traffic included coal, coke and patent fuel (briquettes); Class 2 was 'other minerals' including building materials, stone, sand and gravel, salt, pig iron, iron ore, ashes, manure etc. In 1912, the GW conveyed 33,638,577 tons of Class 1 materials and 10,663,841 tons of Class 2. For comparison that year there were 9,987,839 tons of Class 3 general merchandise.

MINERAL

Mineral traffic originated at many places across GW territory at different times. Iron ore was mined in the Banbury and Hook Norton areas; Westbury and Seend district (Wilts); Gupworthy (Exmoor, Somerset); Heathfield, Lostwithiel; in the Forest of Dean; Bontnewydd (Dolgelly); and in South Staffordshire (Kidderminster/Wyre Forest). Much of this headed for the iron and steel industry in South Wales, the West Midlands (Bilston), Shropshire (Hollinswood), and North Wales (Brymbo). Later, as supplies ran out in some places, a source just to the north of Banbury (Wroxton) was expanded. Increasing trainloads for South Wales ran from the Northamptonshire fields (LMS) via Leamington, and during World War 2, via Yarnton. The 1am Rogerstone to Yarnton H-headcode train of empty iron ore wagons returning to Irthlingborough in Northamptonshire left Rogerstone sidings at 1am behind a '28XX' class 2-8-0, with no intermediate calls, except for water and wagon examination.

Much of the china clay (kaolin), found in Devon (south-west Dartmoor) and Cornwall was sent to Fowey, where special dockside appliances were provided for shipment of the material to many parts of the world (see *GWR Docks & Marine*).

Slate was quarried in North Wales, with deposits at Blaenau Festiniog, Carrog, Dolgelly, Glyndyfrdwy, Llangollen and Tanymanod (within the Ruabon, Blaenau and Barmouth triangle) . There were also slate quarries in Pembrokeshire (the Cardigan, Whitland and Letterston triangle), Devon (around Coryton) and at

Delabole in Cornwall. Tin, copper, arsenic and other metal ores were also found in Cornwall, but were in decline before the end of the C19[th].

Building stone came from Portland/Weymouth and Bath, with granite from Trusham in Devon and from Dartmoor. Limestone in its various forms was used for the manufacture of cement, for agricultural purposes and for road-making. Roadstone was moved from such places as Cranmore (the Mendip Co, Somerset), Christow, Cinderford, Menheniot and Minffordd. A very important source of lime was at Harbury (Leamington), much being dispatched as cement. Rhoose and Aberthaw also regularly dispatched cement by rail. Other building materials, such as sand and gravel, came from Theale, Kidderminster and Buildwas. Salt was extracted at Droitwich, north of Worcester, and at Stoke Works that was on a dead-end branch line from Droitwich Spa.

Where large amounts of material were required, full train loads would be dispatched over long distances. This often happened with iron ore, roadstone and ballast. Trains with other Class 2 materials tended to run shorter distances, to nearby yards, from

A ballast train carrying C-headlamps hauled by outside-framed 'Buffalo' 0-6-0ST No 1566 built at Swindon in 1878 (scrapped 1935). The 14 hopper wagons were vacuum fitted, to Diagram P7. *GWR*

First of two pictures of the same timetabled Down mineral train carrying Stewarts & Lloyds traffic to Banbury. Here the train is near Leamington Spa headed by ROD No 3030 carrying the 1918-36 H-headcode (two lamps to the left on the buffer beam when facing the engine). There is a GW brake van at either end of the train (both to diagram AA2) for ease of reversal on to the LNER at Banbury. *LGRP*

The second picture of the Stewarts & Lloyds mineral train composed of steel hopper wagons and wooden opens. The locomotive this time is 2-6-0 No 4329 of 1913 that again shows the 1918-36 H-headcode of two lamps to the left on the buffer beam when facing the engine. *SLS*

where it was sorted and dispatched to different areas by the wagon-load rather than by train-load.

The term 'ballast' when applied to permanent way traffic included earth and other engineering materials, and all trains run for the Engineering (Permanent Way) Department were called ballast trains. Many were run on an *ad hoc* basis in conjunction with the permanent way department.

Some engineering department vehicles were vac fitted and had oilboxes so, providing that the load did not exceed that specified for a C-headcode train, ballast trains could run at speeds up to

A ROD 2-8-0 hauls a Down mineral train at Lapworth troughs. ROD tenders did not have pick-up apparatus. The locomotive carries the H-headcode that applied between 1918 and 1936.
Real Photographs

A ballast train early in 1938 near Gerrard's Cross loaded with chalk filling for the new London passenger Transport Board (LPTB) car depot at Ruislip. The locomotive is an unidentified 'Grange'. The Toad at the front of the train is boxed in and is a plough van. H-headcode. *G L Lake*

1918-built 2-8-0 No 2872 heads an H-headcode train of Baldwin's wagons loaded with iron ore from Hook Norton for South Wales. The train was photographed at Charlton Kings near Cheltenham on 7 June 1923. *GWR*

The Bitterley Granite Co sidings on the Clee Hill branch, four miles from Ludlow, in November 1922. The line going out of the picture to the right leads to Titterstone Quarry. The double track on the left is an incline descending to the Ddu, Clee Hill and Belfry quarries. A GW signalbox stands at the top of the incline, beyond which tracks climb to the Bitterley sidings, where a GW tank engine stands. *STEAM Swindon*

45mph direct to where trackwork was being done; if the load was exceeded, they ran as Accelerated E/D-headcode trains at speeds up to 35mph.

In 1920, the principal minerals originating on the GW system and carried by the company (at Station-to-Station rates) were:

Material	Tons
Ironstone/Iron Ore	1,366,576
Limestone (non-Agricultural or Road-making)	
	196,536
Sand	161,656
Stone (Road-making)	1,228,586

China Clay was not listed, though 522,913 tons were handled at Fowey that year.

In 1938 mineral traffic originating on the GW was:

Cement and Lime	548,797
Gravel & Sand	199,618
Iron Ore	876,481
Limestone and Chalk	290,126
Road chippings	721,757

China Clay amounted to 454,188 tons, then plummeted over the war years to tens of thousands of tons as former importers were in enemy-occupied territory. After World War 2, tonnages began to increase again, with 234,985 tons being dispatched in 1946 as trade picked up.

A K-headcode goods train headed by a '44XX' 2-6-2T pictured at Marsh Mills, the first station on the branch from the Plymouth main line to Tavistock and Launceston (and to Princetown). The first two vehicles are hopper ballast wagons to Diagram P7, originally built as 12-tonners but uprated to 20 tons by the addition of the plate rails around the top of the wagon in the period from 1904 to 1906. The first wagon No 60254 dates from 1898. *STEAM Swindon*

ROD No 3043 heads a train of mineral hopper wagons at Cheltenham on 21 May 1948. *STEAM Swindon*

A 1907 view of Waun Llwyd Colliery just south of Victoria station on the Ebbw Vale branch that left the Western Valley line at Aberbeeg. The loaded wagons on the hillside supply the mine boiler house. Empty wagons stored on sidings in the foreground are being shunted by a saddle tank. PO wagons whose tip-ends face to the right (down the valley towards Newport) belong to the 'Ebbw Vale Coal, Iron & Steel Co' (EV). GW locomotive coal wagons on the track behind are waiting to be loaded at the corrugated iron shed at the right centre that was supplied by the pit 'screens'. Another saddle tank at the right heads an Up goods train. Further to the right is the Ebbw river. *Commercial postcard*

Cwm Pedol (Pedol Valley) at Garnant, between Ammanford and Brynamman in Carmarthenshire seen at the turn of the 19th/20th centuries. PO wagons belong to David Jones & Sons of Cawdor Collieries (later part of the Amalgamated Anthracite Collieries, registered in Swansea). 16-ton Toad No 56150 was built in 1894 and later diagrammed as AA3. The locomotive is pushing the train owing to the steepness of gradient to colliery. *Commercial postcard*

COAL

There were three types of coal traffic: (i) domestic and industrial landsale coal; (ii) shipment coal from mine to docks for export, for coastwise trade and for bunkering coal-burning ships; and (iii), locomotive coal. Apart from locomotive coal, nearly all of which was carried in the company's own wagons, most coal, coke and patent fuel (briquettes) was carried in private owner wagons belonging to collieries, coal factors or wagon-hire firms.

After the Great Fire of London in 1666, a tax was levied on coal entering the city to pay for the rebuilding, and when railways arrived some 170 years later, charges continued to be levied on coal entering a radius of 15 miles from the General Post Office. Thus, the 1835 Act of Incorporation of the GWR had a provision

that a stone was to be placed on the east bank of the River Colne in the parish of Hillingdon, and 1s 1d paid to the City for every ton of coal brought past this stone (a 'toll gate for coal'); 500 tons per year was exempt for locomotive fuel. Other obelisks were to be found on the north of the main line near West Drayton station, just to the west of where the Staines branch passed underneath, and also on that branch. London coal dues were not abolished until 1889. Transport of coal by the GWR to London alone, which in the year 1846 totalled 4,350 tons, had increased to 1,095,526 tons by 1911.

The South Wales coalfield — where so much of the coal carried by the Great Western came from — had a saucer-like formation, the veins of coal being near the surface at its east (Monmouthshire) and west (West Glamorgan/Carmarthenshire/Pembrokeshire) extremes, and deeper in between (East Glamorgan). Of these, Monmouthshire coal was the softest and most free burning; East Glamorgan yielded harder and drier steam coals; and, western collieries yielded mostly anthracite. While, even from before the Grouping, the largest number of collieries on GW territory was found in South Wales, there was a significant number elsewhere on the system. At regular intervals, a booklet, entitled *List of Collieries on or connected with the Great Western Railway*, was issued by the company. In 1907, the number of collieries connected to the Great Western was listed as:

District	Number of Collieries
Birkenhead	1
North Wales	18
Shropshire	15
South Stafford & Worcester	35
Somerset	22
Forest of Dean	8
Monmouth (Eastern Valleys)	18
Monmouth (Western Valleys)	40
South Wales	162

(The separation of Monmouthshire from South Wales reflects the old status of Monmouthshire as supposedly not being in Wales as it was not part of the Welsh Assizes circuit.) In addition, coal from a large number of collieries connected to other independent or joint railways came on to the GWR for haulage:

Railway	Number of Collieries
Brecon & Merthyr	16
Burry Port & Gwendraeth	16
Great Central	5
Llanelly & Mynydd Mawr	4
LNW	24
Midland	35
Neath & Brecon	14
Rhymney	19
Port Talbot	20
Rhondda & Swansea Bay	9
Severn & Wye Jt	12
South Wales Mineral	6
Taff Vale	54

A few collieries were served by two companies; for example, in the Forest of Dean area, Crump Meadow, Foxes Bridge and Trafalgar Collieries were served both by the GW at Bilson and by the S&WJt at Drybrook Jct.

New collieries continued to open in the valleys above Cardiff, and, by the late C19th, the TVR alone was connected to over 80 mines, whilst the nine million tons of coal carried in 1885 by the Taff had grown to 19 million tons by World War 1. In the heyday of coal, there were some 200,000 people employed in the South Wales coalfield. During the week ending 1 December 1907, the TVR conveyed 404,125 tons of coal that, accounting for returning empties, was equivalent to nearly 14,000 wagons per day.

The nearest collieries to Birkenhead were in North Wales, but it is not generally realised that a significant factor in the development of that port was its ability to provide *South* Wales bunkers coal brought up by train to the Mersey. The 20 Armstrong 0-6-0 tender goods locomotives with 4ft 6in wheels ('Coal Engines' of 1874, Nos 927-946) were employed on this traffic between Pontypool Road and Birkenhead via Shrewsbury in the latter part of the C19th. Another important bunkers coaling port before World War 1 for merchant shipping was Dartmouth/Kingswear that was supplied with South Wales coal (see section on locomotive coal later).

The history of coal traffic in South Wales is complicated by the many standard-gauge railways and docks that, before the Grouping in 1922, were in competition with the GWR. The broad-gauge South Wales Railway seemed more concerned about completing the main line westwards rather than realising the mineral potential of the valleys (or simply underestimated it). Even so, the Forest of Dean Railway and 'feeder' lines to the SWR, including the Ely Valley Railway, the Llynvi Valley Railway and the South Wales Mineral Railway, were broad gauge and would later bring coal on to the SWR. In 1859, a 1¼-mile long broad-gauge branch was laid from the SWR mainline at Long Dyke Jct, Cardiff, to the Bute East dock to gain access to two rented coal tips, from where a great deal of coal was shipped to the GWR locomotive coking plant at Bristol; the invention of the firebox brick arch by Kirtley and Markham of the Midland Railway in the 1860s, by which 'locomotives consumed their own smoke', eventually made it possible to use coal instead of coke.

At Lydney Jct station, there was a railway interchange wharf at which Forest of Dean coal brought down on tramways was tipped into broad-gauge wagons. The SWR provided an outlet by rail for this coal at Llanthony yard (Gloucester docks), where in 1854 it erected one of the earliest hydraulic wagon hoists for the shipment of coal; its capacity was 36 tons, and it was first used to load 120 tons of coal from Nicholson's colliery at Parkend into an Irish schooner bound for Wexford. Coal in the mid-1860s was largely moved from the Forest of Dean area to Swindon, leaving either from Lydney on the west side of the Forest or from Bullo Pill on the east. Completion of Brunel's Chepstow railway bridge in 1853 opened up trade from South Wales, with a couple of daily broad-gauge trains from Neath to Gloucester, Swindon and London. The bridge also gave Lydney coal access to South Wales markets.

After the mixed gauge was completed to Paddington in 1861, through standard-gauge coal trains ran from Pontypool Road via Hereford, Worcester, Oxford and Didcot (the SWR was broad gauge until 1872). The Badminton line opened in 1903 between Wootton Bassett and Filton. It was 10 miles shorter than the alternative route via Bath and had easier gradients, so Newport-London coal traffic could be more heavily loaded between Stoke Gifford and Swindon. Later, in 1925, a new line was opened from Brettell Lane to Oxley sidings, which was a single-line extension of the Kingswinford branch and enabled South Wales coal trains and other traffic to bypass the congested area between Stourbridge and Wolverhampton. At the same time, a large and well-equipped engine shed was built at Oxley to which most of the freight locomotives stabled at the old Stafford Road sheds were transferred.

It is sometimes forgotten that in 1835 Brunel surveyed the proposed TVR. It is rather less well known that the foremost object of the TVR was the conveyance of *iron* from Merthyr for export, although coal later predominated. He had to follow what Parliament and the Boards of Directors required in terms of gauge. The broad-gauge SWR, like his other mainlines, was built for speed whereas the Taff was principally a mineral line to the docks. In evidence to the Gauge Commissioners, Brunel said that at the time he had believed that track radii and gauge should be proportional, so sharper curves along the Taff Vale in comparison with curves along the GW broad gauge meant a narrower gauge in the valleys. In the row between the SWR and GWR over whether the SWR should still go to Fishguard rather than Milford — despite the Irish economic problems of the late 1840s — the Great Western had the impudence to say that the SWR was not as successful as it ought to have been as it had the wrong gauge!

After the Grouping, the number of collieries connected to the GWR now included all those served by the former independent constituent companies (which totalled 158 in the table for 1907) as well as the 220 served by the GW itself in 1907. By the Grouping this overall total had increased a little, with old collieries being worked out and new mines opening. The table below indicates the figures served by the enlarged GWR for 1924 and 1932.

THE SOUTH WALES VALLEYS – SHOWING PRINCIPAL STATIONS & HALTS

James Page

R. Severn

RAILWAYS IN SOUTH WALES

	GW
	LNW
	Midland
	Taff Vale
	Rhymney
	Barry
	Brecon & Merthyr
	Neath & Brecon
	Port Talbot
	Cardiff
	Rhondda & Swansea Bay
	S Wales Mineral
	Alexandra (Newport & S Wales) Docks & Rly

Other Railways:—

GV	Gwendraeth Valley
BP & GV	Burry Port & Gwendraeth Valley
L & MM	Llanelly & Mynydd Mawr
S & M	Swansea & Mumbles
Cam	Cambrian
(GW & RR JT)	Joint lines (as indicated)

1 Sirhowy
2 Tredegar
3 Bedwellty Pits
4 Hollybush
5 Argoed
6 Blackwood
7 Pontllanfraith (HL)
8 Pontllanfraith (LL)
9 Ynysddu
10 Rhymney (B&M)
11 Abertysswg
12 New Tredegar
13 Aber Bargoed
14 Pengam (Mon)
15 Bedwas
16 Machen
17 Pontlottyn
18 Tirphil
19 Brithdir
20 Bargoed
21 Pengam (Glam)
22 Ystrad Mynach
23 Llanbradach
24 Dowlais Top
25 Fochriw
26 Ogilvie
27 Pentwyn
28 Dowlais Central
29 Dowlais Cae Harris
30 Merthyr High St.
31 Bedlinog
32 Pentrebach
33 Troedyrhiw
34 Merthyr Vale
35 Aberfan
36 Abercanaid
37 Abertan
38 Aberdare
39 Travellers Rest
40 Quakers Yd (LL)
41 Treharris
42 Penrhiwceiber
43 Mountain Ash (Oxford St)
44 Mountain Ash (Cardiff Rd)
45 Aberaman
46 Abernant
47 White Hart Halt (up)
48 White Hart Halt (down)
49 Fountain Bridge Halt
50 Waterloo Halt
51 Aber Jc. Halt
52 Aberdare
53 Ynysybwl
54 Trehafod
55 Treforest (TVR)
56 Graig (BR)
57 Treforest (TVR)
58 Treforest (TVR)
59 Treforest Halt
60 Rhydyfelin Halt (HL)
61 Upper Boat Halt
62 Rhydyfelin Halt (LL)
63 Glyntaff Halt
64 Beddau Halt
65 Taff's Well
66 Coryton Halt
67 Whitchurch
68 Rhiwbina
69 Birchgrove
70 Heath Halt (LL)
71 Heath Halt (HL)
72 Llandaff
73 Radyr
74 Llandaff
75 Gilfach Goch
76 Hendreforgan
77 Tonteg
78 Efail Isaf
79 Church Village
80 Cross Inn
81 Pontyclun
82 Tonyrefail
83 Tonyrefail
84 Ogmore Vale
85 Blackmill
86 Pontycymmer
87 Pontyrhyl
88 Llangeinor
89 Nantymoel
90 Betws
91 Llwdy Brongu
92 Bryn
93 Bryn
94 Aberavon Town
95 Maesteg (GWR)
96 Troedyrhiw Garth
97 Llangynwyd
98 Port Talbot Central
99 Blaengwynfi
100 Cymmer General
101 Pontrhydyfen
102 Cwmavon
103 Aberavon Seaside
104 Briton Ferry
105 Briton Ferry Rd
106 Jersey Marine
107 Danygraig
108 Skewen
109 Aberdylais
110 Upper Bank
111 Copper pit
112 Morriston (West)
113 Morriston (East)
114 Clydach on Tawe
115 Glais

Number of Colliries

District	1924	1932
South Wales & Monmouthshire	404	338
Somerset	14	13
Gloucester (Forest of Dean)	18	27
South Staffs & Worcester	26	18
Shropshire	14	13
North Wales	16	7

The number of collieries connected to the LMS in South Wales became:

Merthyr, Tredegar & Abergavenny	9	5
Sirhowy	12	8
Swansea (ex-LNW)	8	5
Swansea Vale (ex-Midland)	38	24

The LNW did not have running powers to take coal from collieries in the Sirhowy Valley directly to Newport Docks so, as explained by Page, a diversionary route to Aber sidings just north of Caerphilly was employed, from where ADR locomotives took over through Machen. After the Grouping, the LMS brought this traffic by the direct route to the end-on junction with the GW at Nine Mile Point station near Risca.

Although the number of individual pits in South Wales continued to be large, in later years they were owned and controlled by only seven or eight combines of coal owners.

Before the Grouping of 1922, there was a plethora of different rates for shipment coal in South Wales depending on the railway company. Some were just for the mileage hauled and tipping was extra, some included the costs of tipping. Rationalisation by the GW was 'neutral' and took the form of a flat rate in between the highest and the lowest rates, such that the total income to the GW remained as it would have been for all the separate companies had the Grouping not occurred.

Collieries were often situated among mountains and river valleys where flat ground was in short supply. Both main lines, and branches off main lines to the pits, were often on steep gradients — perhaps 1 in 40 or 50 for main lines, and 1 in 20 to 1 in 30 for colliery branches. On the seven-mile long Taff-Bargoed joint line that rose at 1 in 40/49, three Rhymney Railway locomotives took 40 minutes to haul 20-wagon iron ore trains. The load of iron ore from Newport to Aberbeeg (for Ebbw Vale) was 32 wagons with a '42XX' in front and a power class A locomotive in the rear ('Dean Goods' or '27XX'/'64XX'/'74XX' pannier tanks).

With normal adhesion, locomotives could travel on gradients up to 1 in 18 without sliding, but they had limited haulage capacity. Very often, trains going up (including colliers' trains) had the locomotive pushing in the rear to guard against breakaways, as at Glyn Corrwg on the old South Wales Mineral Railway. On the ex-TVR Dare branch, the passenger train service terminated at Aberdare, but the line continued as a mineral railway for two miles 27 chains to Bwllfa Colliery. The greater part of this extension was on a rising gradient varying between 1 in 38 and 1 in 30. The maximum single engine load upwards was eight loaded wagons; it was 25 coming down. Although the Clydach Vale pit near Tonypandy was only one mile as the crow flies from the TVR main line, it was 430ft above, and was reached by the Pwllyrhebog cable-assisted incline that rose at 1 in 13 for half a mile. TVR 0-6-0T locomotives, fitted with special boilers designed to keep water over the firebox crown at all times, pushed in the rear. These locomotives had 5ft 3in drivers in order to clear the cable sheaves. The maximum permitted loads were no more than 10 loaded wagons coming down, with 10 empties or five loaded with pitwood going up. In the Western Valley above Newport, the steepest section was the 1 in 28 along the Cwmtillery branch at Abertillery where the maximum load for a power class E locomotive ('42XX'/'52XX', '72XX') was 12 loaded wagons or 24 empties. On the Eastern Valley line to Blaenavon there was a gradient of 1 in 19 on the Cwmnantddu branch that left the main line at Pontnewynydd north of Pontypool Crane Street station; the maximum load was 10 loaded opens or 19 empties. Special double-ended Toads (Diagram AA8 of 1889 in the Wagon index, and their AA24 replacements of 1947) with reduced-profile cabins were used to give the engine driver adequate visibility.

Owing to lack of flat ground, sidings at collieries were often congested and inadequate, and they were not always well maintained by the mine companies. It was necessary to remove loaded wagons and send back empties frequently, otherwise the mine had to stop working. This was one of the jobs of the Control offices (Chapter 12). Whereas docks could store empty wagons and 'wait order' coal in loaded wagons until required, collieries could not, and for this reason in parts of the TVR above Pontypridd there were two Down main lines but only one Up main line, so as to get loaded wagons away from the mines. ('Up' was up the valley, not towards London.) Wagon movement was eased at some collieries by having the inlet for empties from the main line higher up the valley than the outlet, wagons descending by gravity through the loading screens. Shunting was still difficult, however, and often fouled the running lines, interfering with ordinary passenger trains, colliers' trains and passing freight trains.

Finely-broken coal and coal dust was converted into 'patent fuel' briquettes using tar binders. Again, owing to the shortage of flat ground at collieries, the majority of briquette factories were at the docks. Even so, the British Benzol Coal Distillation Co Ltd by-product factory was located at Bedwas Navigation colliery at Trethomas.

There was a great number of signalboxes to control the many branches leading to the many collieries: in the 11 miles of the Rhondda Valley alone, there were 24 cabins. On Sundays, 21 of the 24 were switched out making the whole of the Rhondda into two block sections.

For every ton of coal raised, one ton of pit props, pitwood and general stores had to be supplied back to the mine, which was taken in returning PO wagons. (Pitwood had the bark left on and was cut to 4½-, six-, nine- and 13ft lengths; pit props were debarked and smaller than 4½in in diameter.) As it was difficult to predict requirements, only some pit props went direct to the colliery from the dock, others being stored on the dock estate. In later years there were stacking grounds at Cardiff, Felin Fran (Swansea) and STJ from where distribution to collieries was organised by Control.

The coal industry declined after World War 1. Even so, in 1938, there were 35½ million tons of saleable coal mined from the South Wales coalfield, of which two-thirds went to the various docks for export and bunkering coal.

Empty wagons for Bwllfa Colliery with a Dare Jct (Aberdare) 16-ton brake van No 56124 built in 1894 and later diagrammed as AA3. The ex-TVR Dare mineral line was a two-mile 27-chain continuation of the branch to Aberdare to Bwllfa Colliery. The greater part of this extension was on a rising gradient varying between 1 in 38 and 1 in 30. *GWR/D J Hyde collection*

A 'Dean Goods' 0-6-0 on coal train. The headcode of three lamps across the buffer beam is the 1903-1918 code for a through goods, mineral or ballast train. *SLS*

During and after World War 2, there was open-cast mining of deposits near the surface on the fringes of the South Wales coalfield. The sites were not rail connected, and coal was taken by road to collieries with screens, after which it was conveyed by rail. The coal was not particularly good, but the 500,000 tons/year excavated was a useful addition to the depleted resources at the time. Similarly, in 1946 the two million tons of anthracite duff that had been dumped before the war as being unmarketable at Felin Fran on the Swansea Avoiding lines, was recovered and used.

In 1946, only 22½ million tons of coal was produced in South Wales, of which only a quarter left by sea. While there was a reduction primarily in the export trade (from a pre-war 24 million tons to a post-war six million), the tonnage carried domestically was higher than in 1938 (17 million tons versus 12 million). One-fifth of the saleable coal (about five million tons) went by rail to England, equivalent to 500,000 wagon loads a year, or 10,000 train loads, or one coal train every 45 minutes throughout the year. In addition, there were 500,000 tons of coke and briquettes. Eighty per cent of all this traffic travelled through the Severn Tunnel, the remaining 20% for the Midlands and the north passing through Gloucester or Pontypool Road. All this meant an increase in average length of haul of coal trains from 44 miles pre-war to 57 miles after the war, which also extended the turn-around time of wagons (even though the Wagon Pool remained in operation after World War 2).

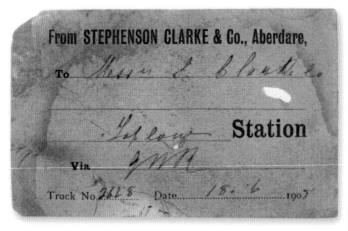

From STEPHENSON CLARKE & Co., Aberdare,

To Messrs L Clarke .o

Taplow Station

Via GWR

Truck No 2628   Date 18. 6. 1908

Wagon label from Stephenson Clarke at Aberdare for a wagon load of coal to Taplow in 1908.

GREAT WESTERN RAILWAY. (3119)
STATION, 194
ADVICE OF COAL, COKE AND PATENT FUEL TRAFFIC.

Mr.
Messrs.

The undermentioned wagons having arrived at this station consigned to you, I have to request that you will please arrange for them to be unloaded at once, and I give you notice that unless they are released on or before (whether the wagons are standing on the sidings available for unloading or in other sidings by reason of your being unable to take delivery). Demurrage will be charged you from that time at the rate of per wagon per day.

For the GREAT WESTERN RAILWAY COMPANY.

FROM	TRUCK NUMBERS.	DESCRIPTION OF TRAFFIC.

THIS ADVICE MUST BE PRODUCED WHEN THE TRAFFIC IS APPLIED FOR.

2,800 pads. 250 bcs.—B.M. 13 1947 69 S.   (SEE BACK.)

A coal train from South Wales on the 1 in 100 climb out of the Severn Tunnel into England. For reasons explained in the text, the 'banker' was attached to the front of the train as far as Pilning; then backed into the Up refuge siding, after which the train pulled forward far enough for the banker to come on at the rear. At Patchway it dropped off. The train locomotive is a straight-footplate '28XX' (from those numbered 2800-2830 built up to 1907). The banker is 2-6-2T No 3159 built in 1907. The STJ Target is No 4 that, in 1933, started duty at 11.20am and finished at 3.20am, with enginemen changing at 7.20pm. *G H Soole*

A Down loaded coke train of Stephenson Clarke (SC) wagons with coke rails on the former TVR line hauled by ex-Barry Railway 0-6-2T, photographed in the 1930s. *Railway Magazine*

'Dean Goods' No 2381 of 1890 at Stourbridge Jct on an Up 'through goods stopping at intermediate stations' (post-1918 J-headcode). Most wagons are wooden-underframe private-owner with grease boxes and contain coal. *LGRP*

'Dean Goods' No 2460 of 1895 on an Up goods (coal and coke) at Handsworth Jct (post-1918 J-headcode). The first wagon with its tip end facing the tender belongs to 'PD' (Powell Duffryn) and has coke rails; three of the remaining five wagons are labelled 'Bowater'. *LGRP*

INDUSTRIAL and DOMESTIC LANDSALE COAL

One landsale coal train had great historical commercial significance. Once the wharf at Dunball, Somerset, downstream of Bridgwater on the River Parrett, was connected to the railway in 1844 'sea coal' from across the Bristol Channel could be distributed by rail further into the West Country than by traditional river navigations. By 1849, the Bristol & Exeter 'Old Dunball Coal Train' departing at 1pm was taking coal on weekdays to Taunton, Wellington, Tiverton etc on its way to Exeter, and from there it was conveyed further westwards by the SDR. This broad-gauge rail traffic was the death-knell of the Bridgwater & Taunton and the Grand Western canals, which (with the dock at Bridgwater) were later taken over by the railway (see *GWR Docks & Marine*).

As the territory covered by the railway expanded, wagons of coal for coal merchants began to be seen in yards at all stations. Domestic coal was often distributed around the system in trains of mixed goods, as were wagons for bigger concerns, such as gasworks. However, dedicated coal trains for large consumers began to be run by the 1860s, and increased in number as demand grew. By the early 1900s, such trains originated at Llanelly, Aberdare and Pontypool Road, with a few from Lydney, Highley, and Ruabon. Coal from the Midlands and Yorkshire came on to the GW via Bordesley and Banbury. The 4.20am Bordesley to Didcot brought to Paddington coal from collieries on the Midland Railway.

The lengths of journey over which industrial and domestic landsale coal was hauled on the GW varied considerably. In March 1936, the following tonnages were carried over the distances shown:

Distances	Tonnage (Thousands)
Up to 1 mile	78.1
Over 1 mile to 10 miles	340.3
Over 10 miles to 20 miles	199.1
Over 20 miles to 30 miles	142.6
Over 30 miles to 40 miles	71.3
Over 40 miles to 100 miles	100.8
Over 100 miles to 150 miles	98.7
Over 150 miles to 300 miles	143.1
Over 300 miles	less than 1

A through Up coal train (F-headcode) hauled by 'Duke' No 3276 *St Agnes* (formerly No 3287) passes through King's Sutton, south of Banbury. The first wagon is a merchandise open with its sheet supporter down and used here to carry coal. *LGRP*

Some of this traffic did not originate at collieries connected to the GW, and arrived from outside the system. In the same month, the tonnage of landsale coal originating on the GWR and carried in PO wagons amounted to some 1,175,000 tons with an average length of haul of 48 miles. The amount of landsale coal carried in GW wagons was only 65,000 tons, with an average journey length of 27 miles.

Among coal trains in the 1927 STT we find the 10.15pm Aberdare to Salisbury (**SX**), transferring on to the SR. This started with J headlamps as it made its way eastwards along the Vale of Neath line, picking up coal traffic at Mountain Ash, Quaker's Yard East, Nelson & Llancaiach East and Maesycwmmer before stopping to pin down brakes at Sirhowy Jct near Pontllanfraith. Here, or earlier if a full through load had been made up before that point, it changed headcode to H. On Fridays it started at 9pm, and on Mondays at 3am. Having turned south at Sirhowy Jct by a spur on to the LNWR (LMS) Tredegar branch near Ynysddu (over which the GW had running powers), it returned back on to the GW by an end-on junction at Nine Mile Point along the main Western Valley line at Risca. A water stop was taken at Rogerstone before the run through Newport to the Severn Tunnel. The difficulty of sometimes arranging passage through the tunnel is shown by the relatively long time it was allowed to stand, if necessary, at STJ (2.43 to 3.30am). Its run through the Bristol area was again punctuated by calls for braking and avoiding other traffic as it descended Filton Bank to North Somerset Jct, to head east for Bath. It came into the No 3 section of the STT, passing Bathampton at 6.11am, and stopping at Freshford Exchange sidings from 6.23 to 6.55am to allow the early Bristol to Weymouth passenger to pass, and where it was also scheduled to receive its banker for the 1 in 75/66 climb from Westbury to Upton Scudamore; if a banker was not available, the number of wagons was reduced to a single engine load for that incline as indicated in the STT. It continued to Trowbridge where it was held from 7.11 to 7.32am to permit the Oxley to Westbury vacuum freight (the 'Crosser') to pass; then held at Westbury from 7.47 to 8.30am (to pick up traffic if the load permitted); then it ran to the Stop Board outside Salisbury (**P** in the timetable) where between 9.45 and 9.50am brakes were pinned down for the descent into Salisbury, arriving at the yard at 9.57am, a journey of nearly 12 hours if running to time. The Mondays only train was examined at Westbury, but on other days examinations were not marked in the STT.

The corresponding return coal empties (with 2-8-0 loco, H-code) departed Salisbury at 11.15am, stopped dead at Upton Scudamore 12.15 to 12.20pm, Westbury from 12.30 to 12.35, passed Trowbridge at 12.47, then was refuged at Bradford-on-Avon from 12.55 to 1.2pm, after which Bathampton was reached at 1.17pm, and the train passed out of the Section at 1.23pm. It eventually arrived at Aberdare at 11.55pm, again running via Bristol, the Severn Tunnel, Newport, and Risca to the Vale of Neath route. The speeds were quite respectable for heavy loose-coupled trains, given the stops and gradients of 1 in 100 or so, the 24-odd miles from Salisbury to Westbury being covered in rather less than an hour. For comparison, the 7.50am ex-Westbury stopping goods (K-headcode) over the same stretch of line did not arrive at Salisbury until 12.55pm, stopping at least half an hour each to shunt at Warminster (where the trainmen were changed), Heytesbury, Codford, Wylye, Wishford and Wilton. A return empties coal train for Rogerstone left Exeter at 8.25am.

An Up coal train from South Wales passing through Little Somerford on the Badminton cut-off in June 1932. 'Consolidation' No 2880 carries the H-headcode. In the year following, the station nameboard was altered to add 'Change for Malmesbury', a connexion having been made to the branch from Dauntsey on the original Brunel mainline to Great Somerford. *STEAM Swindon*

Up train with coal from the north entering Birmingham Snow Hill hauled by No 4917 *Crosswood Hall*. The lamp positions indicate an H-headcode from the period after 1936. *SLS*

For an example of a North Wales coal train, we find in the 1933 STT an Up J-headcode train leaving Hafod siding for Birkenhead at 12.20pm. Hafod — in the GW Shrewsbury Goods Manager's District — was where the Ruabon Coal & Coke Co Ltd had mines. The train next called at Bersham siding (12.27-1.5); at Bersham — in the GW Liverpool Goods Manager's District — the Broughton & Plas Power Coal Co Ltd had collieries. The train then called at Croesnewydd Jct South Fork (1.11-1.30); passed Wrexham at 1.33; stopping dead at United Colliery Siding to pin down brakes (1.37-1.42); passed Saltney at 2.19, Chester Cutting (2.27-3.0), Hooton South (3.23-3.30) and Blackpool Street mileage yard (3.50-4.3) before terminating at Birkenhead at 4.8pm. This train 'Must leave Bersham punctually with whatever traffic is ready. It must not be kept [held up] for traffic'. The return empties departed Birkenhead at 7.50am and called if required at Grange Lane (7.55-8.20) rather than Blackpool Strett, then at all the other stations listed above to arrive at Hafod at 11.33am.

During World War 2, the supply and distribution of landsale coal was controlled by the Government, and previous patterns of supply by train were disrupted. A sequence of Block Coal Trains for public utility services and house coal was instigated, and run on a regular basis. For example, on Tuesday 9 February 1943, the London area was served from collieries via the LNE (ex-GC) line as follows, all consigned to the local gas companies:

Train	Colliery	Consignee (and number of wagons)
via Banbury Jct		
MD14	Old Silkstone	Oxford (46)
MD18	Manvers	Wallingford (6)
		Newbury (20)
		Burghclere (1)
		Wantage Road (5)
		Basingstoke (16)
MD19	Barnsley Main	Taplow (10)
		Slough (26)
		Windsor (10)
MD27	Elsecar	Bristol & Exeter Divisions (47)
via Northolt Jct		
MD38	Brodsworth	Kensal Green (50)
D10	Harraton	Brentford Dock (50)
D13	Easington	Southall (50)

In that week, Oxford received another 46 wagons on the 10th from Fryston Colliery, and 34 more on the 12th from Bolsover. Kensal Green received another two full deliveries via the LNE that week, and Southall three, whilst most of the others mentioned received another two deliveries of a few wagons. Bolsover also made one delivery to Thame (seven wagons) and Marlow (five) that week. Other block coal arrived via Leamington and Oxford New Jct from collieries on the LMS.

SHIPMENT COAL

Of the 57 million tons of coal raised in South Wales in the peak year 1913 (which was 20% of all UK production), 42 million tons were exported, of which 33 million tons was overseas cargo, five million was steamer bunkers coal, and four million tons 'other' (including distribution by coastal shipping).

In 1855, the first train of steam coal from the Rhondda Valley ran down to Cardiff. The quality of steam coal from the Rhondda was superb, and was in demand by navies all over the world. Before Rhondda coal was raised, coal from Llangennech (near Llanelly) was favoured by steam passenger liners, and Llanelly Docks was the first port to ship to overseas coaling stations in distant places such as India, the Red Sea, Africa and South America.

A great deal of coal from the Midlands and the north was brought to Southampton by train over GWR territory. The broad-gauge branch from Reading to the LSW at Basingstoke opened in 1848, and was intended as a short cut for coal to Southampton. However, one transfer from 'narrow' to broad-gauge wagons at Wolverhampton might have been acceptable, but the need to re-transfer the same loads back from the broad gauge to the narrow at Basingstoke could not be seriously contemplated. Thus, mixed gauge was installed from Wolverhampton, via Didcot and Reading, to Basingstoke between 1852 and 1856; this began the demise of the broad gauge. On 9 January 1886, months before regular trains ran through the new Severn Tunnel, an experimental coal train of 14 wagons ran from Aberdare through the tunnel to Southampton, so that 'coal which had been raised at the colliery in the morning was delivered at the port in the evening of the same day'.

While the GWR owned docks at Briton Ferry (1873), Llanelly (1873) and Porthcawl (1884), it owned no docks in eastern South Wales before the Grouping, nor any mineral lines converging on Cardiff. Nevertheless the GW carried an enormous amount of coal traffic for shipment at Newport, Cardiff, Penarth and Barry Docks

A South Wales to Salisbury coal train, having climbed up from the Severn Tunnel to Filton Jct, passes down through Ashley Hill station on 13 July 1929, before the line was quadrupled. Lamps on the 2-8-0 No 2856 (built in 1918) show the H-headcode of two lamps on the buffer beam, one at the centre and one over the right buffer (ie left buffer when facing the engine), indicating a goods, mineral or ballast train carrying a through load to destination. *SLS*

An as-built straight footplate '31XX' 2-6-2T descends the lower Western Valley at Cross Keys (Risca) in 1909. The 45 or so PO coal wagons, all of which have tip ends facing the Down direction, belong to John Lancaster who owned collieries near Ebbw Vale. The headcode of three lamps across the bufferbeam indicated a J-class through mineral train in the 1903-18 code. The locomotive is in original condition (no bunker extension) and, with the toolbox on the running plate, appears to be fitted with a two-way water pick-up. *GWR*

as ordered by the coal factors. The Taff Vale and Rhymney railways carried coal from the valleys immediately to the north of Cardiff, but the coal traffic passing over the GWR in South Wales came from the collieries situated north-west and north-east of Cardiff, ie from the Llynvi, Ogmore and Garw valleys centred on Tondu and the Eastern and Western valleys above Newport. (The Eastern Valley ran through Cwmbran to Pontypool Road and Blaenavon; the Western Valley ran through Risca to Crumlin, Aberbeeg and Brynamman, with a branch to Ebbw Vale from Aberbeeg, all served by the standard gauge Monmouthshire Railway, with connexions to the Alexandra Docks). Before the conversion of the gauge in South Wales in 1872, coal brought from the Eastern and Western valleys had to be transhipped at Newport to pass on to the broad-gauge GWR. It was said that rail transhipment added perhaps 1s 6d per ton to the price of coal.

In 1874, in addition to the two hoists it already leased within the Bute East dock in Cardiff, the GWR leased a third coal tip at the new Roath Basin, reached by an extension of the line from Long Dyke. There were 20-ton wagon weighbridges at all three hoists.

There was a very large tonnage of Newport coal brought to Cardiff, as it was much used for mixing purposes, since Monmouthshire coal had a greater proportion of volatile matter that permitted quick steam-raising.

At Swansea in 1854, the broad gauge Vale of Neath Railway began shipping out coal at tips in the North Dock. To bypass the 1 in 90 gradient on the SWR at Skewen, a new mixed-gauge route 7¾-miles long (the Swansea & Neath Railway of 1863) was built. In 1864 the Vale of Neath itself was made mixed gauge, thus connecting Swansea with the 'narrow gauge outside world' with connexions via Aberdare and Merthyr.

As new docks were built at Swansea, the GW leased quayage and space from the Swansea Harbour Trust to erect its own hydraulic coal hoists: five at the Prince of Wales dock in 1881; one at the Prince of Wales dock extension in 1898; and, a quintet of three fixed and two moveable in the new King's dock in 1910 (see *GWR Docks & Marine*). After the Grouping there was a great deal of reconstruction of coal wagon storage sidings at the South Wales docks when new hoists were installed that could deal with Pole 20-ton mineral wagons.

With fluctuating elements at both ends of the journey (production at the pits, and whether there were ships ready to load at the docks) there was a need for wagon storage sidings. The TVR had capacity for 12,910 wagons in total, distributed as follows: at Aberdare (587 wagons); Stormstown/Clydach (1,037); Coke Ovens/Pontypridd (248); Penarth Jct/Radyr (2,494); Roath Branch Jct /Cardiff (2,240); Roath Dock/Cardiff (1,270); Canton/Cardiff (503); Penarth North Curve/Cardiff (134); Sloper Road/Cardiff (647); Grangetown/Cardiff (305); Penarth Harbour (847); Llandough/Penarth (978); East Branch/Cardiff (872); Crockherbtown Lower/Cardiff (481); and Crockherbtown Upper/Cardiff (267).

The Rhymney Railway had yards at Aber Jct (Caerphilly), Cherry Orchard (Llanishen) and Crwys (Cardiff, north of its Parade station), accommodating between three and four thousand wagons. The Barry Railway's sidings were largely around its Dock (108 miles in length, including the large yard at Cadoxton), with around 50 miles at other locations. The Alexandra (Newport & South Wales) Docks & Railway had more than 50 miles of sidings surrounding its dock facilities at Newport and the Port Talbot Railway provided around 30 miles of sidings, storing over 50,000 tons of shipment coal.

Locomotive coal for overseas railways formed part of shipment coal exports. Colliers belonging to the French Paris, Lyon & Marseilles Railway regularly docked at Cardiff and the *Railway Magazine* in 1905 reported a contract made by the Irish Great Southern & Western Railway for 120,000 tons of 'large Monmouthshire coals' at 11/- per ton free on board, to be delivered over 12 months; it was the third such contract in successive years.

In peacetime, Admiralty coal was carried by sea to the fleet, but in World War 1, owing to the submarine threat, coal was moved by

land. Pontypool Road was the principal assembly point for all the Admiralty coal trains ('Jellicoe specials') of World War 1, all of which were organised through the Admiralty Coaling Agents, Messrs Mathwin of Cardiff. Since the Highland Railway lines between Perth and Thurso were so crowded, it was decided to send coal to Grangemouth on the Firth of Forth, where it was loaded on to colliers bound for Scapa; large quantities also went to Glasgow, Hull and Newcastle (the naval base at Harwich depended on Yorkshire coal). From South Wales the traffic was carried by timetabled trains that were specially signalled for the whole 375-mile journey via Warrington (where the LNWR took over) on to Carlisle, and to final destination by the Caledonian, GSW or the NB railways. The total journey time was no more than 48 hours. For identification, a distinctive label (marked 'P1', 'P2', 'P3' etc) was placed on the buffer beam of the engine, and on both sides of the brake van. In addition to the usual labelling on the wagons, a 6in by 4in yellow waterproof label was fixed in the centre of each side of the wagons at the collieries, so that Admiralty coal might be easily identified, using the same train code.

According to Pratt, another route was from South Wales to Grimsby (Immingham), via Banbury Jct and the GCR. Trains from the Aberdare district were worked locally to Severn Tunnel Jct by 'large tank engines', followed by 2-8-0 or 2-6-0 tender engine haulage beyond, depending upon the route taken and load specified. There were four routes listed from STJ as far as Banbury:

'A' Gloucester, Honeybourne and Leamington
'B' Badminton, Swindon, Didcot and Kidlington
'C' Hereford, Worcester, Honeybourne, Stratford and Leamington
'D' Gloucester, Swindon, Didcot and Kidlington

Of these, the Severn Tunnel (route 'B') was to be used in preference to 'D'. '28XX' engines were specially permitted to run over route 'A' via Cheltenham, Hatton and Banbury, but with a 20mph restriction over the single line Bearley to Hatton section. In addition, empties were permitted to return via Banbury and Cheltenham. '43XX' 2-6-0s could take a maximum of 45 loaded wagons, and the 2-8-0s 54 wagons, both with assistance where necessary.

Later in World War 1, additional routes for Admiralty coal were used beyond Warrington to relieve congestion, such as via Patricroft (L&Y), Normanton (NE) and Berwick (NB). Early in 1918, an average of 80 special trains, totalling 32,000 tons of coal, were being run every week, yet even this was not enough, so 30 more specials were run via Cardiff and Gloucester, and via the Brecon & Merthyr to Talyllyn, there to pass on to the Cambrian system as far as Gobowen, and by the GWR again to Chester for Warrington. By the end of the war, some 5½ million tons of coal had been conveyed, the Admiralty having hired 16,000 wagons for the purpose from wagon hire companies. Every loaded wagon became an empty wagon on return to the collieries in South Wales, and generated an equivalent number of return trains. Maximum trainloads of empties varied between 45 and 60 for the 2-6-0s, and 60 for the '28XXs'.

The lengths of journey over which shipment coal was hauled from colliery to port on the GW in March 1936 was as follows:

Two Down (towards the coast at Cardiff) coal trains, on the four-track ex-TVR main line south of Pontypridd, pass under Walnut Tree Viaduct (ex-Barry Railway) in 1944. The '56XXs' carry the plain 'GWR' style of painting from Caerphilly Works. The single headlamp and target plate are in opposite positions on the two locos (Target No 5/headlamp on left; headlamp/Target C16 on right). The locomotive on left (No 5683?) is running down boiler first: the rule in the Cardiff Valleys was that Up trains should be boiler first, as on right (No 6676?), so as to cover the firebox crown more easily and reduce priming in the exhaust. The first dozen or so wagons in the train on the right are 20-ton Pole wagons. The brake van of an up train of empties is behind the left hand loco. *Western Mail & Echo*

Distances	Tonnage (Thousands)
Up to 1 mile	Nil
Over 1 mile to 10 miles	88.7
Over 10 miles to 20 miles	847.6
Over 20 miles to 30 miles	368.4
Over 30 miles to 40 miles	44.9
Over 40 miles	21.4

In contrast to landsale coal, the average length of haul was just 15.6 miles as opposed to 48. As with landsale, the GWR's use of its own wagons was relatively minimal, with just 9,210 tons conveyed in that month, compared to approximately 1,372,000 tons in PO wagons. Recall that most of these journeys would be under 'Control Engines' (Chapter 12).

The decline of the South Wales coal export trade after World War 1, from 40 million tons in 1913 to 19 million tons in 1938, continued after World War 2 when it fell to nearer six million tons. In 1913 the port of Cardiff itself shipped over 10½ million tons of coal (and another 11 million tons were shipped from nearby Barry in the same year). That was the zenith. Afterwards there was a steady decline and in 1946 coal shipments were only slightly in excess of one million tons per annum; such a comparatively low figure had not been recorded at Cardiff since 1854.

LOCOMOTIVE COAL

The GWR had owned three mines to provide locomotive coal. They were the Gyfeillon colliery on the TVR in the Lower Rhondda, from where coking coal was sent by sea to Bristol via Cardiff in the 1850s. The pit came into the GW's hands in 1854 owing to the failure of its owner to supply coal to Bristol. It was worked by the GW until 1865 and then sold. Ten years later the Directors determined once more to provide their own coal, so the Cilely colliery at Tonyrefail on

the Ely Valley Railway was bought as a going concern in 1874, and the Avon colliery was sunk by Gooch in 1876 at Abergwynfi. However, it was found better to buy coal in the open market and they were sold off (Cilely in 1896 and Avon in 1912). Among other things, large coal (as wanted by the CME's department) was only about half the output of any pit, so the GW was relieved of having to find a market for the concomitant small coal.

In 1908, the GW spent £773,000 on locomotive coal. Prices rose considerably after World War 1. In an address to the Cardiff Business Club in 1924, Sir Felix Pole mentioned the reductions in shipment coal rates just made by the GW in order to help the depressed coal industry. Had railway dock charges remained at the higher levels of 1920, nearly £7.7 million would have been received by the GW instead of the £4.7 million actually charged for the 37 million tons of coal shipped in 1923. He pointed out that the GW purchased about 2¼ million tons of locomotive coal annually, the cost at the pit being about £3 million. So the GW returned to the coal industry a large part of the money it received for conveying shipment coal to the docks.

Nearly all the locomotive coal consumed per year on the GWR came from the eastern section of the South Wales coalfield, and about 60% went to sheds in England. There was a general scheme of regular distribution organised from the GW's Central Coal Office at Pontypool Road, a certain tonnage being allocated to each locomotive depot. Large depots like Old Oak Common and Bristol received about 3,000 tons weekly, whereas at the other end of the scale coal was transferred direct from the wagon to engine in such places as St Ives, where about 20 tons per week were required — or Brixham, with only one ton weekly. In all, there were about 140 coaling stations on the GWR system. Each morning, those collieries contracted to supply locomotive coal for the GW advised the Pontypool Road Coal Office how many empty locomotive wagons they had on hand and how many more they required for the day's loading. In turn, the collieries were informed of the sheds and

Three lamps all on the buffer beam were the positions for the J-headcode between 1903 and 1918. Armstrong goods No 793, built in 1873 and scrapped in August 1912, heads a Down coal train through Bedminster. There are many N6 10-ton locomotive coal wagons, all with one-sided lever brakes. *LGRP*

2-6-2T No 4516 (built in 1908) seen at Wellington (Somerset) on a Down freight showing the pre-1936 H-headcode. The train carries mostly locomotive coal, with a Macaw B loaded with 'round timber' (logs) in the centre and two other bogie bolster wagons towards the rear. This may be a Bristol-Exeter goods. *Real Photographs*

depots to which loaded wagons were to be sent, including variations from the scheduled tonnage to meet the running of special trains and alterations in booked services. In the Northern Division the hard coals of North Wales and the Midlands were mainly used, but in some cases a limited amount of South Wales coal was specially reserved for express work.

The GW preferred coal stages of the elevated platform type rather than mechanical coaling plants, since coal could be issued much more selectively using hand-filled tip wagons. Large lumps of first-grade coal were reserved for express locomotives, coal of lower quality being given to goods locomotives and shunting engines.

Dedicated locomotive coal trains were timetabled as early as 1866, when the broad-gauge 7am ex-Newtown (Cardiff) took coal and coke for the Locomotive Department at Swindon. By 1876, this train (now retimed at 1.15am) had been joined by the 10.45pm Aberdare to Swindon and London. Other trains conveying only locomotive coal listed in the May 1911 *Marshalling Instructions* included the 12.15am Aberdare to Swindon, and the 8.30pm Aberdare to Bordesley Jct carried coal for the Midland Railway, the 45-wagon load being made up with coal for the GCR if necessary (those wagons coming off at Stratford-upon-Avon to be picked up by the 5.50am Worcester to Leamington goods to be dropped off at Banbury). In the 1930s there were three daily locomotive coal trains from Rogerstone hump yard: one to Old Oak Common at 3.20am; a second to Bristol; and, the third to Plymouth and the West Country at 5.15am. Also Aberdare sent a locomotive coal train to Swindon; Tondu sent one to Exeter; and, Llantrisant to STJ

and Bristol. In the same way that dedicated loaded locomotive coal trains were the exception rather than the rule, there were only a few special empty locomotive coal wagon trains. In 1911, one locomotive coal empties train for the Aberdare district was the 10.10pm Southall to Bristol. There is an entry in the 1927 STT for what is indicated as a locomotive coal train (**MO**, RR) departing Trowbridge at 9.25am, arriving at Bradford West Jct at 9.35am with the instruction 'unload coal at pumping station', and this really meant coal for stationary boilers; this same train may be found in the 1899 STT at a slightly different time. There were other such trains across the system, such as the 9.40am ex-Swindon K-headcode 'engine and three trucks of coal to pumping houses between Purton and Swindon' and the 11.13am Gloucester Old yard to Gloucester Docks. The 1914 STT lists bogie locomotive coal wagons between South Wales and Kingswear on Sundays (see *GWR Goods Wagons*). There has been uncertainty about the purpose of such a large amount of coal; the idea that it was for the local gasworks is doubtful. It was most likely bunkering coal for ships, since Dartmouth/Kingswear had become the principal South Devon coaling port for merchant shipping, and until 1914 coal was the port's principal trade (see *GWR Docks & Marine*).

Most often loaded locomotive coal wagons were sent to marshalling yards from the mines and then ran as part of ordinary goods trains running to marshalling yards near the destination; similarly for returned empty wagons. For example, empties were carried by the H-headcode 60-wagon 3.50pm Old Oak Common to Rogerstone. The train carried other traffic too, and the order of all

2-8-0 No 2840 (built in 1912), heading an H-headcode train of 43 loaded locomotive coal wagons, approaches Swindon from Gloucester on 23 September 1945. The coal stacking grounds and stock shed are out of the picture to the right. Note the bogie Siphon on lower-level tracks to the right, along with four-plank open marked with an X (restricted to the lines of the gas works). *GWR/ D J Hyde collection*

wagons behind the engine on leaving was: Newport (High Street), Cardiff, South and West Wales (all detached at Severn Tunnel Jct) and finally Rogerstone. It was possible that important traffic in vac-fitted vehicles was waiting at Reading West to be taken on by the Rogerstone train. Such vehicles would have been dropped off by the 12.55am Paddington to Gloucester E-headcode goods, or the 9.35pm Paddington to Carmarthen (the 'Welshman'), or the 10.30pm Paddington to Cardiff (the 'South Wales Borderer'). When this happened, the Rogerstone train carried E or even C headlamps from Reading. Feeding trains at Reading West Jct with locomotive coal empties were the 2.35pm Southall to Swindon H, and the 6.25pm Hayes to Reading (ex-Slough). It follows that returned empty locomotive coal wagons could be found in the loose-coupled portions of express C-headcode goods trains. Most locomotive coal wagons were loose coupled, although N2/N4 20T local coal wagons were vac-fitted between 1902 and 1934; it is not known

whether these ever ran in the vac portions of fitted goods trains (see Chapter 8).

In 1917 the GW transferred movement of some of its locomotive coal to sea from land, with 400 tons per week being shipped from South Wales to Hayle in Cornwall which, with an additional 800 tons per week sent to Fremington (near Barnstaple, LSWR), provided not only all the locomotive coal needs between Bodmin and Penzance, but also a third of locomotive coal consumed east of Bodmin to Exeter.

During World War 2, the distribution of locomotive coal was controlled by the Government and was moved in complete train loads (block loads) on specified days each week from one pit (or group of adjacent pits) to a single engine shed in England, or group of sheds on a particular route. In comparison with pre-war distribution, some sheds did not get a due proportion of best quality coal, but had to take what the Ministry of Fuel doled out.

There were similar arrangements for SR locomotive coal in block loads from South Wales to Yeovil and Salisbury. In 1941, it was agreed that locomotive coal for sheds west of Bridgwater (about 4,300 tons per week) would be conveyed coastwise from South Wales to Plymouth. Many large depots had emergency stockpiles of coal. That at Swindon of about 30,000 tons began to be used in January 1944 because of shortages. The block load arrangements continued immediately after the war with 64% of locomotive coal still being carried in this way, and 14% in partial block trains.

ROD No 3031 (formerly No 3056), with an H-headcode, descends from Patchway with a locomotive coal empties towards the Severn Tunnel in 1933. *G H Soole*

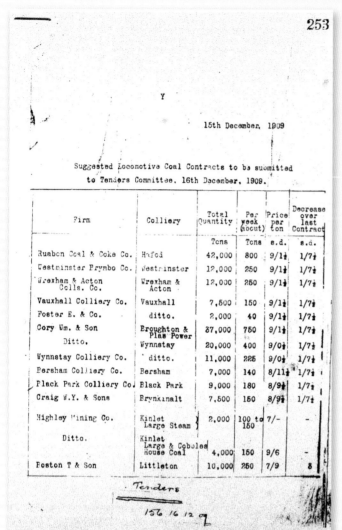

253

Y

15th December, 1909

Suggested Locomotive Coal Contracts to be submitted to Tenders Committee, 16th December, 1909.

Firm	Colliery	Total Quantity	Per week (about)	Price per ton	Decrease over last Contract
		Tons	Tons	s.d.	s.d.
Ruabon Coal & Coke Co.	Hafod	42,000	800	9/1½	1/7½
Westminster Brymbo Co.	Westminster	12,000	250	9/1½	1/7½
Wrexham & Acton Colls. Co.	Wrexham & Acton	12,000	250	9/1½	1/7½
Vauxhall Colliery Co.	Vauxhall	7,500	150	9/1½	1/7½
Foster E. & Co.	ditto.	2,000	40	9/1½	1/7½
Cory Wm. & Son	Broughton & Plas Power	37,000	750	9/1½	1/7½
Ditto.	Wynnstay	20,000	400	9/0½	1/7½
Wynnstay Colliery Co.	ditto.	11,000	225	9/0½	1/7½
Bersham Colliery Co.	Bersham	7,000	140	8/11½	1/7½
Black Park Colliery Co.	Black Park	9,000	180	8/9½	1/7½
Craig W.Y. & Sons	Brynkinalt	7,500	150	8/9½	1/7½
Highley Mining Co.	Kinlet Large Steam	2,000	100 to 150	7/-	-
Ditto.	Kinlet Large & Cobbles House Coal	4,000	150	9/6	-
Boston T & Son	Littleton	10,000	250	7/9	8

Tenders

156 16 12 09

Suggested Locomotive Coal Contracts from North Wales collieries.

G.W.R. LOCOMOTIVE DEPARTMENT - SUPPLY OF COAL UNDER CONTRACTS.

Contractor.	Colliery.	Contract quantity per week Tons.	Week Ended Recd. Tons.	Short Delvy. Tons.	Remarks
LARGE COAL.					
Baldwins Ltd.	Bryn.				
Glyncorrwg Colliery Co.	Blaengwynfi.				
Lysberg Ltd.	Cynon.				
Glenavon Garw Coll's Ltd.	Glynwymmer.				
Penygraig Coal Co.	Penygraig.				
Locket's Merthyr Coll's.	Cilely.				
Lysberg Ltd.	Duffryn Rhondda				
Wm.Cory & Son.	Blaenclydach.				
Wm.Perch & Co.	Windber etc.				
Rickett Smith & Co.	Dyllas.				
Stephenson Clarke & Co.	Nixons.				
Rhymney Iron Co. / Wm.Cory & Son.	Rhymney.				
Tredegar Iron & Coal Co.	Oakdale.				
Burnyeat, Brown & Co.	Sirhowy.				
Ebbw Vale S.I.& C.Co.	Waun Llwyd.				
J.O.Tapson & Co.	North Blaina.				
Stephenson Clarke & Co.	South Griffin.				
Stephenson Clarke & Co.	Six Bells.				
Powells Tillery Co.	Tillery.				
Blaenavon Coal Co.	Blaenavon.				
J.Vipond & Co.	Varteg.				

1914 proforma for 'large coal' supplied under contract for GWR Locomotive Department. *STEAM Swindon*

Unnamed 'Bulldog' No 3419 (formerly No 3709), with the Post-1936 H-headcode, hauls coal empties along the Down relief line in the Thames valley. *SLS*

The coal stage at Whitland, *circa* 1921 pictured with one wooden and two steel locomotive coal wagons. *D J Hyde collection*

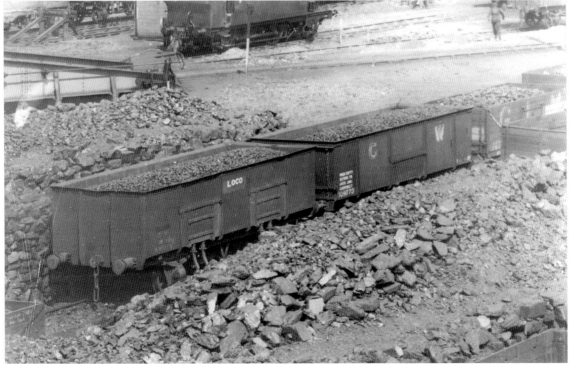

Coal wagons on shed *circa* 1947 among coal stack reserves. Wagon on left is No 83567 from N27; that on the right is No 109770 (a mineral wagon from N23) marked 'When empty return to Aber Junction, Caerphilly'). The GLM private owner wagon to the right has much larger lump coal than the GW wagons. An over-girder locomotive turntable is at the top left. *GWR/ D J Hyde collection*

CHAPTER SIXTEEN

EXPRESS GOODS TRAIN NICKNAMES

IT became the habit of railway staff to give nicknames to 'crack' trains, to simplify their identification in depots and when running. The names were handed down by enginemen, guards and shunters. Nicknames were given to both passenger and express goods services, and a letter from Mr T M Stacey of Tilehurst, Reading, in the August 1904 edition of the *GWR Magazine*, highlighted some of the better-known trains at that time (note that it seems that the same name was given to both Up and Down trains between the same places):

Goods Trains

12.15am from Paddington and 9.50am from New Milford: 'Irishman'

12.35am from Basingstoke and 12.47am from Oxley (Wolverhampton): 'Cherbourg'

3.20am Paddington and 10.40am Didcot: 'Fly'

6.40pm Portobello sidings and 7.30pm Corsham: 'Stoney'

9.35pm Paddington and 1.25am Oxley: 'Old Man'

10.5pm Reading (Low Level) to Oxley sidings: 'Biscuits'

10.15pm Paddington to Plymouth: 'Tip'

10.38pm Paddington and 4.10pm Exeter: 'Pig'

11.35pm Paddington and 8.58pm Bristol: 'Concentrated'

Passenger Trains

12 midnight Paddington to Penzance: 'Owl'

10.50am from Paddington and 10.25am from Penzance: 'Cornishman'

12.25pm Paddington and 8.30am Plymouth: 'Flying Dutchman'

12.15pm Chester and 4.45pm ex-Paddington: 'Afghan'

1.10pm Paddington and 11.25am Plymouth: 'Jubilee'

3pm Paddington and 2.15pm Plymouth: 'Zulu'

3.35pm Paddington and 8.30am Swansea: 'Flying Welshman'

4.55pm Paddington and 11.47am Birkenhead: 'North Star'

Many of these names such as the 'Tip' had been known in broad-gauge days. Some nicknames of goods trains reflected the traffic (biscuits from Huntley & Palmers at Reading; bacon and ham from Exeter; quarried stone from Corsham near the Box Tunnel); the 'Cherbourg' carried traffic between the north and the Continent via Southampton. A few other early nicknames not found elsewhere are given on page 22 of Street.

In 1900 the 'Tip' ran the 115 miles direct to Bristol at 37mph average speed and reached Plymouth at 7.13am in spite of a half-hour stop at Plymouth Laira to detach wagons for Cornwall. Mr Stacey's list did not include all the fast goods trains of the time: the 8.20pm Paddington-Plymouth ran non-stop to Swindon, then called at Taunton, Exeter, Newton Abbot and reached Plymouth at 5.23 am, at an average speed of 34mph. Also, the 9.15pm from Paddington to South Wales ran directly to Swindon at 34mph, then called at Gloucester, before reaching Cardiff at 3.12am where it worked for 50 minutes before heading off to arrive at Swansea before 6am. The 9.15pm was followed from Paddington by the 9.35pm 'Old Man' to Oxford, Birmingham and the north. In those days before the South Lambeth Depot had been opened, many goods trains from Paddington called at Acton (to pick up trucks from Poplar); Westbourne Park (vehicles from Smithfield); and West London Jct (from Chelsea, Brentford, Warwick Road).

The partially-fitted C-headcode trains that began to cover all GW territory in the years up to World War 1 also came to have nicknames. In 1927 the *GWR Magazine* published a letter from the Chief Goods Manager, Mr Elias Ford, in which he reminded readers about these unofficial names, and suggested that there be a competition to name the contemporary vac-fitted express goods trains.

A few nicknames generated by the competition were reincarnations of the names in Mr Stacey's list, but most names were new. Also, whereas in the old scheme Up and Down fast goods trains between the same towns had the same nickname, the C-headcode and Accelerated E-headcode trains in opposite directions were given different names (apart from the Up and Down 'Welshman', between Carmarthen and Paddington). As before, the titles reflected the traffic carried, such as the 'Bacca'

Finding Names for Goods Trains.

AN INTERESTING COMPETITION.

DEAR SIR,—It seems to me that the advantages derived from the practice of applying distinctive names to the Company's express passenger trains would apply also to the naming of the vacuum-fitted express freight trains, about 70 in number.

I believe that certain of these trains have already been given names by the staff concerned in the working of them, as, for instance, the following :—

10.10 p.m. Paddington to Laira, styled " The Tip."

11.40 a.m. Southall to Crewe, styled " The Grocer."

4.0 p.m. Exeter to Penzance, styled " The Flying Pig."

10.5 p.m. Bristol to Paddington, styled " The Cocoa."

It occurs to me that an interesting competition might be arranged, and prizes of £5, £3, and £2, respectively, awarded to competitors who suggest the most suitable names for the trains in question, and perhaps you will be good enough to make the necessary arrangements. The adjudication of the efforts sent in might be left in your hands, aided, if you think fit, by advice from those competent to furnish it.

Yours faithfully,

Paddington.　　　　　　　E. FORD.

THE foregoing letter received from the Chief Goods Manager, makes an interesting appeal to members of the staff who have the gift of finding apt and picturesque names.

Lists of vacuum and accelerated " E " trains are given hereunder. It is not to be supposed that any member of the staff will be sufficiently conversant with the dominant traffics, or other characteristics, to suggest suitable names for all these trains, but some one or more of them will be familiar to a very large number of Great Western employees.

Suggested names may be submitted for any number of the trains, which have been numbered consecutively for the convenience of competitors. All that is necessary is to send to the Editor (a) number of train ; (b) suggested name ; (c) brief statement of reasons for name. Entries may be sent by train or post, and should be addressed to The Editor, Great Western Railway Magazine, Paddington station.

The three best and most suitable names, in order of merit, will be selected by the adjudicators from the entries submitted, and prizes of £5, £3 and £2 awarded to the senders of them. In the event of a winning name being submitted by more than one entrant, the prize in respect of that name will be divided.

Article from 1927 GW Magazine.

VACUUM FREIGHT TRAINS.

Train.	From	To	No.
9.10 p.m.	Paddington	Oxley Sidings	1
9.35 p.m.	,,	Carmarthen Jc.	2
10.10 p.m.	,,	Laira	3
10.30 p.m.	,,	Cardiff	4
11. 5 p.m.	,,	Oxley Sidings	5
11.15 p.m.	,,	Bristol	6
11.35 p.m.	,,	Newton-Abbot	7
12. 5 a.m.	,,	Worcester	8
12.15 a.m.	,,	Fishguard Harbour	9
9.32 p.m.	Old Oak Common	Penzance	10
1. 0 a.m.	Acton	Bristol	11
9.25 p.m.	,,	Llanelly	12
12.15 a.m.	Park Royal	Stourbridge Jc.	13
11.40 a.m.	Southall	Crewe	14
4.30 p.m.	,,	Oxley Sidings	15
9.35 p.m.	Basingstoke	,,	16
8.20 p.m.	Kidderminster	Paddington	33
5.30 p.m.	Newton Abbot	,,	34
11. 0 p.m.	Hockley	,,	35
8.20 p.m.	Birkenhead	,,	36
2.50 p.m.	Penzance	,,	37
7.45 p.m.	Manchester	Bristol	38
8.42 p.m.	,,	Oxley Sidings	39
1.30 a.m.	Oxley Sidings	Basingstoke	40
9.15 p.m.	,,	Bristol	41
9. 5 p.m.	Birkenhead	Cardiff	42
10.50 p.m.	,,	Bordesley Jc.	43

Train.	From.	To.	No.
4.20 a.m.	Westbury	Oxley Sidings	17
12.25 a.m.	Bristol	Carmarthen Jc.	18
6.50 p.m.	Westbury	Birkenhead	19
7.35 p.m.	,,	Manchester	20
10.15 p.m.	,,	Penzance	21
10.50 p.m.	,,	Pontypool Rd.	22
9.45 p.m.	Cardiff	Saltney	23
6.45 p.m.	Worcester	Cardiff	24
8.35 p.m.	,,	Crewe	25
9.10 p.m.	Bordesley Jc.	Birkenhead	26
10.10 p.m.	,,	Swansea	27
2.45 a.m.	Oxley Sidings	Birkenhead	28
4.25 p.m.	Cardiff	Hanwell Bridge Sidings	29
4. 5 p.m.	Exeter	Old Oak Common	30
7.40 p.m.	Bristol	Paddington	31
10. 5 p.m.	,,	,,	32
12.30 a.m.	Paddington	Bristol	53
8.35 p.m.	Carmarthen	,,	54
3.40 a.m.	Banbury Jc.	,,	55

PLYMOUTH DIVISION.

Train.	From.	To.	No.
7.30 p.m.	Penzance	Plymouth	56
4. 5 p.m.	Swindon	Tavistock Jc.	57
10.55 p.m.	Bristol	Laira	58
10.30 p.m.	Reading	,,	59
5.45 a.m.	Pontypool Rd.	,,	60

NEWPORT DIVISION.

11.5 a.m.	Exeter	Pontypool Rd.	61

CARDIFF DIVISION.

7.40 p.m.	Acton	Cardiff S.X.	62

SWANSEA DIVISION.

12.55 a.m.	Cardiff	Swansea	63

BIRMINGHAM DIVISION.

10.5 p.m.	East Depot	Leamington	64
9.5 p.m.	Park Royal	Stourbridge Jc.	65
9.30 p.m.	Neath	Bordesley	66

CHESTER DIVISION.

4.0 a.m.	Oxley Sidings	Crewe	67
11.45 p.m.	Birkenhead	Oswestry	68
12.45 a.m.	Oxley	Birkenhead	69

ACCELERATED " E " FREIGHT TRAINS.

LONDON DIVISION.

7.50 p.m.	Gloucester	Paddington	44
8.5 p.m.	Oxley Sidings	,,	45
7.30 p.m.	Carmarthen	,,	46
11.30 p.m.	Cardiff	,,	47
7.10 p.m.	Victoria Basin	Basingstoke	48

BRISTOL DIVISION.

8.15 p.m.	Paddington	Bristol	49
1.15 a.m.	Penzance	,, (W. Dpt.)	50
10.15 p.m.	Oxley	Westbury S.X.	51
10.50 p.m.	Paddington	Weymouth	52

EXPRESS VACUUM AND ACCELERATED "E" FREIGHT TRAINS

Named goods trains.

Time	From	To	Name
1.05am	Acton	Bristol	The High Flyer
7.40pm	"	Cardiff	The Early Bird
9.25pm	"	Llanelly	The Leek
3.40am	Banbury Jc	Bristol	The Competitor
2.10am	Basingstoke	Wolverhampton	The Cherbourg
9.35pm	"	"	The BBC (Basingstoke, Birmingham, Crewe)
3.55pm	Birkenhead	Smithfield	The Meat
6.05pm	"	Pontypool Road	The Feeder
8.20pm	"	Paddington	The General
9.05pm	"	Cardiff	The Mersey
10.50pm	"	Bordesley Jc	The Birmingham Market
11.35pm	"	Oswestry	The Cambrian Pioneer
11.00pm	Birmingham	Paddington	The Pedlar
9.10pm	Bordesley Jc	Birkenhead	The Shipper
10.10pm	"	Swansea	The Hardware
6.50pm	Bristol	Birkenhead	The Farmer's boy
7.40pm	"	Paddington	The "Bacca"
9.20pm	"	Wolverhampton	The Western Docker
10.05pm	"	Leamington	Spa
10.05pm	"	Paddington	The Cocoa
10.55pm	"	Laira	The Drake
12.25am	"	Carmarthen Jc	The Bristolian
3.50pm	Cardiff	Hanwell Br. Sdgs	The Stock
9.45pm	"	Saltney	The Spud
11.10pm	"	Paddington	The Ironmonger
12.55am	"	Swansea	Port to Port
7.30pm	Carmarthen	Paddington	The Up Welshman
8.35pm	"	Bristol	The Open
11.00am	Exeter	Pontypool Road	The Ponty
4.00pm	"	Old Oak Common	The Flying Pig
12.05am	Gloucester	Cardiff	The Bacon
7.50pm	"	Paddington	The Cotswold
11.00pm	Handsworth	Acton	The Queen's Head
8.20pm	Kidderminster	Paddington	The Carpet
7.45pm	Manchester	Bristol	The "Mon"
8.42pm	"	Wolverhampton	The Early Riser
4.58pm	Marazion	Bristol	The Tre Pol and Pen Flier
10.25pm	Margam	Bordesley	The Tinman
5.30pm	Newton Abbot	Paddington	The Hackney
9.32pm	Old Oak Common	Penzance	The Cornishman
8.05pm	Paddington	Bristol	The Shopper
9.10pm	"	Birkenhead	Northern Flash
9.35pm	"	Carmarthen Jc	The Welshman
10.10pm	"	Laira	The Tamar
10.30pm	"	Cardiff	South Wales Borderer
10.50pm	"	Weymouth	The Jersey
11.05pm	"	Wolverhampton	The Hampton
11.15pm	"	Bristol	The Western General
11.35pm	"	Newton Abbot	The Devonshireman
12.05am	"	Worcester	The Sauce
12.15am	"	Fishguard	Irishman
12.30am	"	Bristol	The Mopper Up
12.10am	Park Royal	Stourbridge Jc	The Stour
2.50pm	Penzance	Paddington	The Searchlight
7.20pm	"	Plymouth	The Pasty
5.40am	Pontypool Road	Newton Abbot	The Laira
10.30pm	Reading	Laira	The Biscuit
11.40am	Southall	Crewe	The Grocer
3.50pm	Swindon	Tavistock Jc	The Rasher
7.10pm	Victoria Basin	Basingstoke	The Cargo
4.20am	Westbury	Wolverhampton	The Moonraker
7.35pm	"	Manchester	The Lancashire Lad
9.55pm	"	Penzance	Western Flash
10.50pm	"	Pontypool Road	The Northern
7.22pm	West Drayton	Wolverhampton	The Drayton
6.35pm	Weymouth	Paddington	The Up Jersey
1.30am	Wolverhampton	Basingstoke	The Southern Docker
2.10am	"	"	The Southerner
2.45am	"	Birkenhead	The Northern Docker
4.00am	"	Crewe	The Northern Exchange
8.15pm	"	Paddington	The Racer
10.15pm	"	Westbury	The Crosser
12.45am	"	Birkenhead	The Flying Skipper
6.45pm	Worcester	Cardiff	The Worcester Fruit
8.35pm	"	Crewe	The "Sparagras"

and the 'Cocoa' from Bristol, and the 'Meat' from Birkenhead. After the Grouping, the GWR had made special efforts to encourage cattle breeders in Canada, and buyers in Britain, to use Cardiff docks: thus the 3.50pm Cardiff to Hanwell Bridge sidings C-headcode goods was nicknamed the 'Stock'. Cardiff was also the principal British port for importing potatoes, and the 9.45pm Cardiff to Saltney (Chester) express goods train was nicknamed the 'Spud'. The choice of 'Moonraker' for the Westbury–Wolverhampton was an inspired reference to the nickname for Wiltshire people, who were supposed to have tried to rake out of a pond the reflection of the moon, thinking it was a cheese. The 'Mopper Up' cleared the last loads for Bristol from Paddington Goods.

The 'names' did not cover all fast goods traffic: among others, the C-headcode 11.0pm Reading to Oxley and 3.50pm Fishguard to Paddington were omitted. Of course vacuum trains introduced after 1927 are not in the list. The nicknames were never used in the STTs. Even so the title 'Irish Goods' (that was not a nickname) is used in the 1933 STT column headings for both the 3.50pm Fishguard Harbour-Paddington (train No 6 in the 1933 STT) and the 12.15am Paddington-Fishguard Harbour. The timings of named trains may have changed after 1927 and may have continued to change in later years as the GW speeded up services (for examples, see the numbering of trains given in Chapter 11).

Most nicknamed goods trains in both the earlier and later lists ran at night. Those that ran during normal daytime hours usually formed quick connecting links with other overnight services. Departures of express freight trains from Paddington Goods were grouped between about 8pm and 1am, with trains for furthest destinations departing earliest. Incoming goods trains to Paddington arrived between about 2am and 7am at Lords Hill Bridge, where the train engine was detached and sent to shed. A pilot engine then propelled vehicles into the shed to be berthed at appropriate platforms.

CHAPTER SEVENTEEN

20th CENTURY GW GOODS TRAINS

Different Classification Trains

EXAMPLES of goods trains from different classes as listed in various STTs are now considered, with examples of their running, and how they fitted into traffic patterns. The list is chronological and consequently not completely alphabetic because Accelerated-E trains existed before the latter were removed to the D classification in 1936 that previously did not concern goods trains. All the following descriptions of the different headcode trains should be viewed as a snapshot of GW goods operations between the wars. The representative examples given in what follows are taken from STTs for different years, but the arrangements for a given train would not have varied much in other years, except perhaps for slight differences in timings where the GW speeded up services, thereby permitting later departures/earlier arrivals of what was essentially the same train. Examples of differences in timing are occasionally given.

Before World War 1, the F-headcode (see Chapter 2) was used mostly for middle distance runs, and not generally for trains between extremities of the system. However, the H code was also used for some non-stop local runs where the load justified it, such as between Acton and Smithfield. Heavy, long-distance mineral trains usually ran with the H-headcode with a '28XX' or 'Aberdare' 2-6-0. Once a full load had been taken on, the train would run through, apart from intermediate calls for water and/or train examination. By far the most numerous classes of goods train were J and K, with the former involving longer distance journeys with intermediate calls. A few K-headcode trains had limited stops after an initial area had been served and these maintained the K lamps for a clear run, though they were still, of course, of lowest priority.

It might be expected that a given loaded wagon, once attached to a fast overnight through train (either where the train started, or having been picked up *en route*), would stay in that train through to destination. However, this was not always the case. Vehicles intended for far-away places had to be kept on the move, otherwise they would not arrive first thing next morning at their destination. But owing to limitations on train length, gradients etc, it was not feasible to keep adding wagons to trains for the furthest destinations at all stops on a journey. Consequently when long-distance trains picked up *en route*, wagons for nearer destinations were dropped off at an intermediate point to make space in the train. Because their destinations were fewer miles away, conveyance by a later train from the intermediate place still got the dropped-off wagons to destination sufficiently early. Particular arrangements about dropping off vehicles at one or more intermediate stations were based on traffic patterns accumulated over many years, and depended on how many wagons it was expected to pick up *en route*.

C-HEADCODE: VACUUM-FITTED EXPRESS GOODS TRAINS

Ventilated and/or insulated vacuum-fitted vehicles for fruit, meat, fish and other perishable traffic were built by the GW from the 1880s, and a limited number of fully-fitted 30-40 wagon trains hauled by passenger locomotives began to be run by the GW from that time, such as meat trains from Birkenhead that ran non-stop the 86 miles to Oxley and the subsequent 139 miles to Acton, thence over the Metropolitan Railway to Smithfield. The four-wheel vans intended for fast running were conspicuous by their being designed with carriage buffers, Mansell wheels, screw couplings and tail lamp irons. They were often attached to passenger trains in ones and twos. Even so, it is probable that they also ran in contemporary loose-coupled express or fast merchandise goods trains and, when formed next to the locomotive, the braking power for the train was increased thus permitting, in theory, faster speeds. To assess the idea of providing a vacuum-fitted merchandise goods service (not just for perishables), a special trial trip was undertaken on Sunday 11 December 1904, that left Acton at 7am and returned from Bristol East depot at 12.45pm. The engine was the almost brand-new 4-4-0 No 3480 *County of Stafford,* (renumbered 3837 in 1912) of Westbourne Park locomotive shed, which hauled the Down train consisting of 22 covered goods vans, nine meat vans, two fruit

The 'Grocer': the 11.40pm Southall-Crewe, C-headcode partially-fitted express goods. The first two iron mink ventilated vans are vac-fitted and have axlebox tiebars to take the strain of more powerful braking than that of loose-coupled trains. Only 11 iron minks had this equipment following their conversion in 1915 to cordite paste vans (see *GWR Goods Wagons*). Returned to ordinary traffic in March 1919, they were allocated in 1927 to Lyons tea traffic and branded 'Return to Greenford', hence their appearance in this train. Curiously the 'Grocer' did not have a train number in the STT. *Moore postcard*

Another view of the 'Grocer', this time hauled by No 4088 *Dartmouth Castle*. The photograph was taken just after the Grouping: the second van still has 25in large GW lettering, the upper lamp iron is still at the chimney rather than the smokebox, and the tender is the original small type (but no locomotive bogie brakes). The three iron minks (fourth to sixth in the train) are from a group of 11 ex-World War 1 cordite paste wagons allocated to Lyons tea traffic in 1927. *D J Hyde collection*

Marshalling Instructions for Through and Important Local Freight Trains—continued.

Formation and Headmarks.	Engine Group.	Traffic Attached en Route.		REMARKS.
		At	To be formed	

WESTBURY—continued.
4.20 a.m. Oxley Sidings "C"
No. 315.
Engine.
●Oxford (CR)
Oxley Sidings vac.
Hockley "
†Bordesley Junction "
Banbury Junction "
Banbury Junction non vac.
†Bordesley Junction "
Hockley "
Oxley Sidings "
	D	†Tyseley C.S.
		Handsworth
			} At one shunt.	Carries "E" Headmarks from Bordesley Junction.
				Load 64 wagons of class 3 traffic or equivalent when necessary, assisted up Melksham and Dauntsey Banks.
				May convey Cornish cattle and perishable traffic for the Gloucester line to Swindon for 12.55 a.m. ex Paddington.
				Feeding trains at Westbury :—
				  2.50 p.m. Penzance. 5.15 p.m. Salisbury.
				  4.27 p.m. Dulcot Siding. 3.35 p.m. Weymouth.
				  11.48 a.m. Frome. 6.40 p.m. Weymouth.
				  6. 0 p.m. East Depot. *5. 0 p.m. Exeter.
				  7. 3 p.m. Castle Cary. ‡8.25 p.m. Swindon.
				  12.25 a.m. Salisbury. 1.10 a.m. Salisbury.
				* Traffic for Banbury Junction and North thereof, in oil box wagons, to be detached at Westbury.
				‡ Important Northern traffic ex Melksham.
				● at Oxford to detach cattle or fruit and vegetable traffic only.
				† Exchange is usually made at Tyseley C.S. from which point traffic is worked to Moor St. by Moor St. shunting engine.
				Connecting trains at Oxley Sidings :—
				  7.20 p.m. Oxley Sidings to Chester.
				  12.0 noon (RR) Oxley Sidings to Crewe.
				Conveys :—
				  P.T. 99 Bridport to Hockley from Westbury to Hockley.
				  P.T. 374 Kingswear to Hockley (M.W.F.) from Westbury to Hockley.
				  P.T. 383 Langport West to Hockley from Westbury to Hockley.
				  P.T. 805 Westbury to Hockley from Westbury to Hockley.

5.0 a.m. to Ludgershall "K"
Local "pick up"
	A	Local Stations		Feeding trains at Westbury :—
				  7.40 p.m. East Depot to Salisbury. 5.0 p.m. Exeter to Swindon.
				  10.35 a.m. East Depot to Salisbury.
				Conveys Burbage traffic to Patney and Chirton on Mondays for 4.30 a.m. East Depot to Reading.
				Connecting train at Patney and Chirton :—4.30 a.m. (MO) East Depot to Reading West Jct.
				Connecting trains at Savernake :—5.55 a.m. Holt Junction to Didcot (MX).
				                 11.10 a.m. ex Savernake (MO).
				Feeding train at Savernake :—1.45 a.m. Reading to Bristol.
				Conveys :—S.T. 794 Westbury to Reading from Westbury to Patney.

AYLESBURY.
9.25 p.m. SX Paddington "E"
9.37 p.m. SO
Engine
Princes Risboro'
High Wycombe
‖Bourne End (CR)
*Maidenhead
Shorts Branch Stations
†Old Oak Common
●Acton
Paddington
	C
	4-4-2
	T
		¶Princes Risboro'
		
		§Saunderton
		 West Wycombe
		
		‡High Wycombe South
		
		Maidenhead
		
		Slough CR
		
		West Drayton
			With wagons on train.
			
			At one shunt.
			" "
			Wagons to stand as under :—
			Old Oak Common.
			Acton.
			Paddington.
			Reading West Junct.
			Reading.
			South Wales.
			Bristol.
			
			With wagons on train.
			Wagons to stand as under :—
			Down Line.
			Old Oak Common.
			Acton.
			Paddington.
			
			In reverse order at one shunt.
			
			With wagons on train.
			
			" " "
				¶ In the event of Princes Risborough being congested and unable to complete the work by 10.20 p.m., the traffic to be picked up at one shunt and the remainder of the necessary shunting undertaken by High Wycombe.
				On Wednesdays efforts must be made at Aylesbury to load cattle traffic in such a manner as will admit of the train being properly formed and dispatched punctually.
				Cattle traffic for stations between High Wycombe and Maidenhead, other than Marlow, must be detached at Princes Risborough or High Wycombe for the 11.30 p.m. Oxford to Taplow.
				Feeding train at Princes Risborough :—6.20 p.m. Auto ex Thame.
				Connecting train at Princes Risboro' :—1.10 a.m. Old Oak Common to Bordesley Jc.
				§ Calls for S.T. work and important goods only.
				† Also calls at High Wycombe North for cattle traffic only.
				Connecting train at High Wycombe :—11.30 p.m. Oxford to Taplow.
				‖ To detach Marlow cattle traffic only.
				* Detach Down Line wagons at Maidenhead. Bristol and South Wales traffic to connect with 1.25 a.m. ex Old Oak Common.
				Feeding train at Maidenhead :—8.17 p.m. ex Loudwater.
				Connecting trains at Maidenhead :—
				  3.10 a.m. Acton to Reading, 3.30 a.m. Old Oak Common to Leamington.
				† Detach Old Oak Common wagons at West Drayton for 10.40 p.m. ex Reading
				Feeding trains at West Drayton :— [West Junction.
				  5.55 p.m. ex Staines. 7.55 p.m. ex Uxbridge.
				Connecting trains at Acton :—4.15 a.m. Acton to Victoria and Albert.
				  5.15 a.m. Acton to St. Pancras and Tilbury Line.
				  6. 0 a.m. Acton to Temple Mills. 6.30 a.m. Acton to Poplar.
				  3.45 a.m. Acton to Smithfield. 4.10 a.m. Acton to Old Oak Common.
				  5.5 a.m. or 7.25 a.m. Acton to South Lambeth.
				● When Acton traffic is detached at Hanwell Bridge Sidings, Smithfield traffic must be taken through to Portobello Up Side, to be picked up by the 4.35 a.m. Acton to Smithfield.
				Train conveys hay and straw traffic consigned to Westbourne Park, which must be kept separate from other Acton and Old Oak Common wagons on train, and must leave Maidenhead between Acton and Old Oak Common wagons.
				If traffic detached Acton, to connect with 4.10 a.m. pilot thence to Old Oak Common and 6.25 a.m. Old Oak Common to Portobello.
				If traffic detached short of Acton, must be worked into Old Oak Common by 6.55 p.m. ex Swindon or 10.40 p.m. ex Reading (extended from Hanwell Bridge Sidings) to connect with 6.25 a.m. to Portobello.
				If connection with 6.25 a.m. ex Old Oak Common not made, Acton Control to arrange work traffic specially to arrive not later than 10.0 a.m.
				Conveys :—
				  S.T. 31 Aylesbury to Paddington from Aylesbury to Paddington.
				  S.T. 32 Aylesbury to Reading from Aylesbury to High Wycombe.
				  P.T. 414 Loudwater to Paddington from Maidenhead to Paddington.
				  P.T. 528 Oxford to Paddington (via Thame) from Princes Risborough to Padd'n.
				  P.T. 720 Staines to Paddington from West Drayton to Paddington.

Marshalling Instructions for Through and Important Local Freight Trains—continued.

Formation and Headmarks.	Engine Group.	Traffic Attached en Route. At	Traffic Attached en Route. To be formed	REMARKS.
BRENTFORD. 6.40 p.m. to Reading "E" Engine Westbury & West of England Reading proper Taplow * Oil box Wagons for 9.35 p.m. Basingstoke Oil box Wagons for 9.35 p.m. and 10.30 p.m. Paddington Reading West Junct. (rough traffic)	A	Southall	Traffic to stand in two roads and to be picked up in two shunts in positions indicated :— *1st Road— Taplow. Reading proper. Westbury and West of England. Urgents for Basingstoke Branch. Oil box Wagons for 9.35 p.m. Basingstoke. †2nd Road— Oil box Wagons for 9.35 p.m. and 10.30 p.m. trains ex Paddington. Reading West Junct. (rough traffic).	Load 60 wagons to Taplow. Connecting trains at Taplow :— 4.0 a.m. Slough to Oxford. Feeding train at Taplow for S.T. :— 2.10 p.m. Reading West Junction to Hayes. Connecting trains at Reading West Junction :— 7.10 p.m. Victoria Basin to Basingstoke. 9.35 p.m. Basingstoke to Oxley 9.35 p.m. Paddington to Carmarthen Junction 10.30 p.m. Paddington to Cardiff ‡10.30 p.m. Reading Low Level to Laira 12.55 a.m. Paddington to Gloucester 1.30 a.m. Reading West Junction to Oxley Sidings 2.20 a.m. Basingstoke to Oxley. 2. 5 a.m. Park Royal to Severn Tunnel Junction 1.45 a.m. Reading West Junction to Bristol 7.55 p.m. Acton to Severn Tunnel Junction (SO) 11.55 p.m. Basingstoke to Oxley Sidings (SO) 11.35 p.m. Reading West Jct. to Oxley Sidings (SO). 10.30 p.m. Reading L.L. connects at Newbury with 10.50 p.m. Paddington to Weymouth and 11.35 p.m. Paddington to Newton Abbot. ‡ If West of England traffic is loaded in Grease Box Vehicles same will work throughout from Reading on 10.30 p.m. thence to Laira. § Reading proper and West of England traffic to be picked up with wagons on train when detaching Taplow wagons. Second pick up to be made between traffic for 9.35 p.m. ex Basingstoke and South Wales wagons for 9.35 p.m. and 10.30 p.m. trains ex Paddington.
		§ Taplow	With wagons on train.	Conveys :— P.T. 423 Maidenhead to Oxford from Taplow to Reading West Junction.
CRIMEA SIDINGS. 2.10 a.m. MX Bordesley Jct. F ' .. Engine †Gerrards Cross †Warwick Leamington †Banbury Banbury Junction †Solihull Bordesley Junction	D	Park Royal Princes Risboro' Banbury Junction Leamington	With wagons on train. At one shunt. In reverse order, at one shunt. At one shunt.	Feeding trains at Park Royal :— 11.20 p.m. Acton 8.33 p.m. Southall. 6. 0 p.m. ex Greenford. 9.30 p.m. Smithfield. 7.30 p.m. Paddington and 8.30 p.m. South Lambeth. 12.45 a.m. Paddington. † To detach only. Connecting trains at Bordesley Junction :— 5.25 a.m. Didcot to Oxley Sidings. 11.10 a.m. Bordesley Junction to Stourbridge Junction.

Remarks bracketed: Must consist of Oil Box Vehicles. May consist of Grease Box Vehicles.

The 'Up Jersey': the 6.35pm ex-Weymouth to Paddington, photographed in the early 1930s. The '43XX' has about 30 wagons on, including two GW Open B vac-fitted wagons with erected sheet supporters and tarpaulins. *LGRP*

vans, three open goods wagons, two carriage trucks and the recently-built Diagram AA2 brake van No 56898, making 31 loaded and eight empties. The return trip comprised 12 covered vans, 12 meat vans, one carriage truck, 15 open goods and the same brake van, being 35 loaded and six empties. Another special trial was run the following Sunday, using the same engine and approximately the same loads.

This experience led to the GWR's idea of 'partially-fitted' express goods trains for general merchandise traffic that ran at average speeds up to 45mph. When introduced, only GW-oil-

No 6853 *Morehampton Grange* heads a C-headcode freight. Shirtbutton on tender. Note that the fitted wagons attached next to the engine are all opens. *D J Hyde collection*

A C-headcode express goods negotiates the reverse curves at Teignmouth just at nationalisation, headed by the last 'Bulldog' in service. 'Bird' class 4-4-0 No 3451 *Pelican* (formerly No 3741) was built in 1910 and condemned in April 1951. *SLS*

An Up freight seen at Angarrack (near Hayle) in May 1940. The locomotive is No 5034 *Corfe Castle*. Note super-elevation of the track. *Railway Magazine*

axlebox vehicles (fitted and unfitted) were permitted and a minimum of a quarter of the wagons had to be vacuum-fitted and connected to the locomotive. (Why only partially-fitted rather than fully-fitted is explained in Chapter 8, where also are given the rules for the proportion of fitted vehicles required that changed over the years.) The first regular vacuum service was introduced on 9 January 1905, running non-stop from Acton (12.28am) to Bristol. The train conveyed vacuum wagons for Temple Meads and Lawrence Hill, worked into Acton from Smithfield (via Paddington) and Poplar. The return was the 8.50pm Temple Meads to Acton and Paddington, again formed with suitable vacuum and other stock. The C-headcode was allotted for this merchandise train; the headcode was already in use for fully-fitted fish, meat and perishables trains.

At a meeting of Divisional Superintendents in March 1905, the introduction of a similar 'fast goods' service to and from

PRIVATE AND NOT FOR PUBLICATION.

GREAT WESTERN RAILWAY.

Circular No. F. 3309A 36.
,, ,, X. 13/7A 36.

PADDINGTON STATION,
LONDON, W.
30th May, 1916.

GENERAL INSTRUCTIONS.
(EUROPEAN WAR.)

CONVEYANCE OF GREASE AXLE BOX WAGONS ON FREIGHT TRAINS.

Numerous cases have occurred where grease axle box wagons containing ammunition, explosives and other traffic have been attached to express freight trains of high speeds and running long distances without stopping, which have had to be detached *en route* through the grease axle boxes becoming hot, and in some cases by the loads having shifted.

It has, therefore, become imperative that only G.W. oil axle box wagons must be attached to trains classified as completely or partially fitted vacuum trains.

To comply with this instruction the present vacuum freight services have been revised, and G.W. oil axle box wagons only must be conveyed by the limited number of trains shown in Schedule " A."

Any grease axle box wagons and Foreign Companies **oil axle box wagons** must work on the trains enumerated in Schedule " B," and on all lower grade trains provided they do not run more than 50 miles without examination.

A printed notice (No. 26), showing the revised timing of the services commencing Wednesday, May 31st, 1916, has been issued.

Conveyance of Explosives.

With reference to the instruction contained in Joint Circular F.3509 A.5. X.13/7 A.5 of April 30th, 1915, as to conveyance of shells and ammunition, Great Western Company's wagons provided with oil axle boxes and containing explosives may be run upon vacuum-fitted trains, provided the load does not exceed 7 tons, and is evenly distributed over the floor of the wagon. To ensure the even distribution of the load Station Agents must get into touch with all Government depots and Contractors forwarding explosives who perform the loading, to instruct their people that this rule must be carried out.

Any wagons containing explosives where the weight of the load exceeds 7 tons must not be forwarded by the trains classified as Vacuum Freight trains (Schedule " A.")

IT IS OF THE UTMOST IMPORTANCE THAT THESE INSTRUCTIONS BE RIGIDLY ADHERED TO.

2

SCHEDULE "A."
VACUUM FITTED "C" HEAD MARK FREIGHT TRAINS.

The instructions on page 91 of the General Appendix showing the conditions under which grease axle box and Foreign Companies' oil axle box wagons are conveyed on Vacuum Freight trains are hereby revised to the extent that the trains shown in this schedule must not in future convey any such wagons, but must be strictly confined to Great Western Company's oil axle box wagons.

UP.	DOWN.
1.30 p.m. Fishguard to Cardiff	7. 5 p.m. Southall to Oxley Sidings
3.20 p.m. Penzance to Paddington	7.48 p.m. Bristol to Manchester
8.10 p.m. Cannock Road to Paddington	7.50 p.m. Worcester to Manchester
8.15 p.m. Birkenhead to Paddington	9.35 p.m. Paddington to Oxley Sidings
8.25 p.m. Manchester to Bristol	9.55 p.m. Paddington to Llanelly
9.30 p.m. Taunton to Paddington	10.15 p.m. Paddington to Laira
10. 0 p.m. Cardiff to Paddington	10.30 p.m. Reading to Oxley Sidings
10.20 p.m. Bristol to Paddington	12. 5 a.m. Paddington to Fishguard
	12.10 a.m. Paddington to Worcester
	12.35 a.m. Acton to Bristol
	2.10 a.m. Oxley Sidings to Crewe

SCHEDULE "B."
TRAINS RECLASSIFIED AS "E" HEAD MARK FREIGHT TRAINS WHICH CAN CONVEY GREASE AXLE BOX WAGONS AND FOREIGN COMPANIES' OIL AXLE BOX WAGONS.

UP.	DOWN.
2.50 p.m. St. Austell to Laira	12.55 p.m. Exeter to Pontypool Road
6. 5 p.m. Newton Abbot to Paddington	9.10 p.m. Bristol to Oxley Sidings
6.10 p.m. Gloucester to Paddington	9.20 p.m. Worcester to Crewe
6.10 p.m. Swansea to Bordesley Jc.	9.32 p.m. Acton to Cardiff
6.15 p.m. Taunton to Paddington	10.15 p.m. Bordesley Jc. to Neath
6.15 p.m. Toddington to Crewe "R.R."	10.38 p.m. Paddington to Cardiff
7.40 p.m. Carmarthen Jc. to Bristol	10.48 p.m. Paddington to Newton Abbot
8.10 p.m. Evesham to Pontypool Rd. "R.R."	11. 5 p.m. Bristol to Carmarthen Jc.
9. 5 p.m. Birkenhead to Cardiff	11. 5 p.m. Paddington to Weymouth
9.40 p.m. Llandilo to Paddington	11.10 p.m. Cardiff to Manchester
11. 0 p.m. Oxley Sidings to Bristol	11.15 p.m. Paddington to Victoria Basin
11.20 p.m. Birkenhead to Hockley	11.35 p.m. Paddington to Exeter
11.30 p.m. Handsworth to Paddington	11.35 p.m. Sth. Lambeth to Sev. Tun. Jc.
12.10 a.m. Cardiff to Paddington	2.10 a.m. Cardiff to Swansea
12.55 a.m. Carmarthen Jc. to Bristol	2.40 a.m. Oxley Sidings to Birkenhead
2.30 a.m. Oxley Sidings to Basingstoke	3. 0 a.m. Basingstoke to Oxley Sidings
	5. 5 a.m. Reading to Hockley
	7.30 a.m. Oxley Sidings to Crewe M.O.

C. ALDINGTON,
Superintendent of the Line.

C. A. ROBERTS,
Chief Goods Manager.

Mr. ....

" .... Station.

Birmingham and the north was discussed. It was not possible to match the Bristol service in speed immediately, 'for want of vacuum-fitted Goods Stock', although some 'twelve large Box Vans per week would be turned out from Swindon Shops when approval was given'. Two trains each way were suggested, the 9.35pm from Paddington to Birkenhead, and 11.5pm to Wolverhampton, returning by a 7pm Birkenhead and a 9.20pm Wolverhampton. The services were introduced on 1 May 1905 'with very satisfactory results, the trains keeping very good time'.

Such was the demand for fitted vehicles for the new fast freights that Wagon Lot 450 was issued at Swindon in September 1904 to equip various existing wagons with the vacuum-brake. Hence many opens and vans were quickly converted, some having only just been built as non-vac vehicles. Some of the wagons eventually converted by the end of 1906 under this Lot 450 had yet to be ordered under subsequent lots!

The success of the existing vacuum non-stop trains from London to Bristol and the north led the Superintendents in July 1905 to consider further extensions in this direction 'when sufficient Vacuum Stock is available':

9.15pm Paddington to Swansea
6.30pm Swansea to Paddington

12.15am Paddington to New Milford
2.45pm New Milford to Paddington

8.30pm Bristol to Manchester
8.30pm Manchester to Bristol (with connexions to and from South Wales)

8.30pm Neath to Bordesley Jct
10.20pm Bordesley Jct to Neath

The Swansea services commenced on 11 September 1905, and Cardiff-Bordesley in early 1906; by the end of that year, 19 such trains were running daily and by 1909, there were 26 express partially-fitted vacuum goods trains serving the whole system, with the number still growing. Compared with previous schedules, hours were knocked off journey times by the 'vacs'. In 1909, goods took nine hours in transit to Birkenhead from London by the best

Line diagram of C headcode train routes.

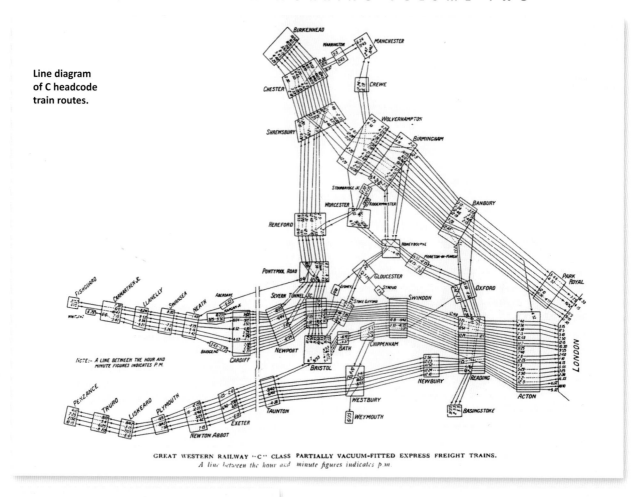

GREAT WESTERN RAILWAY "C" CLASS PARTIALLY VACUUM-FITTED EXPRESS FREIGHT TRAINS.
A line between the hour and minute figures indicates p.m.

TIMEKEEPING and LOADING of GWR VACUUM FREIGHT TRAINS

May 12th 1933

DOWN TRAINS

TRAIN	FROM	TO	TIME DUE	RIGHT TIME OR BEFORE TIME	MINUTES LATE	MAXIMUM ALLOWABLE LOAD WAGONS	ACTUAL LOAD WAGONS	LOADING TAKEN AT
9.10 pm	Paddington	Birkenhead	5.45 am	x	0	45	35	Greenford
9.35 pm	"	Carmarthen	7.15 am		5	64	62	Reading
10.10 pm	"	Plymouth	6.38 am		10	70	69	Newbury R C
10.30 pm	"	Cardiff	4.25 am		43	64	60	Reading
11.5 pm	"	Handsworth	6.38 am		28	60	57	Park Royal
11.15 pm	"	Bristol	3.22 am	x	0	67	46	Old Oak C
11.35 pm	"	Newton Abbot	6.35 am	x	0	70	66	Acton
12.5 am	"	Worcester	4.55 am		5	67	65	Acton
12.15 am	"	Fishguard	1.25 pm	Before Time	at Neath	64	55	Old Oak C (Greenford)
11.30 am	Old Oak C	Crewe	6.19 am	NOT RUN		55		
9.32 pm	"	Penzance	10.15 am	Before Time	at Truro	45	45	Newbury R C
1.5 am	Acton	Bristol	5.22 am		13	67	42	Acton
7.35 pm	"	Cardiff	2.10 am	x		67	54	Acton
9.25 pm	"	"	3.20 am	x		64	45	Reading
12.10 am	Park Royal	Oxley Sdgs	4.50 am		55	60	62	Princes Risboro
12.40 am	Reading	Gloucester	3.27 am	x		67	52	Reading
11.0 pm	"	Oxley Sdgs	3.48 am		5	64	67	Reading
9.35 pm	Basingstoke	"	2.17 am	x		70	40	Moreton-in-Marsh
4.20 am	Westbury	"	11.21 am		19	67	48	Westbury
12.25 am	Bristol	Whitland	6.26 am	x		64	64	Lawrence Hill
6.50 pm	"	Birkenhead	3.20 am		5	50	36	Hereford
7.35 pm	"	Manchester	6.29/7.13am	x		55	27	Hereford
9.20 pm	"	Hockley	2.5 am		5	45	35	Stoke Gifford
9.55 pm	"	Penzance	7.25 am	x		67	61	Bristol West Depot
10.50 pm	"	Pontypool Rd	2.0 am	x		45	60	Lawrence Hill
10.55 pm	"	Newton Abbot	1.50 am	x		67	50	Bristol West Depot
12.50 am	Severn T Jct	Cardiff	1.26 am		4	64	12	Severn T Jct
5.0 am	Little Mill Jct	Swansea	8.18 am		46	45	35	Little Mill Jct
9.45 pm	Cardiff	Saltney	4.47 am	x		58	49	Alexandra Dock Jct
6.50 pm	Worcester	Cardiff	12.30 am		20	64	51	Toddington
8.35 pm	"	Crewe	12.12 am	x		60	49	Kidderminster
9.10 pm	Bordesley Jct	Birkenhead	4.40 am		10	54	53	Oxley
10.0 pm	"	Llanelly	8.34 am	x		45	46	Stourbridge Jct
2.20 am	Oxley Sdgs	Birkenhead	8.15 am	x		54	31	Oxley

UP TRAINS

TRAIN	FROM	TO	TIME DUE	RIGHT TIME OR BEFORE TIME	MINUTES LATE	MAXIMUM ALLOWABLE LOAD WAGONS	ACTUAL LOAD WAGONS	LOADING TAKEN AT
2.40 am	Banbury	Acton	4.52 am		8	70	70	Banbury Jct (Oxley)
3.55 pm	Birkenhead	Old Oak C	11.0 pm	NOT RUN		48	32	Westbury
4.0 pm	Exeter	"	11.32 pm	x		40	40	Westbury
3.5 am	Banbury	"	5.19 am		8	70	65	Banbury Jct
7.40 pm	Bristol	Paddington	1.5 am	x		64	45	Oxford
3.35 pm	Worcester	"	1.25 am	x	5	64	44	Westbury
6.35 pm	Weymouth	"	2.7 am			67	55	Bristol East Depot
5.55 pm	Bristol	"	2.37 am	x		62	55	Bristol East Depot
3.50 pm	Fishguard	"	2.47 am	x		64	30	Banbury Jct
8.20 pm	Kidderminster	"	3.12 am	x		64	43	Oxford
5.25 pm	Newton Abbot	"	3.22 am	x		70	66	Taunton
2.15 am	Banbury	"	4.15 am	x		67	66	Park Royal
7.30 pm	Carmarthen	"	5.7 am	x		58	34	Margam Jct
2.50 pm	Penzance	"	5.50 am		46	70	63	Taunton
8.30 pm	Cannock Rd	"	6.0 am		46	64	64	Banbury Jct
8.20 pm	Birkenhead	"	6.40 am		39	70	70	Queen's Head
4.55 pm	Marazion	Bristol	4.7 am	x		67	51	Exeter
7.45 pm	Manchester	"	6.55 am	x		50	35	Coton Hill
8.40 pm	"	Oxley Sdgs	12.23 am	x		57	49	Crewe
7.10 pm	Victoria Basin	Basingstoke	2.53 am	x		55	54	Tysley
1.10 am	Oxley Sdgs	"	5.3 am		13	40	40	Banbury Jct
9.20 pm	"	Newton Abbot	7.10 am		40	58	54	Hockley
9.45 pm	"	Bristol	5.15 am		22	67	58	Hockley
7.0 pm	Birkenhead	Pontypool Rd	3.5 am	x		50	45	Saltney
9.5 pm	"	Cardiff	5.31 am	x		50	45	Chester
10.25 pm	Margam Jct	Bordesley Jct	6.38 am	x		53	40	Margam Jct
10.30 pm	Birkenhead	"	6.15 am	x		54	52	Coton Hill
11.0 pm	Hockley	Banbury	12.40 am		14	67	64	Tysley
8.10 pm	Oxley Sdgs	"	1.34 am		18	67	66	Tysley
10.40 pm	Langley Green	"	12.19 am		4	64	70	Tysley

arrival versus the former 2.45pm departure and 8am arrival) and the actual acceleration achieved in service was a 10-hour saving. The differences in Up and Down improved timings were influenced by different gradients encountered in different directions.

During World War 1 instances occurred where grease-axlebox wagons, containing ammunition and explosives, were run in express goods trains. Owing to the boxes running hot, or the load shifting, offending wagons had to be detached *en route* thus causing delays. In May 1916, a circular was issued which revised

goods train, and 10¼ hours in the Up direction; Fishguard 11¾ hours Down and nine Up; Birmingham four Down and 4½ Up; Plymouth 8¼ Down and 8½ Up; Bristol 3¼ Down and four Up. In the case of the Up Fishguard goods, the 1909 time was a 8¼ hour (!) improvement on the 1905 timing (9pm departure and 6am

the status of GW vacuum goods services. The trains listed in the table (Schedule A) remained C-headcode and could have only GW vehicles fitted with oil axleboxes. The lower table (Schedule B) listed those former C-headcode trains that were downgraded to E-headcode for the duration. This was the 'ordinary E' classification dating from 1903 (see Chapter 2). The 'Accelerated E' classification appeared in 1923 to solve the same sort of problem of what to do with trains containing foreign axlebox wagons.

Following World War 1, vacuum services were restored and had increased to 40 daily by 1921. To improve continually the service, new GWR express goods trains were introduced, or existing trains accelerated at various times. The C-headcode 4.5pm Exeter to Old Oak Common ('Flying Pig') was accelerated in 1926 to cater for the ever-growing meat traffic from the West of England to Smithfield. With a power group D engine and up to 40 Meat Vans, it served directly, or by connexions, Cullompton, Uffculme, Tiverton and Tiverton Jct, South Molton, Dulverton, Taunton, Chard, Ilminster, Martock, Weymouth, Bridport, Frome, Chippenham and Trowbridge. The train was due into Old Oak at 11.25pm giving transfer to Smithfield just after midnight, six hours earlier than the meat had formerly reached London.

In 1927, a new 'C' headcode train, the 9.32pm Old Oak Common to Penzance (the 'Cornishman') enabled traffic for Cornwall to be sent much later from London; formerly goods had to be sent off in the afternoon. The train was permitted to take 67 wagons to Newbury Racecourse, where re-marshalling took place since only 45 vehicles were permitted beyond: Plymouth and Plymouth District traffic was detached at Newbury to await the arrival of the 10.5pm Paddington-Plymouth (the 'Tamar'); Taunton and Exeter traffic was detached to go forward by the 1.30am Newbury Racecourse-Exeter. Train formation of the 'Cornishman' on leaving Newbury Racecourse was: Penzance, Marazion, St Erth and branch, Hayle, Gwinear Road and branch, Camborne, Redruth, Truro and branches, St Austell and Par. It left at 12.10am and ran non-stop the 142 miles to Newton Abbot in 221 minutes at an average speed of 38mph and was due at Penzance at 10.40am. By 1931, the non-stop section was being run at an average speed of 40mph and in 1933 the arrival time at Penzance had become 10.15am. During 1932 the 'Devonshireman' (11.35pm ex-Paddington behind a '47XX') ran non-stop the 138 miles from Acton to Taunton over the Berks & Hants route. In the same period, the 'Northern Flash' (9.10pm Paddington to Birkenhead, hauled again by a '47XX'), ran the 145 miles over a difficult road with gradients from Greenford to Shrewsbury non-stop at an average speed of 39mph. In 1937, a new express goods departed Birkenhead at 7.45pm for Old Oak Common stopping at Chester (8.45pm) and Shrewsbury (10.45pm). The 153 miles from Shrewsbury were run non-stop. Arriving at 3.45am, it brought London some three hours closer than before, and speeded up connexions with the SR. These partially-fitted GW trains were the fastest and longest non-stop regular freight runs in the country

There were over 70 Class C goods trains daily by the end of the 1930s. Some that commenced their journey as C-headcode trains might be downgraded to D or E services at points *en route*, while others that commenced as less important services were upgraded to C during their journey after having completed loading at intermediate yards. Engine power was very largely the '47XX' and '49XX' classes, though with a few '68XX' and '43XX' on the shorter-

distance trips. The 1936 *General Appendix* laid out the general working conditions for the C-headcode express goods, including the fact that at Stop Boards (see Chapters 10 and 11) '...all freight and mineral trains, even if they are formed partly of vacuum-braked stock, **must always be stopped dead.**' In practice, a nominal one minute was allowed for Class C trains; fully loose-coupled trains stood for longer to enable brakes to be pinned down. The timings of C-headcode trains were based on average speeds of 40 to 45mph, with a maximum of 55mph 'under suitable conditions'. The restriction of using only oil axle box vehicles was emphasised (after 1933 wagons from foreign companies having RCH oilboxes were permitted). The maximum load was 70 wagons, excluding brake van. Whilst minimum and maximum figures were specified, any train of 16 wagons and fewer could have all the vehicles fitted to the locomotive. Fully-fitted trains did not have to halt at Stop Boards nor, after 1933 (Chapter 2), carry side lamps on the brake van.

In the early evening, large busy goods depots may have had fully-loaded wagons that were cluttering up the yard and which were best got rid of. To clear Paddington Goods of such vehicles, C-headcode trains were used to take loaded wagons to Old Oak Common, Acton or elsewhere downline, to be attached to subsequent trains, before heading off on their own journeys. For example, the 8.5pm Paddington to Bristol (the 'Shopper') relieved Paddington Goods of (i) non-vac vehicles intended for Bath and Bristol, dropping them off at Acton to join the 1.5am 'High Flyer' to Bristol which started from Acton; and, (ii) Cardiff and Newport vehicles that were also dropped off at Acton where they waited to join the 'South Wales Borderer' that would itself not leave Paddington Goods until 10.30pm and then call at Acton. This train had also to clear from Reading West all traffic for the Cardiff District, including wagons that had been detached at Reading by the 9.35pm Paddington Goods to Carmarthen (the 'Welshman'). The 'Shopper' for Bristol even took wagons destined for Weymouth and the West of England as far as Newbury Racecourse, to be picked up by later C-headcode trains. Some of the longest overnight fast goods trains, near their destination next morning, would find themselves mixed in with early passenger traffic, so sometimes had to stop to permit such trains to pass.

The timing of trains was often different at weekends, especially on Sundays. Since depots handling merchandise goods did not normally open on Sundays, fast overnight trains that would normally arrive early on Sunday mornings would be stopped at some convenient point *en route* on Saturday nights and stabled over Sunday until the journey resumed at a comparable time late on Sunday night/early on Monday morning. As depots were closed on Sundays, there was no loading of vehicles during the day that would have formed fast overnight trains, so many such trains are shown as **MX**, meaning that they did not run on Monday mornings (they would, of course, function on Monday evenings). The 9.20pm Oxley-Newton Abbot ran only as far as Exeter on Saturdays, and stayed over at Bristol on Sundays. The 10.30pm C-headcode 'South Wales Borderer' Paddington-Cardiff via Swindon and Gloucester was '**SX**' since on Saturdays the train went only as far as Gloucester and carried E-headlamps.

To reduce start-to-stop timings, some C-headcode trains were advantageously routed over the LMS for part of the journey. One example is the 9.20pm Wolverhampton (Oxley) to Newton

Abbot. The 1933 STT shows it passing Birmingham at 11.33, Cheltenham (Malvern Road) at 1.2am, calling at Gloucester between 1.16-1.41am. Then it ran via Standish Jct passing there at 1.52, Berkeley Road South Jct at 2.6, Yate South Jct at 2.24 and Westerly West Jct at 2.31, to return to GW lines and arrive at Stoke Gifford at 2.39am. Similar arrangements are mentioned later on page 203 when discussing F-headcode trains.

The C-headcode was also used for trains carrying fish, meat and perishable traffic (and their empties), cattle and cattle empties, full and empty pigeon basket specials and parcel trains. A C-headcode vacuum empties train was timetabled from west London at 2pm for South Wales (**SO**). Ballast trains often ran as C-headcode using appropriate fitted wagons to enable urgent trackwork repairs to be carried out.

During World War 2 many of the C-class trains were either withdrawn or downgraded for the duration, long non-stop runs being difficult to roster owing to the lack of accommodation for double-home turns. Nevertheless, most services were re-instated in 1945/46.

Here follow descriptions (in greater or lesser detail) of the running of some representative C-headcode express freights in the 1930s.

1.5am Acton to Bristol (Temple Meads), Train No 123, C

At the top of the list of vacuum-fitted services the 1.5am Acton to Bristol (the 'High Flyer'), due 5.22am, the first regular partially-fitted service introduced on 9 January 1905. As explained at the beginning of this section, 4-4-0 'County' locomotives hauled the trial trains, and they continued to do the job in the early days when this train departed at 12.48am from Acton. Later, engines of power class D were rostered and a 4-6-0 'Saint' would often head the train, but No 111 Great Bear appeared regularly as it was restricted to work between London and Bristol owing to its weight and length. It returned with a daytime Up passenger train (or vice versa). By 1938 a 'Hall' was rostered (the light engine leaving Old Oak shed at 12.30am and arriving at Acton West Jct at 12.40) to haul a maximum load of 67 wagons from Acton. On Sundays, the load was increased to 80 wagons and the train downgraded to carry F-headlamps.

The destinations of wagons and their order in the train, on weekdays, were:

Bristol (Temple Meads) Vac
Lawrence Hill Vac
Bath Vac
Bristol East depot (including Midsomer Norton, Keynsham and Avonmouth traffic) Vac and Non-Vac
Lawrence Hill Non-Vac
Bristol (Temple Meads) Non-Vac

Many feeder trains from around London brought traffic to Acton that ended up on this service: for example, the 7.26, 9.9 and 10.31pm from Smithfield (mostly Micas and in later years Meat Containers); and the 7.10 and 8pm from Victoria & Albert Docks, plus any traffic from the East India Docks (imports of meat, butter, fruit, cheese, potatoes etc). Many different feeder trains were scheduled because berthing and unloading of ships at London Docks were unpredictable, plus the fact that certain restrictions applied to trains running through the subway to Bishop's Road on the Metropolitan underground line (usually a maximum of 20 wagons). Goods trains on the Met carried F headlamps and after 1930 were hauled by a '97XX' 0-6-0PT fitted with condensing gear (Wolverhampton and Metro tanks with condensing gear in earlier years). Outlying London goods depots intending to send goods for Bath and Bristol to join the 'High Flyer' via feeder trains were encouraged to use vacuum stock. Often there were vans of biscuits from Chelsea Basin yard for Bristol East depot, brought in by one of the South Lambeth trains.

Other goods trains brought traffic to Acton from Paddington for the 'High Flyer'. The 11.35pm vacuum to Newton Abbot (the 'Devonshireman') brought vehicles for Bath and Bristol before setting out on its own long distance journey. The 6.38pm from Greenford brought several V31/2 'Tevans' from the Lyons factory to add to the train (these had come up with cocoa traffic from Fry's at Bristol), and the 7.30pm ex-Paddington, Ladbroke Grove and Park Royal also brought wagons, including Guinness traffic. Vehicles from St Pancras, Cricklewood and Temple Mills arriving over the North London line, some with East Anglian produce in season, added variety to the train.

After 1930, among vans formed in the 1.5am Acton would have been the long wheelbase, 30ft-over-headstocks V22 Mink G, built mainly for this fast traffic, many of which were labelled 'Paddington-Bristol' or 'Return to Paddington'.

Leaving Acton, the train picked up the Relief line and ran non-stop to Didcot East, where it was scheduled for a brief service stop and to allow the Up Penzance 'Postal' to pass through Didcot. After easing over the Up Main to gain the Down Main, the 'High Flyer' ran through the Vale of the White Horse to Swindon (3.6am). There was a very brief allowance (3.32-3.52) at Thingley Jct (Chippenham), and another at Bathampton to allow the 2.55am Salisbury mail to precede the 'High Flyer' into Bath. The call at Bath Goods was made between 4.17 and 4.40am to detach wagons only; there were no feeding or connecting trains, and local traffic was disposed of generally by road services.

The 'Flyer' then ran the penultimate stage of its journey to Bristol East depot just beyond St Anne's Park station, staying from 4.57 to 5.17. Here wagons would be detached from the centre of the train, and sorted by the depot pilot for various yards in the city. Lawrence Hill traffic went by No 5 Transfer Goods (6.20am) and vans of biscuits from Chelsea were shunted on to the 5.35am East depot to Bridgwater (**MX**) train; this would be hauled by a '57XX' carrying the K headcode. The vans of biscuits were dropped off at Pylle Hill depot, where the Bridgwater train would pick up bacon traffic for conveyance to Yatton, Weston-super-Mare and Highbridge which had been detached from the 8.5am Paddington-Bristol. Other traffic from the 'High Flyer' was taken from Bristol East on services to Keynsham, Radstock and St Philip's Marsh (for Avonmouth). Vehicles were attached at East Depot to the Flyer from the 8.5pm Banbury-Bristol J-headcode goods, which had travelled via Oxford and Swindon and arrived at Bristol at 2.22am. The 1.5am then made its short final leg into Temple Meads Goods.

8.8pm Manchester (Liverpool Road) to Bristol (Temple Meads), Train No 9, C

Another of the 1906 introductions of express freight services was that between Manchester and Bristol (later nicknamed the 'Mon'), running via the North & West route through the Severn Tunnel. In

1933, this train left Manchester at 7.45pm, but by 1938 it was 8.8pm. In what follows, slight differences in timing of the train in 1933 and 1938 are noted. In 1938 the train left Manchester as a D-headcode service, being upgraded at Chester/Saltney to class C for the journey to Bristol. It was hauled by a 'Hall' throughout, working from Manchester (Liverpool Road Goods, ex-LNW) to Temple Meads. GWR engines were available in Manchester being stabled in a part of Patricroft locomotive depot, which was designated a sub-shed of Chester. (But GW locomotives did not work into Manchester Exchange station.) Up until the inter-company goods pooling scheme of 1933, the GWR had warehouse and other facilities at Liverpool Road along with a large staff under a company Goods Agent, with 16 road motors, 129 horse-drawn vehicles and 66 horses. The GW's running powers relevant to this service had commenced with its part-ownership of the Birkenhead Railway, but were modified by later agreements (see *GWR Docks & Marine*).

Compared to the 'High Flyer' Acton-Bristol train, the formation of the 'Mon' was complex, as the service carried wagons both for South Wales and for the West Country, as well as Bristol. The scheduled formation from Liverpool Road was:

Trowbridge Vac
Bristol Vac
Pylle Hill Vac
‡Bristol (West Depot) Vac
‡West of England Vac
Pontypool Road Vac
§Pontypridd, Rhondda Valley, Caerphilly District, Hengoed, Merthyr, Mountain Ash, Aberdare, Glyn Neath, Neath, Swansea, Llanelly (and beyond) all Vac
Hereford Vac
Hereford Non-Vac
†Central Wales Division Non-Vac
†Shrewsbury & Oxley sidings Non-Vac
§Cardiff & Barry District Non-Vac
§Port Talbot & Briton Ferry Non-Vac
§Neath, Swansea, Llanelly & beyond Non-Vac
§Newport Non-Vac
*Weymouth & Salisbury Lines Non-Vac
Pontypool Road Non-Vac
‡West of England Non-Vac
‡Bristol (West Depot) Non-Vac
Bristol Non-Vac

Portions of the train indicated by the symbols were disposed of *en route*: † at Saltney; § Little Mill (just north of Pontypool Road); ‡ Pontypool Road; * Pontypool Road. In addition, the train carried a raft of station trucks from Manchester for North, Central and South Wales (detached at Saltney or Little Mill), and from Birkenhead (attached at Saltney, detached Pontypool Road). The train was restricted to a maximum of 60 wagons to Saltney on weekdays but it was limited to 50 on Saturdays when an additional call was made at Warrington. Leaving Liverpool Road depot, the train had a 21¾-mile journey over LMS metals before reaching joint GW-LMS lines. A short run out of Liverpool Road brought the train through to Ordsall Lane, where it joined the main Manchester to Liverpool line out of Exchange station. The 8.8 ran non-stop thence

through Eccles, Patricroft and Newton-le-Willows, turning south at Earlestown to gain the LMS West Coast main line for the run through Warrington (where it called for some re-marshalling on Saturdays only). Just to the south of Warrington, the train turned off at Walton New Jct on to the old Birkenhead company's line (joint LMS & GW) towards Frodsham, Helsby and Chester. At Chester, it joined the Crewe to Holyhead line to the east of Chester General station, where it stood for a scheduled 18-minute stop (33 minutes in 1933, between 9.25 and 9.58) to allow the 9.15pm Birkenhead to Oswestry local passenger to clear the section ahead.

Leaving Chester station, the train made its way to Saltney Jct Up Yard, due at 10.4pm. Here, the Central Wales, Shrewsbury and Oxley non-vacuum wagons were detached for the 11.15pm departure thence to Shrewsbury. It also took on wagons that had been worked in locally from Warrington and Chester, and left the yard at 10.45pm with a maximum of 50 wagons in the train. A non-stop run to the Stop Board to the north of Coton Hill yard (Shrewsbury) followed (halting between 12 midnight and 12.1am), before the train was held on the loop (12.7-12.22) where the load could be increased up to 55 wagons (but only as far as Hereford). On Saturday nights the train was stabled at Coton Hill until 12.20am Monday. Moving off at 12.20am, the train then ran through the passenger station for a 1¾-hour non-stop run to Hereford (Barton) yard, 52 miles away. A number of southbound fast freights called at Hereford in the early hours, though most ran via the Barr's Court loop rather than Barton. The 'Mon' stopped at Barton yard for 15 minutes (12 minutes in 1933 from 2.5-2.17) to detach wagons for the city and for Gloucester, Cheltenham or Stroud. Vacuum wagons for these latter stations were taken forward by the 7.15am passenger train; non-vacuum wagons by the 7.40am goods.

Departing Barton at 2.21am (2.17am in 1933), the train had an interrupted run, stopping briefly at the board at Llanvihangel summit (3.5-3.6) and again between 3.14-3.15 at the board at Abergavenny (Monmouth Road). From there, a 14-minute run was made to Little Mill Jct for a 30-minute call (26 minutes in 1933, 3.29-3.55am) to detach traffic for the Valleys, South Wales main line, Neath line and Swansea etc, and to pick up Bristol traffic from the 'Mersey' (9.5pm Birkenhead to Cardiff vacuum), which ran just ahead of the 8.8pm. The reason that the 'Mon' called at Little Mill as well as at Pontypool Road (the place where trains normally dropped off wagons for Bristol) was that the 'Mersey' was not scheduled to call at Pontypool Road. Arriving at Pontypool Road yard at 4.3am, the train from Manchester made a lengthy stop to detach all traffic for Bristol (West depot) and the West Country, and for the Weymouth and Salisbury lines (wagons for both being taken forward by the 5.30am Accelerated E [later D] from Pontypool Road to Newton Abbot). Having lightened its load, it then attached Bristol traffic dropped from previous trains originating at Birkenhead, Saltney, Coleham and Worcester before setting off again at 4.50am with a maximum load of 50 wagons.

The route taken out of the yard was via Panteg Jct to Caerleon (with Stop Boards just outside Pontypool Road and Panteg) to join the South Wales main line at Maindee East Jct. STJ was reached at 5.31am, where a wait 'for Severn Tunnel purposes' was undertaken. At 5.51am the train set off into the tunnel, entering it at 5.55 and emerging at 6.7am. It ran up to Pilning (6.13) and

Patchway (6.26), then down the banks with pauses at Filton incline (6.31-6.32), Lawrence Hill (6.43-6.44), Stapleton Road and Dr Day's Bridge Jct before easing into Temple Meads Goods at 6.55am, a journey of a little under 11 hours. At Temple Meads, those vehicles for destinations beyond were taken by transfer trips to East depot, Pylle Hill and Lawrence Hill.

9.10pm Paddington Goods to Wolverhampton (Oxley sidings), via Princes Risborough, C

The maximum loading of the 'Northern Flash' was 54 wagons or 60 wagons when worked by '47XX' class locomotive.

Feeder trains at Paddington Goods were the 5.52pm ex-Acton which included vehicles from the 1.5pm ex-Poplar and the 2.10pm ex-Victoria & Albert Docks with imported goods, and the 5.35pm from Uxbridge bringing Tevans off the 6pm Greenford train. The train stopped at Old Oak Common (9.24-10.0), where additional vehicles from feeder trains would be waiting such as the 6.50pm from Chelsea depot; the 6pm ex-Warwick Road; the 6pm and 7.50pm ex-South Lambeth; and, the 3.26 pm, 3.35pm (SO), 5pm (SO) and 8.39pm all ex-Smithfield.

The formation of the train on leaving Old Oak Common was: Warwick, Leamington, Stratford-on-Avon, Birkenhead, Chester, Market Drayton (all vac); Market Drayton, Wellington, Manchester via Crewe, Shrewsbury, Gobowen and branch, Ruabon and branches, Wrexham, Warrington, Chester, Birkenhead, Wolverhampton (all non-vac). The next call was Ruislip where wagons were attached from the 7.22pm ex-West Drayton which gave connexions from Uxbridge and Greenford. Those wagons destined for Birkenhead were shunted inside the Wolverhampton non-vac vehicles.

Wagons were attached at Princes Risborough from the 4.52pm Taplow-Oxford train. These were vac-fitted vehicles that ran via Bourne End and High Wycombe. At Leamington, in addition to traffic for the town, vehicles for Warwick and Stratford-upon-Avon were dropped off for the 5.45am Leamington-Honeybourne train.

At Oxley sidings the final onward connexions were made. The main part of the 'Northern Flash' was taken on northwards to Birkenhead and stations en route (Chester, Warrington, Wrexham, Ruabon and branch, Gobowen and branch) by the C-headcode 'Northern Docker' that started at Oxley, departing at 2.45am for Birkenhead (due 8.48am). Other connexions were for Wellington (Salop) by the 3.30pm Oxley-Birkenhead; for Market Drayton by the 1.50am Stourbridge Junction-Crewe; and, for Manchester (via Crewe) by the 4.0am Oxley-Crewe. On Sundays connexions at Oxley were to the 11.55pm Bordesley Jct-Birkenhead (the 'Shipper') and 4am Oxley-Crewe (the 'Northern Exchange').

12.5am Paddington Goods to Worcester (via Oxford, Kingham and Honeybourne), Train No 115, C

The maximum load for the 'Sauce' (named after Lee & Perrins Worcester Sauce factory) was 64 wagons between Acton and Oxford, and 50 wagons beyond. All vehicles from Paddington were to be vac-fitted. Intermediate destinations for vehicles on this train were: Kington, Ludlow, Bridgnorth, Tenbury, Kidderminster, Worcester, Withington, Malvern, Hereford, Honeybourne, Stratford-upon-Avon, Evesham, Moreton and branches, Oxford and Thame.

A call was made at Acton where wagons were attached from the following trains: 7.17 and 10.36pm ex-Smithfield (meat vans); 9.15pm ex-South Lambeth; 8pm ex-Victoria & Albert Docks; 6.38pm Greenford to Acton (Tevans); 10.30am ex-St Pancras (LMS); 2.53pm ex-Temple Mills (LNER); 3.45pm ex-Cricklewood (LMS); and the 4.20pm ex-Paddington, the latter being an example of the clearing of wagons from Paddington Goods by earlier trains to Acton where there was more accommodation. Wagons were to be standing in the following order to be attached behind the Thame wagons already on the train: Oxford, Moreton-in-Marsh, Honeybourne, Evesham, Stratford-upon-Avon, Hereford, Malvern, Worcester, Kidderminster and branch, and Hartlebury and branches.

Traffic for Hereford from Acton was given preference over the 'Sauce', and to ensure that all traffic for Hereford would be cleared by this train, some Worcester-bound vehicles would be detached and sent to Park Royal by the 11.20pm pilot goods from Acton, to go forward by the 1.30am E-headlamp Park Royal-Worcester.

A stop was made at Oxford where a parcels van for Worcester was attached from the 12.15am ex-Paddington (passenger) train. Thame vehicles were detached to go forward by the 7am Oxford-Thame passenger train.

The next call was at Moreton-in-Marsh where vehicles would be uncoupled for the 10.5am mixed train to Shipston-on-Stour. The maximum number of vehicles in mixed trains was not to be more than 30, and the speed was limited to 25mph. Goods wagons in such trains were coupled in the rear of passenger-carrying vehicles. At Honeybourne, traffic for Stratford-on-Avon was uncoupled to go forward on the 8am passenger train, and traffic for Evesham by the 6.50am Honeybourne-Evesham.

Upon arrival at Worcester (due 4.55am), the 'Sauce' was split up as follows: traffic for Kidderminster, Tenbury and Bridgnorth was sent by the 7.15am Worcester-Highley; that for Malvern by the 6.40am Worcester-Hereford; for Ludlow and Kington by the 8.15am Worcester-Leominster passenger train; and, for Withington and Hereford by the 6.40am Worcester-Hereford. A station truck conveyed by the main line train over part of its journey was No 403 Paddington-Bridgnorth between Paddington and Worcester (1933 STT).

11.40am Southall-Crewe, C

The 'Grocer' got its nickname from the traffic it carried to the north from the many food industry factories in the Southall area, including vans of tea from Messrs Lyons at Greenford (before the 1927 Competition to name GW vacuum express goods, the train was nicknamed the 'Tea'). The maximum load was 55 vans, all to be fitted vehicles between Southall and Wolverhampton (Oxley). Normal locomotive power used for the 'Grocer' was a '43XX' 2-6-0 class.

Wagon formation on departure was: Oxley, Crewe (LMS), Glasgow, Edinburgh and the LNER (NE Section). The train arrived at Oxley at 3.28pm where it stood until the arrival at 4.15 pm of the 12.50pm Littleton & Badsey to Oxley train (C-headcode, RR, ex-Long Marston), which brought fruit and vegetable traffic in season from the Worcester area. The 'Grocer' departed Oxley at 4.50pm, passing Market Drayton at 5.50pm to arrive Crewe at 6.19pm.

9.20pm Bristol (Temple Meads)-Wolverhampton (Oxley), Train No 216, C (SX, MX), E (SO)

This train, the 'Western Docker', was limited to a maximum load of 45 wagons. In addition to Temple Meads, two other depots, Lawrence Hill and Stoke Gifford, were involved in forming the train. Destinations of wagons when the train departed were, from the locomotive: Cheltenham (Malvern Road); Lye; Stourbridge; Cradley; Brettall Lane; Stratford-upon-Avon; Bordesley Jct and Birmingham district; and, Bilston and Oxley.

On weekdays , assistance was required to get up Ashley Hill to Filton, so the train paused at Stapleton Road between 9.35-9.44pm to attach a banker. An hour (10.2-11.3pm) was spent at Stoke Gifford marshalling yard. Between Yate (passed at 11.18) and Standish Jct (passed at 11.44) the 'Western Docker' ran over LMS metals before passing Gloucester South Jct at 11.56pm. At Hatherkey Jct the train 'shunted for, or followed, another train and also performed work' and departed at 12.7am. Wagons for Lye and Stourbridge were detached at Toddington sidings (north of Winchcombe) for the 7.30pm ex-Cardiff-Worcester train. Honeybourne West Jct was passed at 12.45am before arriving at Stratford-upon-Avon where wagons for Bordesley were detached and the engine took water. Departing at 1.5, the train passed Bearley North Jct at 1.16, Earlswood Lakes 1.38, Tyseley 1.47, and Bordesley Jct at 1.50am.

On passing through Birmingham (Snow Hill) at 1.53am, what had been an Up train from Bristol became a Down train as it went further north. The Bristol-Snow Hill portion of the journey may be found on page 160 of Section 13 of the 1933 STT. Continuation of the route is found on page 7 of Section 13 , where the train is shown standing at Hockley from 1.57-2.30am, where wagons for Wednesbury, West Bromwich, Handsworth and Bilston were detached for the 5.10am from Hockley. A connecting train at Hockley (for Cradley) was the 7.30am Bordesley-Stourbridge Junction. The 'Western Docker' then ran non-stop to Oxley, arriving at 3.9am. Some wagons from the 'Western Docker' continued their journey, after re-marshalling at Oxley, by the 6.50am Oxley-Birkenhead and the 9.45am Oxley-Crewe. At one time, the train was extended to Victoria basin at Wolverhampton. The equivalent Saturday night train (on page 161 of Section 13) was slower (departed Stratford at 1.42; passed Bordesley at 2.32am). Its continuing Sunday morning times north of Snow Hill are on page 55 of Section 13. The train worked at Hockley from 2.38-2.58am, and arrived at Oxley at 3.37am.

E-HEADCODE: VACUUM EXPRESS GOODS TRAINS

E-headcode express goods trains were intended for merchandise, cattle, and fish, meat or fruit all carried in goods vehicles; they did not convey any coal or mineral traffic. They had fitted vehicles on the loco, but fewer than in C-headcode trains and in contemporary 'Accelerated-E' headcode trains (see later), so E-headcode trains were slower than both. There had to be at least four vac vehicles, with more on longer trains. Improvements in timings of E-trains occurred as the years went by. In 1927, the loading of the 9.50pm E-headcode Wolverhampton to Cardiff was restricted beyond Stourbridge Junction to traffic for Newport and Cardiff only and, additionally, the train was diverted to run via Worcester, Hereford, Pontypool Road and Newport, instead of Worcester, Honeybourne, Cheltenham, Gloucester and Newport, giving a three-hour earlier arrival in Cardiff. At that time the bulk of slow mineral traffic to Birmingham from South Wales ran via Honeybourne and Stratford-upon-Avon.

Since the ordinary-E and Accelerated-E trains had the same lamp headcode (and also the same bell code between boxes: five beats given as three pause two) it is not possible to distinguish

An Acton-South Lambeth transfer goods train at Addison Road/Kensington (Olympia). 0-6-0PT No 5757 carries E headlamps. *LGRP*

A transfer freight between Old Oak Common and South Lambeth passes through Addison Road station on the West London line in the 1930s. The locomotive is '57XX' No 8764 and carries the E-headcode. There is a container on a flat wagon immediately behind the loco. *D J Hyde collection*

No 7808 Cookham Manor passes Wilmcote (between Stratford-upon-Avon and Henley-in-Arden) on an E-class freight train in September 1943. The cab-side window is sheeted over to reduce firebox glare at night in the blackout. *A G Atkins collection*

between them in photographs unless the time that the picture was taken and the relevant section of the STT is to hand. In 1936, the Accelerated-E classification was abolished and those trains moved to an expanded D-headcode, leaving just the 'ordinary' class E as described in this section, the definition for which now also included ballast trains with a minimum of four vacuum vehicles connected to the engine.

9.10pm Llandilo Jct (Llanelly) to Bordesley Jct, Train No 68, E

There were 'Express Goods and Tin Plate' trains running daily between Llanelly and Shrewsbury as early as the 1880s, and also between Swansea and Birmingham, though it was not until just before World War 1 that an afternoon fast goods ran to the Midlands from Carmarthen Jct. In 1936, this service started at Llandilo Jct for Stourbridge Jct and was extended to Bordesley Jct by 1938. It was formed:

Bordesley Jct Vac
Hockley Vac
Shrewsbury and beyond Livestock Vac

Hereford Vac
Worcester Vac
Alexandra Dock Jct Tank Wagons Non-Vac
†Saltney
†Shrewsbury
Stourbridge Jct Non-Vac
Hockley Non-Vac
Bordesley Jct Non-Vac

Saltney and Shrewsbury vehicles (†) were only added 'if necessary to make up the load'. On Saturday nights, this train was much reduced in length and worked by a 'Bulldog', and was stabled at Canton, Cardiff until Sunday night.

The train left Llandilo Jct at 9.10pm behind a scheduled '43XX' with a non-stop 13-mile run along the Swansea District line to Felin Fran, limited to 56 wagons unassisted owing to the climb to Llangyfelach. At Felin Fran, it picked up traffic from Swansea and the Pantyffynon districts, then, remaining on the Swansea Avoiding lines, it ran via Jersey Marine Jct North to rejoin the South Wales main line at Briton Ferry followed by a non-stop leg to Cardiff with an unassisted 53-wagon limitation up to Pyle.

A brief call was made at Cardiff at midnight to change enginemen and guards before setting off through Cardiff General station along the main line to Alexandra Dock Jct. At this Newport yard, it dropped off tanks and, when necessary, Saltney traffic, then picked up further traffic for Worcester and the Midlands before proceeding to a stop at Newport station to allow the E-headcode Cardiff to Banbury to pass ahead for a call at East Usk Jct. With the Banbury clear, the train ran up to Maindee Jct to join the North & West route for a fast run to Abergavenny station. With the 3½-mile, 1 in 85/82/95 climb to Llanvihangel ahead, a bank engine was positioned in the rear, dropping off at the summit. Following a brief pause at Pontrilas, the Bordesley train continued to Red Hill Jct, where a call was made to pin down the brakes for

The third-built Collett 0-6-0 of the '2251' class, No 2253, shortly after construction at Swindon, heads the 6.55pm (SX) E-headcode goods from Hayes to Reading West Jct; it was photographed just after starting its journey at Dawley on 16 August 1930. *Ken Nunn collection/LCGB*

'28XX' No 2833 (built in 1911) heads an E-headcode freight. The chimney lamp iron is now on the smokebox door. *A G Atkins collection*

the descent into Hereford (Barton), where a call was made to drop off and pick up traffic.

Leaving Barton, the train ran on to Ledbury to take on another banker for the 1 in 80 climb beyond, then stopped at Colwall to pin brakes down for the 1 in 80 descent to Malvern Wells. Another call was made at Malvern Link to prepare for the descent to Leominster Jct, followed by the run into Worcester (Tunnel Jct) to drop off traffic. Starting again, the train ran the 22 miles to Stourbridge Jct in 56 minutes, start to stop, where a long call was made to detach vehicles containing traffic for West Midland and Birmingham destinations, which would be taken forward by local services through Kidderminster via Old Hill.

The penultimate leg commenced with a stop at Oldbury & Langley Green to allow two local passenger trains to overtake before the train followed the second to Hockley to offload vac and non-vac vehicles. With a clear run scheduled, the train then made its way through Snow Hill station to Bordesley Jct, due at 10.25am, after some 13¼ hours on the road.

9.50pm Wolverhampton (Victoria Basin) to Cardiff, E

This is a train that requires many different Sections of the STT to trace its path. Its departure at 9.50pm and its journey through Stafford Road (10pm), Cannock Road Jct (10.8), as far as Priestfield to arrive at 10.18pm may be found in two places: (i) Section 13 of the 1933 STT, page 110; and (ii) Section 15, page 66. But its continuation from Priestfield departing at 10.50 will be found only in Section 15. It halted at Blowers Green sidings (11.10-11.38pm) and stopped at the Stop Board at Round Oak & Wednesbury from 11.45-11.48, followed by some time at Stourbridge Jct (12.8-1.15am). Journeying on, it passed Kidderminster at 1.32, Hartlebury at 1.40, Droitwich at 1.52 and Worcester (Tunnel Jct) at 2.3am, to arrive at Worcester Rainbow Hill Jct at 2.4am where the enginemen and guard were changed. Section 12 of the STT, page 11 has now to be consulted to find the continuation of the train that left Rainbow Hill at 2.8am. It passed Malvern Link at 2.29, Malvern Wells at 2.36, Colwall at 2.43 and exited Ledbury Tunnel at 2.53am (no entry time is given in the STT). The train stood at Shelwick Jct from 2.24-2.29 and passed Barrs Court at 3.33, before stopping 'if required to detach' at Hereford 'Worcester sidings' between 3.35 and 3.43am. It worked at Hereford Barton from 3.46-4.9 and then passed Red Hill Jct at 4.17 before halting at the Llanvihangel Stop Board from 4.57-5.0, and also at the Abergavenny Stop Board between 5.11-5.15. Work was done at Little Mill Jct (5.35-6.0) before pulling into Pontypool Road passenger station to take on locomotive water (6.8-6.18am). A pause was made at Maindee Jct North (6.41-6.53) before arriving at Newport at 6.58am where wagons could be detached if required before leaving at 7.10 to arrive in Cardiff at 7.35am. The final leg of the journey on the main line between Newport and Cardiff is printed in Section 7 of the STT, page 8. On Saturday nights the train was stabled at Worcester until 2.10am Monday.

1.10am Salisbury to Cardiff (MX, E) (MO, F) (via Westbury, Bath, Bristol East depot and Severn Tunnel Junction)

The reason for two different headcodes for this train was due to a ruling that colliery empties were permitted beyond Westbury *only* on the Monday train and not on other days. The Monday train with lots of empty coal wagons was slower and could not take the

E-headcode, and therefore carried the inferior F-headcode. Maximum load was 64 wagons Class 3, or 42 Class 1, or 86 empties. locomotive power assigned was D (see Chapter 6).

Marshalling order destinations for this train from Salisbury were: Bristol East depot (**MO**); Newport High Street; Severn Tunnel Junction; Newport Dock Street; Cardiff (cattle traffic); Cardiff (goods shed traffic); Westbury; Taff and Rhymney sections; Cardiff District; and destinations further west in Wales.

Having negotiated the Stop Board at Upton Scudamore (1.58-2.3am), the first call for this train was Westbury (2.11-2.55) where LNER wagons ex-Salisbury were detached to be sent to Banbury by the 4.20am Westbury-Oxley sidings (the 'Moonraker', with the E-headcode). If there were too many LNER wagons to be cleared, the rest were taken by the 5.20am ex-Hackney yard (Newton Abbot) or by the 6.25pm ex-Westbury, both to Banbury Junction and both carrying the J-headcode. On Mondays only, vehicles for Bristol were left for the Salisbury train by the 6.40pm Weymouth-Paddington (Up 'Jersey') that had arrived at Westbury at 10pm.

A stop was made at Trowbridge (3.6-3.20, **MX**) where milk or dairy produce and bacon traffic from Devizes and Holt Jct bound for West Wales were attached. These vehicles would be taken as far as Severn Tunnel Jct where they would connect with the 12.5pm H-headcode to Landore. They were shunted into the train between the Newport High Street and Newport Dock Street vehicles. Wagons were also added at Trowbridge for Newport and Cardiff districts.

The next stop was Bath where more shunting took place and more vehicles were added, to give the following formation upon leaving: Severn Tunnel Jct; Newport High Street; Taff and Rhymney sections; Cardiff District and westwards; Cardiff goods depot and Newport Dock Street. Additional Cardiff and Newport vehicles had been brought to Bath by the 1.55am (**MX**) Chippenham-Bristol East depot (J-headcode), and other vehicles for South Wales with perishable traffic had been brought by the 8.45am Didcot-Bristol East depot K-headcode local pick-up goods. This particular batch of wagons was coupled between the Newport High Street and the Newport Dock Street wagons already on the train. It seems that the different Newport vehicles were to be kept as far apart as possible on this train. Bristol East depot was the next call where vehicles with produce from the Channel Islands for the Bristol area would be detached on one of the reception roads in the yard before the train continued its journey towards the Severn Tunnel. Filton was passed at 4.51am, five minutes were allowed for pinning down the brakes at the Stop Board just after Patchway Tunnel on the descent to the tunnel in addition to the 10 minutes (5.8-5.18) at Patchway 'for Severn Tunnel purposes', ie to attach a banker/pilot.

At Severn Tunnel Jct (5.42-6.18), vehicles with perishable goods from Devizes, Holt Jct and the Didcot-Bristol pick up goods train would be dropped off, to go forward to Landore and Swansea district by the 12.5pm STJ-Landore H-headcode train. Wagons attached to the train at STJ were from the 12.10am Paddington-Fishguard express goods (the 'Irishman') with C-headlamps and were for Newport where the Salisbury train stopped from 6.42-6.50am. Traffic for Newport Dock Street, Alexandra Dock etc was detached at Ebbw Jct, and Taff Vale and Rhymney traffic was detached at Rumney River Bridge/Roath sidings Cardiff (7.12-7.42). The train terminated at Cardiff Newtown Goods where connecting trains were: 11.35am Cardiff-Ely Valley; 10.10am Cardiff-Tondu K-headcode; and, the 9.50am Rumney River Bridge-Radyr Jct.

ACCELERATED E-HEADCODE: VACUUM EXPRESS GOODS TRAINS

With few exceptions, all GW goods wagons (both fitted and unfitted) were equipped with OK oil axleboxes from the start of the C20th. Other companies also equipped some of their goods wagons with oilboxes, but many of these were packed with waste and horsehair. While much better than grease boxes, these foreign oilboxes could still run hot. The GWR did not permit such vehicles to run in its partially-fitted C-class vacuum trains, so that they had to be conveyed in trains of the next class below, ie E-headcode. It followed that delivery of supposedly urgent goods carried in wagons having foreign oilboxes was delayed in comparison with the service provided for goods conveyed in GW vehicles.

In order to speed up such freight, the GW 'Accelerated-E' category of goods train was introduced in 1923 in which foreign oilbox wagons could run. These trains had to have from 10 to 15% of vacuum vehicles connected to the loco, and were timed at about 5mph faster than E trains. In comparison with C-headcode trains over the same route they were, in essence, given more time to start and stop. The 25 or so 'Accelerated E' trains were indicated in the timetables with a distinctive 'iron cross' symbol ✠ alongside the letter E.

As with all other goods trains, the headcode might be changed *en route* depending on vehicles attached or detached. Improvements in the goods service could be made by upgrading a train in the timetable. In 1928, for example, the F-headcode 12.10am Gloucester to Cardiff (which formerly carried general merchandise and coal) was re-scheduled to carry no coal, reclassified as 'Accelerated E', and retimed to arrive 40 minutes earlier. Again in 1928, following reclassification from E to 'Accelerated E', the 2.10am Basingstoke to Wolverhampton (the 'Cherbourg') got to Birmingham 40 minutes earlier, which was important for the Continental and Channel Islands perishable goods ex-Southampton.

Some years after the Grouping, the other main-line companies began to build open wagons and vans on RCH-standard underframes that had a design of oil axlebox that was comparable in performance to the GW oilbox. In 1933, such wagons were permitted to run in GW C-headcode trains. Foreign oil boxes packed with horsehair or waste remained in service, however, as did wagons with grease boxes (particularly PO vehicles). The need for 'Accelerated E' trains was, therefore, still necessary.

8.30pm Exeter to Cardiff, Accel-E

The evening Exeter to Cardiff started life as a fast goods in the early 1890s, but was downgraded to ordinary goods around the turn of the century. The train was running as an E from World War 1, but only upgraded to 'Accelerated E' in 1934, under which code it ran until late 1936 (after which it carried lamps of the new D headcode). The formation of this train from Exeter was:

Cardiff Shed Vac
Newport (Dock Street) Vac
Newport (High Street) Vac
Northern Non-Vac
Taunton Non-Vac
Newport (High Street) Non-Vac

Newport (Dock Street) Non-Vac
Cardiff Non-Vac
West Wales Non-Vac

The wagons for Taunton and its branches (Barnstaple, Minehead and Chard) were not to exceed 15 in number. Scheduled engine power for this train was a '43XX', with 40 wagons maximum leaving Exeter yard, many collected from trains ex-Newton Abbot.

The first part of the journey involved a gentle and almost continuous climb to Tiverton Jct, some 15 miles and 35 minutes distant. Wagons were attached here from local branches and from the early afternoon all-stations pick-up goods from Exeter. Forty minutes were allowed for marshalling, and also to permit the C-headcode 4.25pm Penzance to Paddington perishable (the 'Searchlight') to pass ahead. The 8.30pm left Tiverton at 9.45pm, the maximum load now being 60, just about the limit for a '43XX' over Whiteball with Class 3 traffic.

It entered Whiteball Tunnel at 10pm and after one minute at the Stop Board at the top of Wellington bank it took the main line through Norton Fitzwarren, to be diverted around the goods loop to the south of Taunton station where another call was made between 10.35 and 11.5pm. Traffic attached came from local branch lines, while wagons for services to Bristol and Westbury as well as local lines were detached. The train was now formed:

Cardiff Station Truck Vac
Cardiff Shed Vac
Newport (Dock Street) Vac
Newport (High Street) Vac
St Philip's Marsh Non-Vac (if required)
Rhondda Valley Livestock and Perishables Non-Vac
Newport (High Street) Non-Vac
Newport (Dock Street) Non-Vac
Cardiff Non-Vac
West Wales Non-Vac

In 1934, on leaving the yard, the 8.30pm from Exeter followed the Up Postal along the recently-added relief line as far as Cogload, then called at Bridgwater between 11.30pm and midnight to pick up local feeder traffic. A subsequent call (CR) was made at Highbridge to pick up livestock traffic for St Philip's Marsh. A non-stop run was then made to Bristol, where the train called at West depot between 1.37 and 2am for examination and water purposes (EW in the STT), and again at Pylle Hill (2.11) to change enginemen and guard. If there were livestock traffic for St Philip's Marsh, the 8.30pm would take the Bristol relief line, and regain its route again via Marsh Jct and North Somerset Jct; otherwise it ran via Temple Meads and South Wales Jct. A bank engine came on at Stapleton Road at 2.21am for the 1 in 75 Filton incline, the climb starting at 2.35am. At the top, the banker was detached as the train waited (2.45-3am) for the 10.30pm Paddington to Cardiff C headcode vac freight ('South Wales Borderer') to pass ahead from the Badminton route towards the tunnel, and also for it to be overtaken by the Class E Bristol East depot to Aberdare service.

The call at the Stop Board between Patchway Tunnel and Pilning lasted for five minutes, from 3.5 to 3.10am, followed by the Severn Tunnel banking procedures at Pilning Jct with an extra locomotive in front (3.18-3.42). The tunnel was entered at 3.48

Marshalling Instructions for Through and Important Local Freight Trains—continued.

Formation and Headmarks.	Engine Group.	Traffic attached on Route.		REMARKS.
		At	To be formed	

BRISTOL (West Depot)—contd.
 	
9.35 p.m. Tavistock Junction "E" ✠
Engine
Through Vacuums for Laira
Newton Abbot and Branches
Cornish
Plymouth and District
	D	Hackney (when necessary to make up full load).	With wagons on train.	Headmarks may be reduced on Saturday nights only by arrangement between Bristol and Exeter Controls.
				Load 64 Class 2 and 3 traffic to Newton Abbot—50 beyond.
				Feeding trains at West Depot :—
				   No. 10 Transfer 8.0 p.m. ex Pylle Hill.
				   No. 11 Transfer 1.30 p.m. ex Temple Meads.
				   No. 2 Transfer 6.45 p.m. ex Temple Meads.
				   No. 12 Transfer 1.25 p.m. ex East Depot.
				   2.45 a.m. ex Worcester (3.30 a.m. Mondays).
				   12.50 p.m. ex Severn Tunnel Junction.
				Feeding trains at Newton Abbot :—
				   2.15 p.m. Moretonhampstead.
				   3.25 p.m. Kingswear and 7.10 p.m. Paignton.
				Connecting trains at Hackney :—
				   4.45 a.m. Newton Abbot to Torre.
				   6.10 a.m. Newton Abbot to Kingswear.
				   6.55 a.m. Newton Abbot to Totnes.
				   11. 5 a.m. Newton Abbot to Moretonhampstead.
				   10.20 a.m. Newton Abbot to Ashburton.
				Connecting train at Tavistock Junction :—
				   4.35 a.m. Tavistock Junction to Ponsandane
				Connecting trains at Laira :—
				   6.25 a.m. Laira to Plymouth.
				   6.35 a.m. Laira to Tavistock.
				   7.43 a.m. Laira to Plymouth.
				   7.45 a.m. Laira to Sutton Harbour.
				   8.20 a.m. Laira to Friary.
				   7.50 a.m. Laira to Devonport.
				   9.35 a.m. Laira to Yealmpton (WSX).
				   9.35 a.m. Laira to St. Austell.
				   9.55 a.m. Laira to Launceston.
				Traffic for Plymouth District and for Stations not served by 4.35 a.m. Tavistock Junction to be worked to Laira by 4.5 a.m. transfer.

Marshalling Instructions for Through and Important Local Freight Trains—continued.

Formation and Headmarks.	Engine Group.	Traffic attached en route.		REMARKS.
		At	To be formed	

PENZANCE.
1.15 p.m. Bristol "E" ✠
Engine
Station Trucks
From Truro :—
Engine
†Exeter S.T.
†Exeter Goods
Bristol S.T.
Bristol (Canons Marsh)
Taunton and District Meat and Cattle
Bristol Depots
Common User Empties
†Newton Abbot and Branch from Stations at which 6.50 p.m. Marazion does not call.
†Exeter
§Northern traffic
‖Reading
London District rough traffic
Laira
From Laira :—
Engine
Canons Marsh Vacuum
Station Trucks
Taunton and District Meat and Cattle
Canons Marsh Non-Vacuum
L.M. & S. Line via Bristol
Bristol Depots
	D To Truro. 2-8-0 Truro to Laira. E From Laira. D	Marazion
		St. Erth
		Hayle
		Gwinear Road
		Camborne
		Drump Lane
		Truro
		*Grampound Rd. (CR)
		Bodmin Road
		Laira
		Newton Abbot
			With wagons on train.	Runs at accelerated "E" speed from Truro.
				Load, 64 wagons Newton to Bristol.
				Calls locally as between Penzance and Truro.
				Feeding trains :—
				  St. Erth—11.50 a.m. ex St. Ives.
				  Gwinear Road—2.2 p.m. ex Helston.
				  Drump Lane—2.50 p.m. ex Penzance to Paddington.
				  Truro—3.15 p.m. ex Falmouth. 1.35 p.m. ex Camborne.
				      2.30 p.m. Carn Brea Yard. 2.55 p.m. Newquay to Truro (MWF.)
				  Bodmin Road—2. 0 p.m. ex Truro. 4.30 p.m. ex Bodmin.
				†Detached at Laira for 4.45 a.m. Laira to Exeter.
				§Connecting train at Laira :—4. 5 a.m. Laira to Exeter.
				‖Connect at Laira with 12.40 a.m. Laira to Reading.
				*For Hide and Skin traffic.
				Feeding trains at Laira :— Feeding trains at Newton Abbot :—
				  6.45 p.m. ex Devonport. 3.25 p.m. ex Kingswear.
				  8.16 p.m. ex Plymouth. 2.35 p.m. ex Ashburton.
				  5.15 p.m. ex Sutton Harbour. 7.10 p.m. ex Paignton.
				  11.45 a.m. Yealmpton to Laira (WSX.) 2.15 p.m. ex Moretonhampstead.
				  12.15 p.m. ex Doublebois. 5.20 p.m. ex Ivybridge.
				  3. 0 p.m. Launceston to Laira.
				S.T. and Canons Marsh traffic must be formed next to engine from Laira.
				On Mondays and Wednesdays conveys Live Stock traffic for South Wales from stations West of Laira and Launceston Branch.
				Connecting trains at Taunton :—
				  6.45 a.m. Taunton to Barnstaple.
					7.30 a.m. Taunton to Yeovil.
					May convey Up and Down side traffic (including Avonmouth tanks) from West Depot to East Depot on Sunday mornings.
					Connecting train at East Depot Mondays :—2.15 a.m. East Depot to Cardiff.
					Conveys :—
					  P.T. 276 Falmouth to Bristol (T.Th.S.) from Truro to Bristol.
					  P.T. 364 Kingsbridge to Bristol (M.W.F.) from Newton Abbot to Bristol.
					  P.T. 371 Kingswear to Bristol (M.W.F.) from Newton Abbot to Bristol.
					  P.T. 390 Launceston to Bristol from Laira to Bristol.
					  P.T. 494 Newquay to Bristol from Bodmin Road to Bristol.
					  S.T. 611 Penzance to Bristol from Drump Lane to Bristol.
					  S.T. 613 Penzance to Exeter from Drump Lane to Laira.
					  S.T. 689 St. Austell to Bristol from Bodmin Road to Bristol.

An Acton-Newbury Accelerated-E headcode goods on the Berks & Hants line headed by 1906-built 4-4-0 *County of Chester.* There is a string of eight Mica meat vans behind the first three wagons. *A G Atkins collection*

and exited at 4am. On clearing the tunnel, a call was made at Severn Tunnel Jct to detach the banker. The train also called at the STJ marshalling yard to put off the Rhondda traffic (4.6-4.40).

At this time (1934), the route between the western outskirts of Severn Tunnel Jct and Newport (East Usk Jct) was still only double track, and the 8.30pm ran along it in front of the 1am Paddington to Swansea express passenger. The Exeter goods was held at Newport East to allow the Paddington to overtake and enter the station, after which the Accelerated-E train moved through into Newport Goods, where the two High Street sections (now together) were detached. After that brief call, the train moved down to Ebbw Jct, where the Dock Street portions were removed.

The final nine miles to Roath sidings were then completed with a 6am scheduled arrival; from there, traffic was dispersed onwards to Newtown Goods and destinations beyond by six other services originating in the Cardiff area.

10.15pm Oxley to Westbury Accel-E

This is a train that changed Up and Down directions many times during its journey. As shown in section 13 of the 1933 STT, page 110, having departed Oxley, it passed Wolverhampton station in the Up direction at 10.15pm, and paused at Wednesbury (10.32*10.50; * meaning not to perform work) and at Queen's Head (11.9-11.50), and travelled on the relief line to arrive at Hockley at 11.57pm. Departing at 12.15am and now classified as being in the Down direction (Section 13, page 124), the train ran through Snow Hill at 12.19 to Tyseley (12.26-12.46). Bearley West Jct was passed at 1.23, Stratford-upon-Avon at 1.31, Honeybourne East Jct at 1.47, and the train stopped for a bank engine at Honeybourne South Jct. Now becoming an Up train (Section 15, page 41), it paused at Moreton-in-Marsh from 2.19-2.49, and then passed Kingham at 3.3, Yarnton at 3.33 to arrive at Oxford at 3.40am (**CR** for cattle only). Section 4, page 12, shows the train arriving at Didcot Foxhall Jct in the Down direction at 4.1am and standing until 4.16, after which Steventon was passed at 4.22, Wantage Road on the relief line at 4.31, to come to a stand at Challow (4.38-4.47am). The train remained at Swindon Transfer sidings from 5.16 to 5.40, before moving on to Chippenham (6.11-6.26, **L**) as found in Section 3, page 12. (**L** indicted that the train could stop only to detach traffic.)

Thingley Jct was passed at 6.32am, Melksham (6.41-6.55, **L**), Holt Jct (**CRL**), Trowbridge (7.7-7.25, **L**) arriving at Westbury at 7.37am.

D-HEADCODE: EXPRESS VACUUM GOODS TRAINS

When the 1936 *Appendix to the Rule Book* was issued, the Accelerated-E trains were moved to a newly-expanded D-headcode. The new D-headcode took the lamp positions of the former H-headcode (two lamps on the buffer beam, one at the centre and one the left side facing the engine). The old D-headcode covered just empty coaching stock and had a bell code 2 pause 2 pause 1. That bell code was retained for coaching stock in the new D-headcode, but express vac goods trains running under the new D-headcode had bell code 2 pause 2 pause 3. Since the positions of headlamps of pre-1936 H-headcode trains and post-1936 D-headcode freight trains were identical, it follows that in undated photographs it will not always be clear whether the train is an H (1918-1936) or a D (after August 1936). If the headlamps are painted white (introduced in December 1936), it will most likely be a D-headcode; if red, an H, but between August and December of 1936, and until stocks of red-painted lamps were used up, it could be either.

The new type of partially-fitted Class D goods train ran at a maximum speed of 35mph. The engine's vacuum was connected to at least four wagons on trains of up to 40 wagons, increasing to a minimum of 11 on 70-wagon trains, with not more than half of the train's total being the maximum figure. While grease axlebox wagons continued to be permitted on this type of train, it was under restricted loading conditions, whereby such vehicles could carry no more than half of their registered capacity, the load being evenly distributed, and special attention was to be given to inspections of them *en route*. With the introduction of class D, the Accelerated-E class was withdrawn, although of course the original E-headcode itself remained in use.

Around 20 D trains were running daily in the late 1930s, with a '49XX' or '68XX' usually at the head.

2.10am Basingstoke to Oxley sidings, D

Following the addition of standard gauge to the broad-gauge rails between Oxford and Basingstoke in 1856, through running of goods trains between the North of England and the LSWR became possible. There were no regular GW narrow-gauge passenger services to the South Western at that time; it was the passage of freight without transhipment that was of particular value.

By the late 1930s there were three partially-fitted trains each way — one C, one E and a D — the classification depending upon the load. The 'BBC' (Basingstoke, Birmingham, Crewe) C-headcode

A farm removal undertaken by the GWR on 29 September 1936 was from Bletchington (between Oxford and Banbury) and Crudgington (between Wellington and Market Drayton in Shropshire). The train is hauled by 'Star' 4-6-0 No 4044 *Prince George* carrying the new D-headcode that was introduced in August 1936 to replace the former Accelerated-E classification. The removal concerned 130 head of cattle, all the farm equipment, and the contents of four households. The whole operation was completed in one day. *GWR/D J Hyde collection*

train No 152) left at 9.35pm and on weekdays ran effectively non-stop (apart from gradient Stop Board and water requirements) from Reading West Jct via Oxford, Honeybourne and Tyseley to Oxley. Another train (that departed at 6.55pm in 1925) was permitted to carry either the C- or E-headcode depending on the urgency of the traffic and the axleboxes of the vehicles.

The D (former Accelerated-E) headcode 'Cherbourg' (train No 151) left Basingstoke at 2.10am some five hours after the 'BBC' but took the different route via Reading, Oxford and Banbury. In both cases, the trains departed from Basingstoke in the Up direction, but became Down trains beyond Reading.

The 2.10am ex-Basingstoke was formed:

Oxley sidings Vac
* Banbury Livestock
* Tanks, Netley to Banbury
¶ Bordesley Livestock
 Hockley
 Banbury Jct (to include †Moor Street, †Bordesley Jct and
‡ Leamington)
 Oxley sidings Non-Vac
 Reading West Jct (Loaded wagons only)

Traffic was dispersed *en route* according to the designations: * at Oxford; † ‡ Banbury Jct; ¶ Tyseley Carriage sidings. Feeder services at Basingstoke were nearly all from the Southern Railway, including those that arrived at 3.12, 6.12 and 8.43pm from Southampton docks.

The train started from Basingstoke with a 'Hall', with a maximum load of 70 wagons as far as Banbury. Its first stop was at Reading West Jct, at the Down Old yard (2.44-3.15am), where the

rearmost portion was removed (to be picked up by trains calling there such as 10.30pm C-headcode Paddington-Gloucester and Cardiff, 12.55pm E-headcode Paddington-Gloucester and 6.25pm J-code Westbury-Banbury). Traffic was attached at Reading from Winchester, and from the 6.25pm ex-Hayes F-code, 6.40 ex-Brentford E-code, and 9pm pilot goods from Reading's King's Meadow low-level yard. The 'Cherbourg' set off, passing Didcot East at 3.43, to call briefly at Oxford (4.2-4.12am) to detach livestock traffic and petrol tanks for Banbury (to be taken forward by the 2am Reading West Jct to Oxley train that called later at Oxford, and to be dropped off at Banbury South). Traffic from local area trains was also picked up at Oxford.

The 2.10am passed through Banbury station and called at Banbury Jct to detach traffic for Bordesley Jct, Moor Street, Leamington, and the LNER. It worked for some 50 minutes for marshalling, adding wagons from the LNER line, perishable traffic for the North of England and Scotland from Trowbridge and Calne, which had arrived on station truck No 141 from Chippenham, motor cars from Cowley and paper traffic ex-Littlemore brought from Oxford by the 6.50pm Newton Abbot-Banbury (J-lamps). The load onwards was a maximum of 60 wagons.

It was held briefly at Leamington to allow the 6.25am local passenger for Wolverhampton to clear ahead, and again at Acock's Green where it caught up with that same train. The 'Cherbourg' stopped at Tyseley Carriage sidings if required, to drop off livestock for Bordesley, and to allow the 7.40am Solihull passenger to pass; the load now was a maximum of 58. It was held at Snow Hill station to permit the Solihull passenger to depart ahead, before easing forward through the tunnels to reach Hockley yard.

A 50-minute call was made there to carry out work, and to allow the busy morning suburban traffic to abate.

Having completed its work at Hockley, the Basingstoke headed for Handsworth, where there was yet another traffic check for a terminating local empty passenger train, before having a clear run to Stow Heath, then Wolverhampton, where it was held to allow the 7.56am Evesham to Shrewsbury passenger to overtake it. With the Evesham clear, the train made its way into Oxley yard, where much of the stock was transferred onwards to Crewe (by the 4am 'Northern Exchange)'; to Birkenhead by the 3.30 and 6.50am trains; and to Wellington (Salop) by the 7.20am Oxley-Coleham.

When this train was an Accelerated-E goods, the timings in the 1933 STT were slightly different from those above taken from the 1938 STT, in particular the amount of time allowed for work at stations: at Banbury Jct in 1933 it called from 5.9-5.34am; at Tyseley from 6.49-7.8; and, at Hockley from 7.26 to 7.42 to drop off only. It took the relief line at Soho & Winson Green and passed Handsworth at 7.52, and terminated at Oxley at 8.10am. In the reverse direction between Oxley and Basingstoke in 1938 were the C-headcode 1.30am (the 'Southern Docker') and the E-headcode 2.10am (the 'Southerner').

F-HEADCODE: EXPRESS GOODS TRAINS

The earliest version of this headcode concerned 'Express Cattle or Express Goods Train Class B'. Later was added 'These Head Lights may also be carried by Full Train Loads of Ballast or other Materials for Engineering purposes if running intact long distances'. That combined description is found in the 1927 STT. Merchandise traffic was conveyed, but mineral traffic and/or empties were also carried. In 1936, its description was changed to 'through fast freight train not running under C, D or E lamps, with through load'. In other words, Class F trains had no fitted wagons attached to the loco, and were marshalled with wagons for the first stop on the engine, for the last on the brake van, and wagons attached at intermediate points being lined up in reverse order.

In the late 1930s, there were around 120 Class F trains running daily, over both short (eg Gloucester to Kemble and Welshpool to Shrewsbury) and long distances. '43XX's were common on these trains, with some '68XX', while a few '28XX', '30XX' and '72XX' goods engines were also rostered.

There were 'working arrangements' whereby GW express goods trains were advantageously routed through Ashchurch (on the LMS Bristol to Birmingham line) from Lansdown Jct (Cheltenham), at the end of the GW/LMS joint line, to Abbot's Wood Jct at Worcester. Trains so routed during weekdays in 1936 – it so happened that they were all F-headcode – were the 4.40pm Cardiff to Worcester, the 9.55pm Cardiff to Oxley (including the same train on Saturdays) and the 9.50am Stourbridge Jct to Cardiff; on Sundays it was the 12.55am Worcester to Bristol. Routing of these trains did not exercise running powers, but balanced other working arrangements whereby LMS trains travelled over GWR metals principally from Avonmouth through Henbury and Stoke Gifford to the LMS line at Yate.

Most goods trains in the Central Wales district were K-headcode, but there were a few F-headcode. For example, at 2.10am a Down F-headcode left Welshpool for Machynlleth, calling 18 miles further on at Moat Lane Jct (3.1-3.15), after which came a single line section with a 1 in 52 descent to Llanbrynmair at the

Marshalling Instructions for Through and Important Local Freight Trains—continued.

Formation and Headmarks.	Engine Group.	Traffic Attached en Route.		REMARKS.
		At	To be formed	
OXFORD—continued.				
6.50 a.m. Severn Tunnel Jo. "F" ..	D	Yarnton	} At one shunt.	Load 70 wagons.
Engine		*Gloucester (D.B.S.)		Conveys odd wagons to Honeybourne for Worcester and South Staffordshire district attached at Oxford Road.
†Cheltenham				† C.R. at Malvern Road to detach only.
Gloucester				*†Gloucester Docks Branch Sidings to make up load for Severn Tunnel Junction, East Usk Junction and Pontypool Road.
Severn Tunnel Jct.				Feeding train at Gloucester :—
				11.35 p.m. (2.5 a.m. MO) Swindon to Neath.
				Connecting trains at Severn Tunnel Junction—
				For Eastern Valleys 4.20 p.m. Severn Tunnel Junction to Pontnewynydd.
				Western Valleys 8.55 a.m. Exeter to Rogerstone.
				Newport } 4.40 p.m. Stoke Gifford to Cardiff.
				Cardiff }
				Pontypool Road, 10.50 p.m. Bristol to Pontypool Road
7.45 a.m. Moreton-in-Marsh "K" ..	A	Local Stations		Feeding trains at Oxford :—
Local "pick up"				1.30 a.m. Park Royal to Worcester.
				4.52 p.m. Taplow to Oxford.
				8.15 p.m. Thame to Oxford.
				8.55 p.m. Swindon to Oxley Sidings.
				5.25 p.m. Fairford to Oxford.
				5.59 p.m. Abingdon to Oxford.
				4.55 a.m. Didcot to Oxford.
				Connecting train at Moreton-in-Marsh :—
				10.10 p.m. Moreton-in-Marsh to Honeybourne.
				Conveys:—
				S.T. 155 Bristol to Worcester from Oxford to Moreton-in-Marsh.
				S.T. 526 Oxford to Hockley from Oxford to Moreton-in-Marsh.

'Aberdare' No 2665 of 1902 on an F-headcode through goods passing Hatherley Jct (Cheltenham) just after the Grouping. First wagon is lettered GN, second LMS, third LBSC, and the fourth GW. All except the GW open have grease axleboxes. *LGRP*

Below: F-headlights on a 2-6-2T No 6110 in 1946. The train is composed mainly of PO wagons, whose condition reflects longer intervals between repairs during World War 2. *W Beard*

No 4976 *Wenfield Hall* shunts at Helsby Jct, Cheshire, on the GW/LMS joint line. The loads on the first two open wagons and on the bogie Macaw of this F-class train are sheeted over, and the load on the bogie Crocodile at the right is very large and shored up by baulks of timber. *Ian C Allen*

No 3830 *County of Oxford* (built in 1912 so no re-numbering) heads a Down freight near Dawley Jct signalbox (near Hayes & Harlington) on 16 August 1930. The headcode is class F. The van next to engine is followed by a long GW Open C tube wagon. *Ken Nunn collection/LCGB*

A Down F-headcode goods seen at King's Sutton, south of Banbury, just after the Grouping. The second to fourth wagons in the train are piled high with timber. In the background, on the left, there is an LSWR van. The locomotive, *Guy Mannering,* was built in July 1904 as 4-4-2 No 184 at the time of comparisons with the French 4-4-2s and was rebuilt as a 4-6-0 in August 1912 when it became No 2984. *LGRP*

A 'Dean Goods' carries the F-headcode on the former Cambrian Railways single-line section between Aberdovey and Machynlleth. *H W Burman*

'Aberdare' 2-6-0 No 2629 of 1901 heads an F-headcode, class B, express goods ex-Bordesley Jct near Hatherley Jct, Cheltenham, on 24 September 1924. *H G W Household/Swindon Museum*

2-8-2T No 7209 seen near Oxford hauling an F-headcode freight in wintry conditions. *A G Atkins collection*

'43XX' No 5359 passes King's Sutton just before the Grouping; the locomotive became No 8359 with increased weight on the pony truck after 1928. The Toad behind the locomotive has large GW lettering and a white roof that has not yet gone grey with smoke and dust. The headcode is F — the middle lamp on the buffer beam is obscured in the picture by the vacuum pipe. *LGRP*

top of which was a Stop Board where the train stood between 3.45-3.50 for pinning down brakes. 10 miles further on at Cemmes Road, the train crossed another Up F-headcode goods before terminating at Machynlleth at 4.40am. The Up F-headcode train had left Machynlleth at 4am on the single line for Newtown, calling at Llanbrynmair (5.48-6.0), then at the Stop Board (6.20-6.25) before the descent into Carno to arrive at 6.34am. Departing at 6.47, the train missed out stations at Clatter and Pontdolgoch before calling at Caersws (7.7-7.30). Double lines were met at Moat Lane Jct where the train stopped (7.34-8.5) before it ended its journey at 8.20am at Newtown.

Another F-headcode goods train in mid-Wales was the following:

4am Moat Lane Jct to Talyllyn, F

The train departed at 4am. After eight miles, its first stop was Llanidloes (4.26-4.35) as listed on page 140 of Section 14 of the 1933 STT. It stopped if required to detach traffic at Rhayader, before meeting the Stop Board above Elan Jct (1 in 60-70 falling gradient) where brakes were pinned down. Builth Wells, 34 miles from Moat Lane, was the next stop (6.5-6.17) but it was timetabled to call at the previous station (Builth Road, ex-Cambrian and LNW mid-Wales line, from 5.50 to 5.59) when required to put off dolomite traffic for the LMS, or to pick up in one shunt traffic for the LMS via Three Cocks Jct. Three Cocks (ex-Cambrian and Midland railways from Hereford through Hay-on-Wye) was 14 miles after Builth Wells and was the next stop (6.55-7.30). The train paused at Talgarth (7.40-7.50) where traffic was detached as required, before terminating at Talyllyn at 8.10am.

6.30pm Bristol to Weymouth, F

The 6.30pm ex-Bristol East depot was a typical cross-country goods train. It started as an Up train in book 4 of the STT and continued as a Down train in book 3. It ran a 92-mile journey, and beyond Trowbridge it called for work only at principal yards. This train took traffic originating in the Bristol area, and also traffic brought in from the Worcester area attached *en route* at Honeybourne, Gloucester and Stoke Gifford. Scheduled for '43XX' haulage, the train was limited to a single-engine load for Bradford Bank (62 wagons). It was formed thus:

Westbury†
Bruton*
Witham
Yeovil
Maiden Newton
Bridport Branch
Dorchester
Weymouth

Leaving at 6.30pm, it ran non-stop via Bathampton (7.3pm) and the Bradford Junctions to Trowbridge (7.29-8.5), where it was required to pick up any 'late-loaded' traffic for London (†), to be attached next to the engine and detached at Westbury to be picked up by the 6.35pm Weymouth to Paddington C-headcode goods (the 'Up Jersey'). It also paused at Trowbridge for the passage of the 6.57 Bristol to Salisbury passenger that called at Trowbridge (7.52-7.54) and the Swindon to Weymouth milk empties before running to Westbury where it stood from 8.20 to 8.30pm.

The next call was at Witham, where both local and Bruton traffic (indicated in the STT by an asterisk *) were detached, the latter to connect with the following morning's 8.40am Westbury to Weymouth. It also picked up traffic from trains off the Wells branch. Then on to Yeovil Pen Mill (10.14-10.30), to detach traffic for local (including SR) and Langport branch destinations, as well as picking up any wagons loaded locally.

Having passed under the Southern main line, the 6.30pm started a gentle climb towards Yetminster, where it stopped (10.41-10.45) for the banker to help on the four-mile haul up Evershot bank, that had a significant portion as steep as 1 in 51. The next call was Maiden Newton (11.16-11.24), to detach local and Bridport branch traffic, followed by the eight-mile run to Dorchester to detach wagons for local destinations (11.45pm to 12.10am). The run to Weymouth was interrupted by a call at the Stop Board (12.20) near the northern entrance to Bincombe Tunnel to pin down brakes before the descent of 1 in 52/50 to Upwey Jct, followed by another section of 1 in 74 to Radipole. The train was scheduled to terminate at Weymouth Jct yard at 12.34am, with connexions on to Portland and Abbotsbury.

2.10am Crimea sidings (Paddington) to Bordesley (MX), F

The train ran over the Relief mainline passing Old Oak Common

West Jct at 2.20am where it took the line to Park Royal that was reached at 2.26 (page 180, Section 1 of the 1933 STT). Greenford East Loop was passed at 3.1am, South Ruislip at 3.9, and High Wycombe at 3.49 before coming to a halt at Princes Risborough at 4.14. Departing at 4.40am, the train passed Ashenden Jct at 5.3, Bicester at 5.25 and then halted at Aynho Jct (5.48-5.59am) to let other traffic through. Banbury (6.12-6.24) and Banbury Jct (6.30-6.55) were called at before stopping at Leamington to do work (7.42-8.32). Between 8.39 and 8.46 the train was at Warwick and work was subsequently done at Hatton. Leaving at 9.20am, Lapworth was passed at 9.30 before the train paused at Acocks Green & South Yardley (9.50-9.55) to be overtaken. Bordesley Jct was reached at 10.10am (page 15, Section 13 of the STT).

G-HEADCODE: LIGHT ENGINE, or LIGHT ENGINES COUPLED TOGETHER, or ENGINE & VAN

This was not a train code as such, but the class covering either light engine movements or, particularly, engine and brake van transits to and from yards. These were very much part of the overall traffic pattern, and were a vital part of the coal traffic arrangements in South Wales as the pair were dispatched on either a regular basis or on demand as 'Control Trains' to collieries, yards or docks (see Chapters 12 and 15). Targetted engines might typically leave shed and run straight to the van sidings at Abercynon, Cathays, Ferndale, Radyr or Treherbert to pick up their van for the day's work.

Again, when the amount of traffic after a country cattle market or horse fair was sufficiently heavy to justify a special train for which a loco, brake van and guard had to be ordered out from a major station, the G-headcode would be used.

Perhaps surprisingly, on page 52 of Section 13 of the 1933 STT, the G-headcode is given for a return empty auto train to Banbury (also in Section 1 for a return auto departing West Ealing at 7.53 pm, arriving Southall at 8pm) but the expected D-headcode is given for identical trains elsewhere (eg Section 1, page 101).

H-HEADCODE: THROUGH GOODS TRAINS (Carrying Through Load to Destination)

Class H trains were the long-distance loose-coupled goods services that carried nearly all types of traffic — heavy coal and mineral

A mixed train in 1938 at Pontrilas, on the Golden Valley line, is soon to set off on the 19-mile journey to Hay-on-Wye. Three mixed trains and two passenger trains ran on weekdays. The 0-4-2T shows the light engine G-headcode but all trains on this branch were supposed to carry the passenger B-headcode. According to the 1933 STT, brake vans on this branch did not carry sidelamps. *J D Hewitt*

2-6-2T No 5542 shunts at Minehead. Café Strand visible in the background is to the north of the goods yard. The date of the photograph is unknown, but there were two Up (to Taunton) goods trains per day in 1933, one at 12.35pm arriving Taunton at 4.37pm and the other departing at 3.35pm and arriving at Taunton at 7pm. Both called at all stations on the 25-mile long branch and carried K-headlamps. The locomotive shows the G-headcode for a light engine and van. *SLS*

services, empties, and some general merchandise. In the early years of the C20[th] they would typically be hauled by 0-6-0 tender engines. By the 1930s, '28XX' locomotives (and '72XXs' in the late 1930s) handled over half of the 140 or so daily H goods trains of that time. Despite the use of 'through load to destination', some H trains carried loads for intermediate points (the headlamp code was dictated by the STT and was, perhaps, not always consistent). The position of the lamps for H-headcode trains changed in August 1936 from two lamps on the buffer beam on the left facing the engine, to two on the right of the buffer beam facing the locomotive (see comments under the D-headcode).

1am Rogerstone to Yarnton, H

The train was made up of empty iron ore wagons returning to Irthlingborough (LMS) in Northamptonshire. It left Rogerstone sidings at 1am behind a '28XX' class 2-8-0, and had no intermediate calls, except for water and wagon examination.

The first leg was via Gaer Junction to Newport (High Street) station, where a stop was made on the through road to allow the F-headcode 8.45pm Margam to Worcester (H-headcode when conveying grease axlebox tank wagons), that was going to run ahead of it along the same route, to gain headway. With the Worcester train some seven minutes clear ahead, the 1am set off for a non-stop run through Severn Tunnel Jct station and alongside the River Severn to its next stop, Lydney, where it was refuged to allow the 12.45am Cardiff (Pengam) to Banbury E-headcode express freight to pass. This latter train had left East Usk sidings some 24 minutes after the 1am had departed the Newport area, but by the time the 1am had reached Lydney it had narrowed the gap to 14 minutes, and was allowed to overtake on its non-stop run to Gloucester. The 1am was further held at Lydney to allow the 3.5am Lydney to Oxford coal train, another class H, to move ahead.

The next leg was short, to Bullo Pill, where the train was held for 20 minutes to take water, and for the first intermediate examination to take place. Setting off again, the 1am was next held at Gloucester station to allow the 4.40am Class E to Cheltenham from Gloucester Transfer sidings (located alongside the Cheltenham Loop that fed into the Gloucester South Jct area) to pass ahead of it. Moving on to Engine Shed Jct, the Rogerstone train was held again to allow the 4.40 Gloucester sufficient headway on the (then) single Up line to Cheltenham. When clear, the 1am followed the 4.40 until the latter turned off on to the St James's branch, after which the train had a clear run ahead to Toddington, where the train was held for 20 minutes for its second water and examination stop, some 30 miles after the first.

Routed on to the OWW line at Honeybourne, the 1am had to manoeuvre between junctions as there was no direct connexion from Gloucester to Oxford. The train firstly ran ahead through the junctions until the brake van was clear of East Loop Jct at the Stratford end of East Loop box, then halted. The waiting bank engine then moved forward on to the brake van, and the whole train reversed along the North loop (with the banker leading) towards Honeybourne station, where it stopped, and the banker removed.

The 1am remained at Honeybourne for almost an hour whilst other movements took place around it. These included a couple of freights that were calling at Honeybourne yard, and a passenger train (the first Up express of the morning, 6.45am Shrub Hill to Paddington that called at all stations to Handborough). Once the express had reached Chipping Campden, the 1am left Honeybourne to follow along behind, running non-stop to Yarnton, due at 9.1am. The '28XX' was removed, and the train went on behind an LMS locomotive for the remainder of its journey via Bletchley to the Northamptonshire iron ore fields. This was one of

ACTON—continued.

Formation and Headmarks		Engine Group	Traffic attached on Route		REMARKS
			At	To be formed	
3.10 a.m. MX Reading "F" 5.45 a.m. Sundays "K" Engine West Drayton and Branches Slough Taplow and Wycombe Branch Maidenhead Twyford and Branch Reading Goods Reading West Junction	..	C 4-4-2 T	Slough †Taplow †Maidenhead	} With wagons on train.	Load 80 wagons. Feeding trains at Acton :— 12.55 a.m. Paddington for Maidenhead traffic. 12.41 a.m. Smithfield. 9.15 p.m. South Lambeth. 10.30 a.m. St. Pancras. 2.53 p.m. Temple Mills. 3.45 p.m. Cricklewood. 8. 0 p.m. Victoria and Albert. 9.30 p.m. Plaistow. Connecting trains at West Drayton :— 6. 5 a.m. to Staines. 6.20 a.m. to Uxbridge. Feeding trains at Slough :— 2.0 a.m. ex Paddington for Maidenhead traffic ex O.O.C. 8.43 p.m. Windsor to Slough. 9.30 p.m. West Drayton to Slough. †Must not convey surplus Northern empties from Taplow and Maidenhead. Feeding trains at Maidenhead :— 8.17 p.m. Loudwater to Slough. 9.25 p.m. Aylesbury to Paddington. Connecting trains :— At Slough :—5.45 a.m. and 8.55 a.m. to Windsor. At Taplow :—4.0 a.m. Slough to Oxford. At Twyford :—5.48 a.m. to Henley Branch. At Reading West Junction :—8.35 a.m. Local train to Didcot. 9.15 a.m. to Basingstoke. 1.45 a.m. Old Oak Common to Leamington (MO). 2.5 p.m. Reading West Junction to Tyseley for Tank Cars. Conveys :— P.T. 721 Staines to Reading from Slough to Reading.
7.45 a.m. Stoke Gifford "H" Engine Reading Reading West Junction †Swindon and West of England Newport Cardiff Stoke Gifford	..	D	Reading West Jct. Swindon	With wagons on train. At one shunt.	Load 75 wagons. Feeding train at Acton :—4.41 a.m. Smithfield. Conveys tank wagons for Bristol and Avonmouth. Locomotive and Carriage Department Stores Vans work on the 3.50 a.m. Old Oak Common to Reading West Junction to connect at that point with the 7.45 a.m. Acton. Feeding train at Swindon :—3.40 a.m. Banbury Junction to Bristol. †Weymouth Line and West of England traffic to be detached at Swindon. Connecting trains at Swindon :— 8.45 a.m. Didcot to Bristol (tank wagons). 1.20 p.m. Swindon to Weymouth (Cattle). 4. 5 p.m. Swindon to Laira. It is important that this train should connect with 4.40 p.m. SX, 9.35 p.m. SO, Stoke Gifford to Cardiff. Connecting trains at Stoke Gifford, 6.35 p.m. Stoke Gifford to Llandilo Junction. 1.20 p.m. Acton to S. Tunnel Junction

Marshalling Instructions for Through and Important Local Freight Trains—continued.

Formation and Headmarks.		Engine Group.	Traffic attached on Route.		REMARKS.
			At	To be formed	
STOKE GIFFORD—contd. 4.40 p.m. Cardiff "J"/ (9.35 p.m. SO) Engine †Severn Tunnel Junction Newport (High St.) §Newport (Dock St.), Alex. Dock, etc. Cardiff and District	..	..	A	Severn Tunnel Junction East Usk Junction Ebbw Junction	With wagons on train } At one shunt.	Conveys Pontypool and Hereford district traffic (ex Avonmouth) Stoke Gifford to Severn Tunnel Jc. when necessary. Feeding trains at Stoke Gifford :— 7.45 a.m. ex Acton. Connection to be maintained. 11.45 a.m. ex Avonmouth (for Hereford traffic). Feeding train at Severn Tunnel Junc. :— 2.5 a.m. Park Royal to Severn Tunnel Junc. † Including wagons for B. & M., Rhymney and Taff Vale sections to connect with 5. 0 a.m. Severn Tunnel Junc. to Pont Shon Norton. Feeding train at Severn Tunnel Junc. :— 8.45 a.m. Gloucester to Severn Tunnel Junc. § Detached at Ebbw Jct. Connecting trains at Cardiff :—Ely Valley, 7.40 a.m. ex Cardiff. Bridgend and L. & O. Section—3.50 a.m. ex Cardiff. Conveys S.T. 289 Gloucester to Cardiff from Severn Tunnel Junc. to Cardiff.
5.10 p.m. Tyseley "H" Engine Stratford-on-Avon Earlswood Lakes (CR) Shirley (CR) Hockley Bordesley Junct.	..	..	D 26XX	Toddington Stratford-on-Avon	} At one shunt.	Runs via Standish Junct. Feeding trains at Stoke Gifford :— 4.45 a.m. ex Taunton. 11.45 a.m. ex Avonmouth and Bristol transfers. May convey banana traffic Avonmouth to Lye, to connect with 3.5 a.m. Bordesley Junc. to Stourbridge Junc.
6.35 p.m. Llandilo Junct. "H" Engine Briton Ferry ‡Swansea Docks Felin Fran Llandilo Junct. and beyond or Port Talbot Felin Fran Llandilo Junction and beyond	..	..	D	Train runs via Felin Fran.		Feeding trains at Stoke Gifford :— 7.45 a.m. ex Acton. 7.35 a.m. ex Southall. 10.30 a.m. ex Swindon. ‡ Detached at Briton Ferry. Connecting trains at Felin Fran :— 6.15 a.m. Swansea Docks to Pantyffynnon. 2.40 p.m. Felin Fran to Pantyffynnon. 4.15 p.m. Felin Fran to Tirydail.
8. 5 p.m. Old Oak Common "H" Engine † Stores Van from Swindon Acton Old Oak Common	..	..	E	Swindon Hanwell Bridge	Reverse order at one shunt. At one shunt.	Load 60 wagons to Swindon, 90 Class 1 traffic beyond. † Conveys Swindon to Old Oak Common Stores van formed on engine. Feeding trains at Stoke Gifford :— 9.25 a.m. ex Margam Junc. 2.30 a.m. ex Llandilo Junc. Feeding train at Swindon :—6.15 a.m. Aberdare to Reading.

A 'Goods train carrying through load to destination' (1918-36 H-headcode of two lamps to the left on the buffer beam facing the engine) approaches Lea Mount Tunnel, Dawlish in 1919. ROD 2-8-0 No 3004 is in the condition as bought from the government, including Westinghouse brake pump mounted on the off-side of the smokebox, Ross pop safety valves and side chains on the front buffer beam. *Railway Magazine*

very few GW goods trains to run via Yarnton and the LMS before World War 2, the majority being routed via Leamington.

Although this service took eight hours to complete its 111-mile journey on GWR metals, some 2½ hours of that were stationary to allow traffic of greater priority to overtake.

11.55pm Laira sidings to Reading West Jct, H

In complete contrast to the 1am Rogerstone H, the 11.55pm Laira to Reading West Jct carried out a great deal of work *en route*. It was scheduled for haulage by either a 'Grange' or a '43XX', and was formed thus:

Empty Vacuum Stock
x Tavistock Jct
¶ Tavistock Jct (for 11.30pm Truro)
† Exeter
** Tiverton Jct, (CR, Suns)
§ Taunton
I Livestock for Bruton and Frome
Westbury
Newbury
a Southall, inc Brentford and West Ealing
Newton Abbot and branches
• Reading, including 'shorts' to Hayes
a Acton and Old Oak

The formation from Laira was geographical, with the wagons travelling furthest at the rear of the train. It was formed from traffic carried to Laira by a number of trains from Cornwall, and more from Plymouth itself. Also included were vehicles for Taunton that were unsuitable for the preceding 6.30pm C-headcode Drump Lane (Redruth) to Bristol, and also traffic for Acton and Old Oak unsuitable for vacuum services, indicated by 'a' in the above list.

To trace the path taken by this train requires inspection of three books of the 1933 STT (No 6, page 75; No 5, page 62; and, No 3, page 52). This will illustrate some of the inconsistencies that can occur within different books of a given STT, particularly what the station name(s) at the head of a column may mean. Do they mean where the train is going to, or where it has come from? At the start of a journey, it will be the destination station. Near the destination station, it will be where it has come from. In between when more than two STT books are involved, it may be either. In

2-6-0 No 6305 (built in 1920) hauls a pre-1936 H-headlamps goods at Frome, *circa* 1932/3 (ATC installed). The first van is LMS; there are then five GW Minks to Diagrams V21/23, V12, V21/23, V4 and V18. These are followed by two LMS vans, another GW, another LMS and then two GW Minks before a GW Toad followed by the rest of the train. *LGRP*

A southbound unfitted H-goods near Hatherley Jct (Cheltenham) hauled by 2-8-0 ROD No 3017 on 1 May 1937. The headlamps still painted red but are in post-1936 positions. *H G W Household/Swindon Museum*

An Exeter-Rogerstone through coal and coke empties pictured at Patchway in 1937. No 6820 *Kingstone Grange* carries the post-1936 H-headcode of two lamps to the right on the buffer beam facing the engine. *A G Atkins collection*

Book 6, this train is described as the 11.55 Reading Goods, as it is in Book 5; but in Book 3, it is the Laira Goods.

Moving off from Laira, the first of the intermediate calls to drop off and pick up traffic *en route* was made at Tavistock Jct (12 midnight–12.30am), just under a mile up the main line. Here, wagons that were destined for the 1.15am Plymouth (Millbay) to Avonmouth H-class train were removed (**x**), as were those for the 11.30pm Truro to Banbury Jct. (¶, J-headcode), which meant that neither of those trains had to call at Laira. During the 30-minute call at Tavistock Jct the train took on additional traffic from Cornwall and then set off through Plympton and up the 1 in 42 Hemerdon bank. The engine alone could take just 24 general merchandise wagons up the incline, and was therefore banked by the Tavistock Jct night banker (9.30pm, No 3 engine duty), which, along with the concurrent 1.50am duty (No 1), assisted all up freight trains until around 6am. As the banker dropped off, the

11.55pm continued unassisted to the stop board at the top of Rattery bank (1.16-1.20), some 300 yards beyond Rattery signalbox. Four minutes were allowed here for pinning down wagon brakes, and following the 4¼-mile descent to Totnes (for which 14 minutes was allowed start to stop, average running speed about 22mph), another four-minute call was made to release them (1.34-1.38). At the same time, the Totnes No 3 banker was run to the rear of the train to assist it up the range of gradients (as much as 1 in 37) over the 4½-miles to Dainton summit. Again, 14 minutes was allowed for the journey, with a halt at the top (1.53-1.57) to pin down the brakes for the two-mile descent to beyond Stoneycombe. The Divisional Boundary at Ashburton Jct had been passed at 1.40am. It was then mostly a level run over the mile or so to Aller Jct (2.7-2.10) where the brakes were once again released for the run to Newton Abbot station yard (2.15-2.25) to drop off three station trucks for Exeter and Paignton, before running the short distance to Hackney yard for its next work.

At Hackney between 2.28 and 3am, the task was to drop off traffic for the Kingswear line and local branches, and to pick up goods brought in from the same places. Some 25 minutes were permitted for this, after which the train set off along the river and coast sections to Exeter, with a maximum load of 62 class 3 equivalent (merchandise) wagons.

The yard at Exeter was between the passenger station and the river, just beyond the engine shed, and 20 minutes (3.50-4.10) were allowed for exchange of traffic. In addition to detaching wagons for local and connecting services (including for the SR), a raft of wagons for the North of England via the Severn Tunnel was dropped off, to be taken on to Bristol by a later service. The preceding 6.30pm C-headcode from Drump Lane (Redruth) to Bristol had dropped off wagons for Taunton at Exeter since it ran non-stop to Bristol, and these too were attached to the 11.55pm (†).

Oil-burning 2-8-0 No 3865 heads an Up H-headcode freight on the South Wales main line west of Cardiff in 1946. This photograph shows that, when first converted, oil-burning '28XXs' ran with their original running numbers before being changed to the '48XX' series. The sliding metal panel on the cabside window is a remnant of a wartime measure to reduce glare from the firebox during the blackout. *J G Hubback*

2-8-2T No 7204 hauls an Up H-headcode goods at Churchdown (between Cheltenham and Gloucester) in 1939. Previously red, headlamps were painted white after December 1936. Three Macaw Bs and an open wagon carry steel-bar traffic. *LGRP*

Below: In the summer after nationalisation, on 3 May 1948, '2884' class No 3825 with side-window cab stands and takes water on one of the through roads at Gloucester station heading an H-headcode freight. *SLS*

Oil-burner No 4807 (formerly No 2848) climbs Dainton Bank with a west-bound freight on 15 July 1947. The mixed goods train has sheeted opens (none using sheet supporters) and a Macaw B in view. *C F H Oldham*

Unnamed 'Bulldog' No 3419 (formerly No 3709 and built in 1906) hauls a post-1936 H-headcode goods at Wootton Bassett. The leading four vehicles are cattle wagons. There are some very tall tarpaulined loads in open wagons further down the train. *D J Hyde collection*

The train entered Whiteball Tunnel at 5.5am and ran along the main line all the way to Taunton where it took the goods loop lines to the south of the passenger station to detach its Drump Lane traffic, and where wagons from Minehead, Barnstaple and Chard were put on (5.32-5.55).

With a maximum load of 70, the train set off for Cogload Jct and the Berks & Hants route, which was pretty clear of other traffic at that time of the morning. Its next call was Castle Cary (7.4-7.7), to attach a banker to help over the 1 in 81 Brewham bank facing it. Four miles later, at Bruton, it called when required to detach livestock traffic from Cornwall, and might also run via the Frome loop to detach livestock at the station when required (Clink Road was passed at 7.48 when not calling at Frome station).

A call at Westbury was next (8.1-8.50), to detach any local and Salisbury traffic, and to pick up wagons from the Weymouth line. It was now entangled with the morning passenger traffic. After the 6.50am express from Weymouth had left Westbury at 8.39am, the 11.55pm ex-Laira was scheduled to have a clear run to Patney (where it would call when necessary to pick up any livestock traffic). Savernake was passed at 10.2 and Bedwyn at 10.12, then on to Newbury for the next timetabled stop (10.37-11.15). Here, wagons were detached for the Didcot and Winchester lines, and others picked up for Reading, including any from Tile Mills Siding (between Aldermaston and Theale) brought in by a Down local goods.

Its last intermediate stop was at Theale (11.47am to 12.14pm), where some traffic for Reading, including 'shorts' (•) for Hayes only, was detached for a following London train. It then ran to West Junction yard to terminate at 12.28am, its traffic being disposed of on to other services mostly bound for stations to Old Oak Common, Basingstoke and Reading's Coley goods branch.

6.10pm Pontypool Road to Oxley goods, H
The start of this train as far as Worcester Tunnel Jct is found in Section 12 page 71 of the 1933 STT; the continuation is in Section 15 page 6. In Section 12 it is called the 'Oxley sidings goods'; in Section 15, the 'South Staffordshire goods and livestock'. The first stop is Abergavenny (6.37-7pm) where work is done and the train overtaken. The Stop Board at Red Hill Jct (1 in 92 falling grade)

caused a five-minute halt, after which the train pulled into Hereford (Barton) at 8.11. It left at 9pm to travel just a mile to Worcester sidings where it stayed from 9.5 until 9.27. At Ledbury a banker was attached for the 1 in 70 climb to Colwall where there was a Stop Board for the 1 in 80-90 descent through Malvern Wells and another at Malvern Link (10.47-10.51). The train then proceeded to Worcester Tunnel Jct where it remained from 11.15-11.40pm. It called if required at Kidderminster at 12.20am before working at Stourbridge Jct from 12.45-1.50. Kingswinford Jct and siding was called at, again if required, before pulling in to Round Oak (2.9-2.30) for work. More shunting was performed at Dudley (2.46-3.20), Bilston (3.33-3.43) and Stow Heath (3.49-4.46) before Wolverhampton Low Level station was reached at 4.52am. The Pontypool Road goods then pulled into Oxley at 5.20.

J-HEADCODE: THROUGH GOODS TRAINS (Stopping at Intermediate Stations)
This class was very similar to H-headcode trains, the essential difference being the number of intermediate stations called at, though J-headcode trains also tended to travel shorter overall distances than H. Should longer distances be involved, a train starting off as a J would often be upgraded to H or even F at an appropriate point. According to the STTs, J trains were rather more common than H in the early years of the C20th. Perhaps confusingly, the J code was also used to convey through loads over shorter distances without intermediate stops, regardless of their description. To add to inconsistency, the code was used for local or pick-up duties over quite long distances, eg Banbury-Old Oak Common, and Neyland-Carmarthen, rather than the K-code. Again, the J-headcode was used for the docks transfer train departing Gloucester Old yard at 6.30am, passing Over to arrive at Docks Branch sidings at 6.42am. This train was limited to 54 wagons.

9.30pm St Blazey to Tavistock Jct (Plymouth), J
This train cleared from St Blazey a mixed load of wagons many destinations. It utilised one of St Blazey's '42XX' class 2-8-0Ts, which worked the Fowey line china clay services. The whole journey was contained on page 73 of Section 6 of the 1933 STT. The formation on leaving St Blazey was Reading and London,

Rough Traffic (ie unsorted)
    Bristol
    LMS via Bristol
    Newton Abbot and branches
    Common Users
    North Staffs District
    Northern, via Severn Tunnel
    Eastern Valleys
    West Wales
    Newport
    Cardiff

The load was restricted by the various gradients as far as Liskeard to 38 class 2 (mineral) or 48 class 3 (general merchandise) wagons, or a combination thereof (see Guard's Ready Reckoner, Chapter 11). Setting off from St Blazey yard at 9.30pm, the train ran non-stop to Liskeard for a five-minute water stop (10.25-10.30), picked up the single line token at Saltash to go over the Royal Albert Bridge at 11.2, passed Keyham at 11.11 and then stopped at Plymouth North Road again for water (11.17-11.22). It passed Lipson Jct at 11.27 and was due into Tavistock Jct at 11.35pm at which point the train was divided up: (a) trains for Severn Tunnel Jct took the Welsh and Northern traffic; (b) a transfer train took any wagons for North Staffs back to Laira to be attached to Bordesley trains; (c) Avonmouth services took Bristol and Newton Abbot traffic; and, (d) the 11.55 p.m. Laira to Reading West H-headcode train took the rough traffic for Reading and London.

6.50am Carmarthen Jct to Aberdare, J

In contrast to the St Blazey goods above, many J-class trains such as the 6.50am Carmarthen Jct to Aberdare called at far more stations *en route*. In 1938, this train was scheduled for a '72XX' class 2-8-2T. In the 1933 STT, it may be found initially on page 57 in Section 10, and subsequently on page 30 of Section 11. It conveyed the following traffic:

    Llandilo Jct
    Felin Fran
    †Aberdylais
    †Resolven
    Glyn Neath
    Hirwain
    Aberdare and beyond
    *Hirwain Pond

Over the easy coastal section to Llanelly, the engine could take 96 mineral (class 2) or 100 general merchandise (class 3) or empties, the maximum number of wagons permitted in normal goods trains. Apart from traffic loaded locally, wagons for this train arrived at Carmarthen on trains from Fishguard Harbour and Neyland. Departing at 6.50am, the train passed Llanelly at 7.43 and had a clear run to Llandilo Jct East, where it called for its first work (7.47-8.25), dropping off vehicles for various trains to Old Oak Common, Pontypool Road, Severn Tunnel Jct and Gloucester, as well as for local services. Wagons were picked up off trains from Pembrey, Neyland and Whitland. Since after this stop its purpose was to convey traffic along the Vale of Neath line, no traffic was taken on for intermediate stations between Llanelly and Neath.

The 6.50 set off on the Swansea Avoiding Lines from Llandilo Jct, passing Morlais Jct South at 8.43, again with a clear road for its next call at Felin Fran (9.35-10.15). In the 1933 STT it also called at Llangyfelach (9.7-9.20). At Felin Fran local and Swansea traffic

Chaired sleepers in the six foot between a permanent way train and an H-class goods at South Ruislip seen in 1949. The train is headed by 2-8-0 No 2850 built in 1913. *C R L Coles*

Marshalling Instructions for Through and Important Local Freight Trains—continued.

Formation and Headmarks.	Engine Group.	Traffic attached on Route.		REMARKS.
		At	To be formed	
NEWTON ABBOT—continued.				
6.0 a.m. Bristol West Depot "J" .. Engine Exeter Taunton including Forest of Dean Bristol Depots L.M. & S. via Bristol	D	Exeter Taunton	} With wagons on train.	Load 60 wagons from Taunton. Feeding train at Newton Abbot :— 6.50 p.m. ex Marazion. 2.15 p.m. ex Moretonhampstead. 12.30 a.m. ex Kingswear. 7.10 p.m. ex Paignton. 5.20 p.m. ex Ivybridge. Connecting train at Taunton :— Forest of Dean traffic—6.0 a.m. Taunton to Lydney next day.
11.20 a.m. Ivybridge "K" .. .. Engine Brent Kingsbridge Branch Wrangaton Ivybridge	C (45 XX)	Totnes Brent	} At one shunt.	Feeding trains at Newton Abbot :— 4. 5 p.m. Swindon to Tavistock Junction. 7.40 p.m. Bristol to Newton Abbot. 10.30 p.m. Avonmouth to Laira. 11.35 p.m. ex Paddington. 10.30 p.m. ex Reading. 8.10 p.m. ex Severn Tunnel Junction. 10.55 p.m. West Depot to Laira. 8.30 a.m. ex Oxley Sidings. 10.10 p.m. ex Banbury. Connecting train at Brent :—Kingsbridge Branch 2.10 p.m. Connecting train at Ivybridge :—2.40 p.m. Newton Abbot to Laira. Conveys :— S.T. 501a Newton Abbot to Plymouth from Newton Abbot to Ivybridge.
2.40 p.m. Laira "J" ... ... Engine Plymouth District	D	Brent Ivybridge	} At one shunt.	Feeding trains at Newton Abbot :— 3.45 a.m. West Depot to Newton Abbot. 8.30 a.m. ex Oxley Sidings. 8.10 p.m. ex Severn Tunnel Junction. 7.15 a.m. Exeter to Heathfield. 10.10 p.m. ex Banbury. 9. 0 a.m. ex Exeter. 7.40 p.m. West Depot to Newton Abbot. Calls Cornwood for S.T. purposes. Feeding train at Ivybridge :—11.20 a.m. Newton Abbot to Ivybridge. Connecting trains at Laira :— 2.30 a.m. Laira to Plymouth. 7.30 a.m. Laira to Sutton Harbour. 7.40 a.m. Laira to Friary, Southern Railway (South Western Section). Convey :— S.T. 137 Bristol to Plymouth from Newton Abbot to Laira. P.T. 370 Kingsbridge to Plymouth from Brent to Laira. P.T. 501a Newton Abbot to Plymouth from Ivybridge to Laira.

Marshalling Instructions for Through and Important Local Freight Trains—continued.

Formation and Headmarks.	Engine Group.	Traffic Attached en Route.		REMARKS.
		At	To be formed	
READING WEST JUNCTION.				
1.30 a.m. MX Oxley Sidings "J" .. Engine Oxford North End †Banbury Banbury Jct. Leamington Bordesley Jct. Hockley Wednesbury Oxley Sidings	B	Oxford North End Banbury Junction Leamington Bordesley Junction	With wagons on train. At one shunt. At one shunt. With wagons on train.	†From Oxford only. Feeding services at Reading West Junction :— 6.40 p.m. Brentford. 6.25 p.m. Hayes. 7.30 p.m. Newbury to Reading West Junction. 6.25 p.m. Reading Central. 7.45 p.m. ex Newbury. 9.35 p.m. Basingstoke to Oxley Sidings. Feeding trains at Oxford :— 4.52 p.m. ex Taplow. 8.15 p.m. ex Thame. 5.25 p.m. ex Fairford. 5.59 p.m. ex Abingdon. 3.55 p.m. ex Moreton. Connecting trains at Oxford :—1.30 a.m. Park Royal to Worcester, 9.35 a.m. Oxford to Bordesley Junc., 5.50 a.m. Oxford to Witney and 12.30 p.m. Oxford to Fairford. Connecting trains at Oxley Sidings :— 3.5 p.m. to Croesnewydd and 3.50 p.m. to Crewe. 5.30 p.m. and 7.20 p.m. to Shrewsbury and beyond, respectively. Conveys :— P.T. 347 Holt Junc. to Hockley from Reading W. Junc. to Bordesley. P.T. 423 Maidenhead to Oxford from Reading W. Junc. to Oxford. S.T. 668 Reading to Hereford " " " " " " S.T. 676 Reading to Worcester " " " " " "

Marshalling Instructions for Through and Important Local Freight Trains—continued.

Formation and Headmarks.	Engine Group.	Traffic attached en Route.		REMARKS.
		At	To be formed	
NEWTON ABBOT—continued.				
7.30 p.m. St. Blazey "J" ...	E 2-8-0 T	Totnes	At one shunt	Feeding trains at Newton Abbot :—
Engine				9. 0 a.m. Exeter to Newton Abbot. 8.10 p.m. ex Severn Tunnel Junction.
†Laira				2.15 p.m. ex Moretonhampstead. 8.30 a.m. ex Oxley Sidings.
Bodmin Road				10.10 p.m. Banbury to Newton Abbot. 7.40 p.m. West Depot to Newton Abbot.
Lostwithiel				Feeding train at Totnes :—2.35 p.m. ex Ashburton.
Par				† Reduce load only, to consist of traffic for St. Germans, Menheniot, Liskeard
St. Blazey				Connecting trains at Laira :— [and Doublebois.
				Plymouth—3.20 a.m. ; Doublebois—5.0 a.m.
				Connecting trains at :—
				Bodmin Road—7.40 a.m. to Bodmin. Par—6.5 a.m. Par to Newquay.
10. 0 p.m. Marazion "J"	D	Truro	With wagons on train.	Conveys :—P.T. 166 Buckfastleigh to Plymouth from Totnes to Laira.
Engine				Traffic on this train to be formed in station order.
†Tavistock Jct.				Feeding trains at Newton Abbot :—
Truro				5.45 a.m. Pontypool Road to Laira. 7.40 p.m. W. Depot to Newton Abbot.
‡Scorrier				9. 0 a.m. Exeter to Newton Abbot. 7.15 a.m. ex Exeter.
‡Redruth				10.10 p.m. ex Banbury. 8.10 p.m. ex Severn Tunnel Jct.
‡Camborne				2.15 p.m. ex Moretonhampstead. 8.30 a.m. ex Oxley Sidings.
Carn Brea				† Reduce load at Tavistock Jct. by taking off traffic for St. Austell and below
Gwinear Road				‡ Detached at Truro. [to connect with 4.35 a.m. thence.
*Hayle				Connecting trains at Truro :—
St. Erth				Falmouth Branch—6.55 a.m. to Falmouth.
Marazion				Scorrier—7.10 a.m. ex Truro.
Penzance				Redruth and Camborne—2.0 a.m. ex Plymouth.
				* Detached at Gwinear Road for 2.0 a.m. ex Plymouth. [Helston.
10.20 p.m. Severn Tunnel Jct. "J" ...	D	Exeter Bridgwater	} At one shunt.	Connecting trains at Gwinear Road :—11.10 a.m. Mixed, Gwinear Road to Lond, 62 to Bridgwater, 60 beyond.
Engine				Feeding trains at Newton Abbot :—
Eastern Valleys				1.20 p.m. ex Laira. 7.10 p.m. ex Paignton.
*Western Valleys				3.25 p.m. ex Kingswear. 6. 8 a.m. ex Laira.
Newport				2.15 p.m. ex Moretonhampstead. 6.50 p.m. ex Marazion.
Cardiff				2.35 p.m. ex Ashburton.
Severn Tunnel Junction				* From Bridgwater only when necessary to make up a load.
				Feeding trains at Bridgwater :—
				2.35 p.m. ex Yeovil. 8.30 p.m. Exeter to Cardiff.
				1. 5 p.m. Exeter to Bristol.
				Connecting trains at Severn Tunnel Jct. :—
				Eastern Valleys—10.15 a.m. ex Severn Tunnel Jct.
				Western Valleys—As ordered by Cardiff Control.
				Newport, Cardiff,
				Llantrisant, } 9.50 p.m. Victoria Basin to Cardiff.
				Bridgeud
				West Wales—12.5 p.m. and 1.35 p.m. ex Severn Tunnel Jct.

Marshalling Instructions for Through and Important Local Freight Trains—continued.

Formation and Headmarks.	Engine Group.	Traffic attached en Route.		REMARKS.
		At	To be formed	
ST. BLAZEY.				
3.5 a.m. MX Tavistock Jnc. "J"	E 2-8-0 T	Par Liskeard	} At one shunt.	Feeding train :—
Engine				At Liskeard :—2.35 p.m. ex Looe.
†Forest of Dean				Connecting trains at Tavistock Jct. :—
Reading and London Rough traffic				Reading and London—12.40 a.m. Laira to Reading.
Eastern Valleys				Eastern Valleys } 1.20 p.m. Laira to East Depot to be detached at Newton
Newport				West Wales } Abbot for 10.20 p.m. ex Newton to Severn Tunnel Jct.
Cardiff				Newport }
West Wales				Cardiff } 1.20 p.m. Laira to East Depot.
North Stafford District				North Stafford District—3.10 p.m to Oxley Sidings.
				† To connect Tavistock Junction with 6.50 p.m. Marazion to Newton Abbot.
SALISBURY.				
12.25 a.m. (MX) Aberdare "H" ...	E	Westbury Rogerstone	} At one shunt.	Load, 60 empties from Salisbury. Not to convey Eastern Valleys traffic.
Engine				Salisbury to confer with Westbury Control as to other traffic being put on this train to make up a full load.
†Northerns				Feeding train at Westbury :—
Aberdare				12.0 noon Weymouth to Severn Tunnel Jct.
				† Northern wagons to be put off at Westbury.
				L. & N.E. wagons via Banbury Junction, in oil boxes to be cleared by 4.20 a.m. Westbury, other wagons via Banbury Junction by 5.20 a.m. ex Newton Abbot or 6.25 p.m. ex Westbury.
				Carries "J" Headmarks from Sirhowy Jct.
				Terminates at Severn Tunnel Jct. on Sundays and leaves 2.15 a.m. Mondays.
				Empties for Messrs. Stephenson Clarkes & Cory Bros. to be kept separate.

Marshalling Instructions for Through and Important Local Freight Trains—continued.

Formation and Headmarks.	Engine Group.	Traffic attached en Route.		REMARKS.
		At	To be formed	
WEYMOUTH—continued.	D	Dorchester		Connecting trains at Yeovil:—
2. 0 p.m. Swindon "J"		Maiden Newton	With wagons on train.	5.40 p.m. Yeovil to Durston. 9.30 a.m. to Langport West.
Engine		Yeovil		10.30 a.m. to C. M. Bank.
Yeovil		Witham		Booked at Evershot and shunts wagons in position for 3.35 p.m. ex Weymouth.
Durston Branch		Frome (CR)	At one shunt.	‡ Wagons suitable for 4.20 a.m. Westbury to Oxley Sidings.
Witham and Wells Branch		Holt Junction	" " "	Feeding trains at Witham:—
‡Westbury & North of Didcot		Melksham (SX)	" " "	10.35 a.m. Cranmore to Witham.
Chippenham				1.35 p.m. Dulcot Siding to Witham.
Gloucester Line				Connecting train at Witham:—
Swindon Stores				8.55 p.m. Witham to Wells (mixed).
M. & S.W.				* Wagons unsuitable for 4.20 a.m. Westbury to Oxley Sidings.
Highworth Branch				Connecting trains at Chippenham:—
East of Didcot				8. 0 p.m. St. Philip's Marsh to Paddington.
*North of Didcot				1. 0 a.m. Westbury to Swindon.
Shorts to Didcot				8. 5 a.m. Chippenham to Calne.
Swindon Goods and Mileage				9.32 a.m. Chippenham to Corsham.
				Connecting trains at Swindon:—
				8. 5 a.m. Swindon to Gloucester.
				1.10 a.m. Swindon to Didcot.
				4.25 a.m. Swindon to Oxley Sidings.
3.35 p.m. Westbury "F"	A	All stations except		Connecting train at Witham:—
Local "pick up"		Maiden Newton		8.55 p.m. Weymouth to Bristol.
	D			Connecting trains at Westbury:—
				6.40 p.m. Weymouth to Paddington.
				4.20 a.m. Westbury to Oxley Sidings.
				1. 0 a.m. Westbury to Swindon.
				11.55 p.m. Cardiff to Salisbury.
				Conveys:—
				P.T. 785 Wells to Paddington, Witham to Westbury.
				P.T. 803 Weymouth to Bristol, Weymouth to Witham.
				P.T. 805 Weymouth to Hockley SX (transfer shed), Weymouth to Westbury.
				P.T. 806 Weymouth to Paddington, Weymouth to Westbury.
				P.T. 807 Weymouth to Padd'n MO (empties shed), Weymouth to Westbury.
				P.T. 809 Weymouth to Reading, Weymouth to Westbury.
				S.T. 811 Weymouth to Smithfield from Weymouth to Westbury.
				S.T. 813 Weymouth to Swindon, Weymouth to Westbury.
				S.T. 815 Weymouth to Westbury, Weymouth to Westbury.
				S.T. 856 Yeovil P.M. to Salisbury S.R., Yeovil to Westbury.

0-6-0PT No 5760 on a short Down goods (J-headcode) emerges from one of the tunnels along the line at Dawlish in 1936. *LGRP*

was detached and outbound wagons added on to the train before it continued along the District lines via Jersey Marine Jct North (10.28) as far as Neath Jct box on the R&SB line, alongside Neath engine shed. There, the train reversed back to Neath River Viaduct and down the loop to Cardonnel Jct, to pick up the Vale of Neath line. Moving forward again, the 6.50 passed under the South Wales Main Line at Neath Riverside and entered the yard at Neath Jct (Vale of Neath) at 11.13, where the wagons for Aberdylais and Resolven were dropped off to be taken on by the first local service.

Leaving at 11.40am, next was a 30-minute run along the gradual climb to Glyn Neath, where more traffic was detached (12.10-

Outside-framed 0-6-0 Armstrong standard goods No 1094, built in 1870 and superheated when reboilered, heads a J-headcode stopping goods at Hatton. *LGRP*

A through train of coal empties is headed by 2-6-2T No 5189 bearing the J-headcode. Some of the private-owner wagons belong to 'Baldwin' and to 'Crump'; Baldwins Ltd owned the Aberbaiden Colliery near Bryndu between Kenfig Hill and Tondu. *HMRS*

43XX' No 4310 of 1911 (still with circular cab spectacles above firebox) is seen at the head of an Up domestic coal train carrying the J-headcode as it emerges from Wood End Tunnel, between Earlswood Lakes and Danzey, on the line between Birmingham and Stratford-upon-Avon. Notice 'whistle' sign for trains entering the tunnel. *LGRP*

12.35pm). Thereafter, the climb became steeper, and the '72XX' was limited to 55 mineral, 69 merchandise or 92 empties. (See Chapter 10 for tests on wagon brakes down this bank.) Hirwain Pond was five miles further up the 1 in 50/47 incline, where a call was made to drop off empties including those for local anthracite collieries such as Rigos, Aberpergwm, Rock, and Cwmgrach & Empire (in 1933, the train was not scheduled to stop at Hirwain Pond). Then on to Hirwain (1.5-1.15), for further wagon detachments, and a stop at Gelli Tarw Jct (1.24-1.35) to pin down brakes before the 1 in 50 descent and approach to Aberdare arriving at 1.50pm.

Traffic for beyond Aberdare was mostly destined for the Vale of Neath route to Penar Jct (between Pontllanfraith and Crumlin) and along connecting routes.

10.15am Hereford Barrs Court to Shrewsbury, J

This is an example of a joint goods train that was worked by the LMS according to the 1933 STT. (A similar train but worked by the GW, was the K-headcode 12.5pm from Hereford Worcester sidings to Shrewsbury.)

The first stop was Leominster and was of long duration (10.45am-12.20pm). Woofferton was reached at 12.45, having called if required at Berrington & Eye for tranship traffic. It left at 1.10 and had another long stop at Ludlow from 1.25-2.47. Then to Onibury (2.59-3.38) and Craven Arms & Stokesay (3.50-4.15). Marsh Brook was called at if required then Church Stretton (4.45-5.0), followed by three more **CR** stops at Leebotwood, Dorrington and Condover. Coleham was passed at 5.40 and the train terminated at Shrewsbury at 5.45pm.

A straight-footplate '28XX', No 2854 (built in 1913), hauls the J-headcode 4.50pm from Bristol West depot to Laira goods at Uphill. *D J Hyde collection*

A 'Through goods stopping at intermediate stations' (J-headcode) pictured at Hooton on the Birkenhead Joint line after the Grouping. 0-6-0PT No 1551 was built as a saddle tank at Wolverhampton in 1880 (scrapped September 1933). The three-plank open behind the locomotive is owned by Llysfaen limestone quarries in Denbighshire and the next wagon by Parkinson's. These private-owner wagons still have grease axleboxes. There is an LMS brake van in the middle of the train. *LGRP*

No 6848 *Toddington Grange* seen at Oxford in the late 1930s on a J-headcode stopping freight. Shirtbutton on tender. *D J Hyde collection*

No 6848 *Toddington Grange* heads a through J-headcode goods stopping at intermediate stations. *D J Hyde collection*

K-HEADCODE: LOCAL PICK-UP GOODS TRAINS

The lowest priority goods train was the local or pick-up goods. K-headcode goods trains were timetabled all over the GW system serving separate sections of the main lines including all the intermediate yards and stations along a route, and along virtually all branch lines. Local pilot and trip workings also carried this headcode. For many wagons, these were the first and last movements in the goods chain.

Fitting a local goods train into faster traffic was not easy, as it was not only slow, but also invariably had work to do at smaller wayside stations which could block the line, so that a good time allowance was necessary for it between refuge points.

One of the shortest (both in mileage and time) K-headcode goods in the 1933 STT is the 4.15pm Carmarthen Goods that terminated at Carmarthen station at 4.20. Examples of straightforward K-headcode goods trains would be the Margam-Cornelly train, found in Section 7, page 85 of the 1933 STT. Another would be the 9.5am goods and coal from Reading West Jct to Basingstoke, that passed Southcote Jct at 9.14; Mortimer (9.31-10.7 to do work and to allow the 9.46am passenger to Basingstoke to overtake); Bramley (10.17-10.55); arriving at Basingstoke SR station at 11.10am. This is found on page 17 of Section 3 of the 1933 STT.

K-headcode trains that ran comparatively short distances would often return back after arrival at destination with the same locomotive. For example, Stourbridge Jct to Priestfield was about 10 miles and the **MX** 4.10am arrived at 6.28, having called at Brettell Lane, Kingswinford Jct, Round Oak and Dudley. It returned from Priestfield back to Stourbridge at 7.10am.

9am Gloucester 'T' sidings to Swindon, K

This train served all yards between Gloucester and Swindon, and since it was on the road for 5½ hours, was allocated a tender engine, usually a '43XX'. Wagons were marshalled in station order for all yards between Stonehouse and Swindon (but no wagons for Swindon Locomotive Works were conveyed). It will be found as an Up train in Section 7 of the STT page 83 (details here are for 1933; in 1938 the train started at 9.18 am).

The train originated in 'T' (Transfer) sidings, that area of yard alongside the Cheltenham loop that fed into the Gloucester South Jct area, and was formed by wagons off daily goods trains from Wolverhampton, Worcester, Bristol and Bullo Pill. It followed the 7.37am Severn Tunnel Jct to Swindon passenger at South Jct. Running for some 25 minutes to its first stop, Stonehouse (9.25-9.58), it followed the departing Chalford auto into the station, then crossed into the yard to perform work, and also to clear the Up Main for the following 9.20am Cheltenham to Paddington express.

The load was not to exceed 42 wagons on leaving Stonehouse, and the 9am moved the half-mile up the line to call when required

229

Marshalling Instructions for Through and Important Local Freight Trains—continued.

Formation and Headmarks.	Engine Group.	Traffic attached en Route.		REMARKS.
		At	To be formed	

SWINDON—continued.
8.25 p.m. Westbury "K" ...
Engine
Dauntsey
Chippenham and Branch
Melksham
Holt Junction
Trowbridge
Westbury
	A	Dauntsey
		Chippenham
		†Melksham
		Holt Junction
		Trowbridge
			At one shunt.
			In reverse order at one shunt.
			
			At one shunt.
				To pick up milk vans at Goods Yard Box, Swindon.
				Feeding trains at Swindon :—
				  3.0 a.m. Oxley Sidings to Swindon. | 11.5 a.m. Banbury to Stoke Gifford.
				  Calls at Wootton Bassett when required.
				† Including important Birmingham and Northern traffic.
				Feeding train at Chippenham :—5.40 p.m. ex Calne.
				Connecting trains at Holt Junction :—
				  2.10 a.m. Bristol to Reading. | 9.53 a.m. Holt Junction to Devizes.
				  5.55 a.m. Holt Junction to Didcot. |
				Feeding train at Trowbridge :—7.40 p.m. East Depot to Salisbury.
				Connecting trains at Westbury :—
				  4.20 a.m. Westbury to Oxley Sidings | 8.50 a.m. Westbury to Weymouth.
				  7.50 a.m. Westbury to Salisbury. | 9.30 p.m. Avonmouth to Salisbury.
				Conveys :—S.T. 58 Bath to Westbury from Trowbridge to Westbury.
				  S.T. 180 Calne to Westbury from Chippenham to Westbury.
				  S.T. 739 Swindon to Newbury from Swindon to Holt Junction.

8.35 p.m. (SX) Severn Tunnel Jct. "J" 1.15 a.m. (MO) to Bassaleg "H" Engine ‡Chepstow (CR) Gloucester †Bullo Pill Locomotive Empties Severn Tunnel Junct.	D	Gloucester T. Sdgs. (MX) Lydney (CR) (MX)	With wagons on train. At one shunt.	Runs via Gloucester. Conveys wagons from Gloucester to connect with 5.0 a.m. Severn Tunnel Junction to Pontypridd. ‡ Detach Beer traffic from Cheltenham when required. † Detached at Gloucester for 8.45 a.m. Gloucester D. B. Sidings to Severn Tunnel Junction. Connecting train at Severn Tunnel Junction :— 9.5 a.m. Severn Tunnel Junction to Llandilo Junction.

11.35 p.m. (SX) Neath "F" ...
Engine
Bridgend
Gloucester
Bullo Pill
Lydney
†Severn Tunnel Junct.
Newport Dock St.
Cardiff
Swansea Div. beyond Neath
Margam Jct.
Port Talbot
Briton Ferry
Swansea Docks
Neath
	D	Gloucester T. Sidings
		Gloucester D. B. Sidings
		  (CR)
		Lydney (CR)
		
		Bridgend
			With wagons on train.
			
			In reverse order at one at one shunt.
			With wagons on train.
				Conveys Stores ex Swindon Factory. Starts from Loco. Yard.
				Runs via Gloucester.
				† Detached at Gloucester.
				Feeding train at Gloucester :—
				  3.30 p.m. Swindon to Gloucester.
				Connecting trains at Gloucester :—
				  Bullo Pill
				  Lydney } 8.45 a.m. Docks Branch Sidings to Severn Tunnel Jct.
				  Severn Tunnel Jct. including Pontypool Road and Eastern Valleys—6.50 a.m. ex Oxford.
				  Newport Dock St. and Cardiff—1.25 p.m. Gloucester to Cardiff.
				  Felin Fran and beyond—8.50 p.m. Gloucester to Llanelly.
				  Swansea Valley Junction
				  Landore
				  Swansea High Street } 3.25 a.m. Gloucester to Landore.
				  Gowerton

at Jefferies Siding, with wagons of coal inbound, and bricks outbound. Any Jeffries traffic for Down line stations was taken on to Stroud for conveyance back to Gloucester. At Stroud (10.8-10.27), Jefferies' traffic was detached and traffic left by an earlier Up goods train was attached. An auto train (stopping from 9.39½ to 9.41) and a through Up goods train called at Stroud during this period, before the pick-up was permitted to proceed.

The next call was at Brimscombe (10.37-11.11) where a brief stop was made for yard work, followed by another at Chalford (11.17-11.27). The remote goods yard at Coates, on the Down side, was next for a short call (11.47-11.57) before moving on to Kemble (12.2-12.29pm). All these stops were of sufficient duration to deal with a handful of wagons at each. Minety station yard followed, where a more lengthy call was made not only to carry out work, but also to allow passage of the 11.40am Cheltenham to Paddington express (stopped Swindon 1.4-1.14pm) and the 1.1pm Kemble to Swindon local (stopped Minety 1.11-1.14) passenger trains. Another protracted stop was made at Purton between 1.40 and 2.25 (**W**) both for yard work and also to allow the 11am Cardiff to Swindon Parcels to pass, (**W** meant that on Saturdays the train ran five minutes earlier from Purton; in 1938 the symbol had been changed to **R**) before taking the final leg through Highworth Jct Swindon yard, due at 2.40pm, with its traffic connecting with both Up and Down main line services.

8.10am Oxley sidings Wolverhampton to Crewe, K

This local goods train took the branch from Wellington, usually with a '43XX', a type of locomotive often used on goods trains over that line during the 1930s. It was formed in station order for all yards from Codsall to Crewe.

The train was mainly fed at Oxley by trains from the south, but also locally from Herbert Street Goods and Victoria Basin. Leaving the yard at 8.10am, the 1933 STT, Section 14 page 15 gave the train's first call at Codsall (8.27-8.37) for 10 minutes before moving on to Albrighton, where a longer stop was made (8.45-10.24). Apart from the local work, this long call was mostly for operational purposes to allow passage along the Down Main of (i) the 8.33am fast passenger from Snow Hill to Birkenhead; (ii) the 9.2am Wolverhampton to Birkenhead local passenger (stopped Albrighton 9.17-9.18); (iii) the 9.45am F-headcode Oxley to Crewe freight; and, (iv) the 9.26am Snow Hill to Shrewsbury local passenger. After this last train, the 8.10 moved out to follow it, with time now in hand to call at Cosford sidings and Ruckley sidings if required before arriving at Shifnal yard. (According to the 1938 STT, the train might be refuged at Ruckley about this time when trial engines were being run from Stafford Road to Shifnal, although in the 1933 STT, Section 14 page 21, these were timed to leave Stafford Road at 2.20pm; be at Codsall 2.31-2.33; Albrighton 2.42-2.44; and, arriving Shifnal at 2.59pm.) Fifty minutes was allowed at Shifnal for local work (11.10am to 12 noon), and to permit the passing of the 9.30am Worcester to Crewe local passenger train and the 9.10am Paddington to Birkenhead express passenger.

Setting off from Shifnal at noon, the next short call was to the sidings at Hollinswood (12.15-12.30) for local work, then to Oakengates for a longer lay-by (12.37-1.30),

An Up K-headcode stopping goods pictured at King's Sutton south of Banbury. The outside-framed Armstrong standard goods 0-6-0 is No 890 of 1874, now fitted with a Belpaire boiler. It was condemned in December 1925. *LGRP*

where the 12.10pm Wolverhampton to Wellington passenger would overtake.

From Oakengates, it was a 10-minute run to the yard beyond Wellington station for the next stop (1.40-2.15pm). Here, traffic was dropped off, while more was picked up which had been left by the early morning train from Shrewsbury to Much Wenlock, which did not call at intermediate stations on the branch.

Leaving the yard at Wellington, the train made its way across the main lines and on to the double-track Crewe branch. The first call was made at Crudgington (2.29-2.49), backing traffic into the yard on the far side of the running lines, then into the single goods siding alongside the Down main at Ellerdine siding (2.56-3.11), and into the yard on the far side at Peplow (3.16-3.30). There, the 8.15 was refuged in the yard to allow the passage of the Bournemouth and Portsmouth Harbour to Manchester portion of the Bournemouth to Birkenhead express passenger, which had been detached at Wellington and had left there at 3.17 pm, rapidly catching up with the 9.10am over the branch during the previous 20 minutes. (The Bournemouth was not allowed to convey any 'tail traffic' [vans of perishables, cattle trucks, horseboxes etc] to and from Market Drayton.)

The next stop, Hodnet, was marked '3.37 • 4.15', where • meant 'to shunt for, or follow another train, and also to perform work'. Thus the 38 minutes time allowance included yard work and passage of the 3.40pm Wellington to Crewe passenger, which called at Hodnet between 4.3 and 4.4pm towards the end of the scheduled goods stop. It then followed the passenger train to Tern Hill where it paused from 4.23 to 4.25, after which came the principal station on the line, Market Drayton. This stop from 4.44-5.15pm was followed by others at Adderley (5.27-5.37), then Audlem (5.44-6.10), after which the train ran to Nantwich Jct (6.23) to join the LMS line between Shrewsbury, Whitchurch and Crewe. Although it left GWR metals at the junction, it still called at Nantwich LMS Goods (6.25-6.45) to allow another Great Western local passenger to overtake it (the 5.40pm Wellington to Manchester London Road that called 6.38-6.39). The K-headcode goods also called at Willaston, the final intermediate LMS station on the line, to drop off cattle traffic when required. The train then terminated at the Great Western sidings at Gresty Lane at 6.55pm.

The Camerton-Westbury pick-up goods approaches Limpley Stoke on 12 March 1937. The single lamp of the K-headcode on 0-6-0PT No 8747 is painted red which is not surprising as white-bodied lamps began to be introduced only in December 1936. Immediately behind the locomotive are an LMS van, a NE van, a 'Bristol' private-owner seven-plank open, four loaded private-owner five-plank coal wagons and a GW mink, followed by the GW Toad. *R S Carpenter*

A double-headed K-headcode pick-up goods on the lines of the former Cambrian Railways soon after the Grouping. The leading locomotive is 'Duke' No 3256 *Guinevere* (formerly No 3257) built in 1895. Behind is ex-Cambrian Railways 4-4-0 'Large Belpaire Passenger' locomotive No 1014 (Cambrian No 94) built by Robert Stephenson & Co. *SLS*

2-6-0 No 6301 approaches Clink Road Jct near Frome with a K-headcode stopping goods in the early 1930s. *LGRP*

2-6-0 No 8328 on a K-headcode pick-up goods heads to Bristol near Upwey Jct on 7 July 1939.The 65 locos numbered in the '83XX' series were converted from '53XXs' from 1928 by altering the front end so that the pony truck took more weight (11 tons), thus relieving the leading driver flanges that wore on the sharp curves of West Country lines. *A G Atkins collection*

'43XX' No 4359 of 1914, showing the K-headcode, is coupled to an outside-framed 0-6-0PT that perhaps has failed. The bolster wagon No 153215 on left has diamond-frame bogies. *LGRP*

CHAPTER EIGHTEEN

SPECIAL TRAFFIC

IN a 1937 lecture at the GWR (London) Lecture and Debating Society, D H Hawkeswood and F G Dean defined *special traffic* as 'traffic requiring special arrangements either for its collection, loading, dispatch, conveyance, or delivery'. That is, facilities beyond the usual road cartage collection and delivery services provided for merchandise goods conveyed between stations by trains comprising the normal type of open wagon or van, and also beyond the minimal facilities provided for mileage traffic in depot yards.

For some special traffic, special vehicles were provided by the railway, particularly for goods that had to be well-ventilated or refrigerated during the journey. These special vehicles were not too different from other goods wagons and were within the loading gauge. Very heavy items (large castings, for example) could also be carried on special strengthened wagons, but still within gauge and run in ordinary goods trains. Other within-gauge traffic such as sheet glass in crates, and building materials such as slates, was traffic that required careful handling. But sometimes loads would not fit with within the loading gauge and fell in to the category of *exceptional loads* that had to be run in special trains.

One type of special traffic was perishable and seasonal goods (fish, meat, flowers and vegetables) that would become rotten and lose value if dealt with like ordinary merchandise traffic. Most seasonal traffic was recurrent and regularly timetabled, such as the autumn sugar beet trains to the two factories on the GW at Kidderminster and at Allscott (Salop). During the British sugar beet campaign (that lasted about three months), the Kidderminster factory took in about 1,800 tons of beet per day, loaded in open wagons. Transport of Christmas trees was another seasonal traffic.

Many other types of special traffic were 'one-offs' but within gauge. Trains that conveyed objects that were out-of-gauge were clearly special, but trains that conveyed goods that were normal and within gauge could be exceptional in the sense of carrying very unusual traffic, such as a train of 20 glass-lined tanks, each on a flat wagon, taken to Trowbridge in 1938 for the bottling store at Usher's Wiltshire Brewery. In 1931 what was claimed to be the biggest consignment of lager ever despatched in the UK was sent from Wrexham to London Docks. A special train of vans took 1,700 ice-covered casks for ocean-going liners. The consignment was sent under the GW Registered Transit scheme (see *GWR Goods Services*). Timetabled beer trains were rare, but the 1927 STT gives the 12.30am Bordesley-Winchester beer train (**RR**) halting at Newbury from 5.35 to 5.50am, before passing over the Didcot, Newbury & Southampton line. The 3.15am (**SO**) transfer from Reading West to Basingstoke returned wagons that had conveyed beer back to the SR. The last surviving GW manure wagon (R1 in the diagram index) was marked 'for conveyance of beer traffic and returned beer empties only to and from Hockley'. In the late C19th, the 11.48am Bristol to Reading goods called at Bradford on Avon when required 'to pick up beer for Marlborough'.

Transport of a menagerie from St Ives to Salisbury was special. A report of the event in the 1929 *Railway Magazine* punned between the types of circus animal conveyed and the GW's use of animal names in its telegraph code ' … sixteen Crocodiles, two Pythons and two Scorpions … ' were railway vehicles that were used. The Pythons (covered carriage trucks) had to be specially

A flywheel carried on Morel No 41977, a wagon specially built without a centre floor section for ships' propellers and large wheels. *GWR*

The body of refurbished carriage for the narrow-gauge Vale of Rheidol line mounted on a Macaw Z wagon photographed at Swindon Works. Shirtbutton GWR insignia. Note the white-painted rectangular water tank wagon No 419 to a DD Diagram, marked 'Locomotive Water', on left in front of the engine smokebox. *GWR/D J Hyde collection*

strengthened to carry elephants. Some of the cages were rather wide so a special path was mapped out with two sets of running lines being kept clear for the train. Travelling cranes were provided by the GW at departure and destination. A carriage was marshalled in the train for the people in charge of animals. The train itself was in charge of an inspector and two guards.

The transit of special traffic could often be planned ahead, but sudden demands for special trains could occur. Christian Barman in *Next Station* tells the tale of a ship carrying 1,600 tons of grapefruit bound for a port in the north-east which developed engine trouble and put in to Plymouth. At very short notice, the GW provided five special trains, which enabled the cargo to reach its destination earlier than it would have done by sea.

Telegraph codes for special traffic are given in Chapter 3.

In the following chapters, special traffic is described under the headings of: (i) Fruit, Flowers and Vegetables; (ii) Bananas (from Avonmouth); (iii) Livestock Trains and Agricultural Traffic (cattle trains; cattle markets and horse fairs; agricultural shows; foot and mouth disease; farm removals); (iv) refrigerated traffic (pork, beef, mutton and rabbit traffic from the West Country; meat and poultry imported from overseas and Ireland *en route* to Smithfield market); (v) fish (from the West Country and Wales); and, (vi) dangerous goods (explosives; inflammable liquids; corrosive and poisonous substances; compressed and liquefied gases; substances liable to spontaneous combustion). Chapter 25 is separately devoted to 'exceptional loads' that were outside the loading gauge.

Brentford Docks often dealt with special loads like this motor launch on 17 April 1930. The vehicle behind the loading crew, agent and owner was Crocodile E No 41958, Diagram C9, built in 1923 that had a capacity of 35 tons. In 1945, this wagon and one similar (No 41957) were strengthened to take 30 tons distributed in the well rather than the previous 20-ton limitation. *GWR*

The view along the length of a train of motor car vans with the end doors open for road vehicles to drive through from an end loading dock at Morris Cowley on 20 August 1936. The first vehicle is a brand-new G31 Mogo No 105708. Note the wheel bars carrying the wagon running number and rubber-covered chains for securing cars. The vehicles behind are another Mogo and the longer vans coded Asmo. *GWR/D J Hyde collection*

A train of Morris cars for the November 1938 Glasgow Motor Show. The train of G26/G32 Asmo vehicles from Cowley is headed by 4-4-0 No 3832 *County of Wilts* (built in 1904; No 3475 before the nominal date of renumbering of 1 January 1913). It has been pointed out that the train in this posed picture seems to be facing in the wrong direction for Glasgow. Furthermore the headcode of a single lamp is for an inferior J-class train, rather than the C-headcode that would be expected for a fitted train. *GWR/D J Hyde collection*

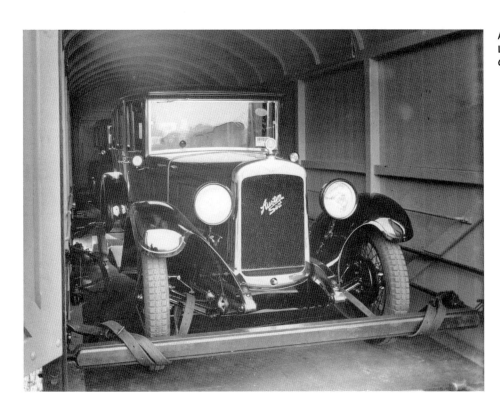

An Austin Six car in an Asmo at
Longbridge, Birmingham.
GWR/D J Hyde collection

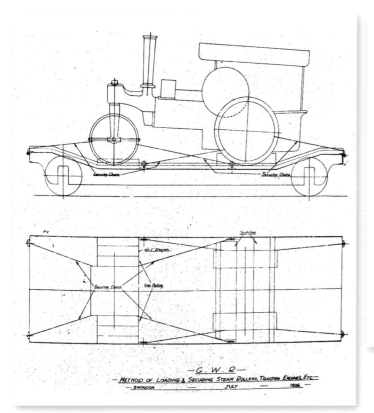

LOADING OF STEAM ROLLERS AND TRACTION ENGINES.

The following instructions must be observed :—

Loading.

    10-ton "Loriot K" to carry rollers and engines not exceeding 6 tons.
    12-ton "Loriots" to carry rollers and engines not exceeding 8 tons.
    15-ton "Loriots" to carry rollers and engines not exceeding 10 tons.
    20-ton "Loriots" to carry rollers and engines not exceeding 16 tons.
    25-ton "Loriots" to carry rollers and engines not exceeding 18 tons.
    35-ton "Rectanks" to carry rollers and engines exceeding 10 tons.

    Subject to examination by the Chief Mechanical Engineer's Inspector before dispatch, rollers and engines not exceeding 12 tons in weight may be loaded on the following 15-ton "Loriots" :—
    "Loriots D" Nos. 42138 to 42155.
    "Loriots E" Nos. 42156 to 42164, 42202 to 42205.

    NOTE.—The wheel base of the roller or engine must not exceed the length of the well of the vehicle upon which it is loaded.

    In the event of the standard load gauge dimensions being exceeded, full particulars must be furnished to the District Goods Manager, in accordance with the standing instructions.

Securing Load.

    Scotches must be fixed at the front and rear of the back wheels. The front wheels should not be scotched fore and aft, but should be substantially packed with 10 in. by 5 in. sleepers at the sides only.

    The method of securing with binding chains, illustrated below, must be employed.

    The brakes of the rollers must be put on tightly before transit.

Securing Railway Vehicle.

    Before unloading or loading a steam road roller or traction engine, the Foreman or person in charge must see that the brakes of the railway vehicle are securely applied and that scotches are placed behind all wheels of the vehicle.

    On no account may the chains be placed or bound over the front forks.

    Driving or Fly wheels must be thoroughly secured by ropes, and specially examined for the purpose of seeing that they are securely keyed on the shaft.

Left and above: Swindon drawing showing method of loading and securing steam rollers and traction engines etc on Loriot well wagons. *GWR*

Barrels of Welsh whisky being loaded at Frongoch (near Bala) in undiagrammed 3-plank open No 39630 built on Lot 325 in 1884. *D J Hyde collection*

Christmas trees being loaded into GW Minks; the checker with his portable desk checking invoices. *D J Hyde collection*

GW wagon No 41724 for glass in crates coded Coral A (Diagram D2, built 1908) shows the method of securing plate glass between packing and the moveable partitions on the vehicle. Note the DC II brake at left end on this side of the wagon. *K Ettle*

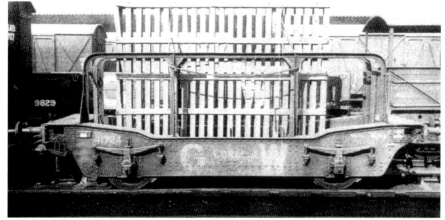

Carriages for London Underground being taken on their own bogies from the Birmingham Railway Carriage & Wagon Works at Smethwick using a GW match truck No 48657; this had a special coupling to adapt to the lower Tube coaches. The match truck was newly painted and the labelling cannot be seen in full and is tantalisingly labelled '4 tons. To be returned to the Birmingham Railway ... ' and ' These wagons ... '.
GWR/D J Hyde collection

Another London Underground coach *en route* from the Birmingham Railway C & W factory using another match truck No 32061 having a special coupling. The labelling is in very small writing in the centre of the wagon, but has a similar message to that on No 48657 in the adjacent photograph.
GWR/D J Hyde collection

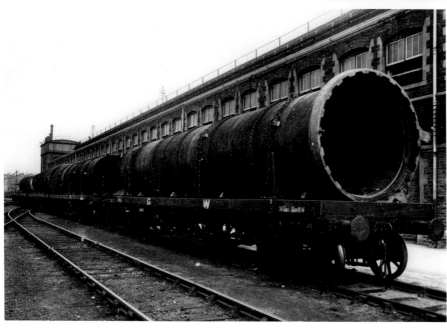

Some special traffic concerned the GW itself ('railway domestic special traffic'). Here are cylinders, about 90 ft long by 6ft 9 in internal diameter, for the Hayes creosoting plant photographed at Swindon on 19 August 1933. The nearer cylinder is loaded on Diagram J23 Macaw E bogie bolster wagon No 84476, that had started life as a J14 Macaw B in 1915, then in 1917 was strengthened to carry military traffic by having extra underframe bracing added (J18), and was finally put back into merchandise traffic with bolsters reinstalled in 1919 becoming J23. Between the bogie bolster vehicles, four-wheel Macaw bolster wagons were used as match trucks.
D J Hyde collection

At Hayes, trollies loaded with untreated sleepers were run in to the cylinders (up to 600 sleepers at a time) that were then evacuated to draw in heated creosote from a storage tank, after which pressure (up to 200psi) would be applied to inject the preservative. *GWR/D J Hyde collection*

A GW Simplex four-wheel petrol shunter chained to Loriot E No 42162 (built in 1908), photographed at Swindon Locomotive factory. No 23 was built in 1925 and mostly worked at Bridgwater Docks. The cab has been removed to comply with the loading gauge. *Real Photographs*

CHAPTER NINETEEN

FLOWERS, FRUIT & VEGETABLES

A LARGE proportion of special freight traffic was seasonal movements in fruit, flower and vegetable crops. Nearly all such traffic was worked by special goods trains for which special allocations of wagons had to be provided. Regulations provided for the thorough cleaning of all vehicles between successive loadings of plums, apples, beans, peas, brussels sprouts, asparagus, tomatoes, broccoli, potatoes etc. The season for flowers (narcissi, gladioli and wallflowers in particular) from the Scilly Isles and West Cornwall was roughly January to April. Next came the Cornwall and Jersey potato crops, followed by Guernsey tomatoes. The Worcester fruit season (apples and plums mainly) began as early as June and lasted through to September, and Channel Islands tomatoes followed after.

In the C19th, one solution to the requirement for speed to get perishable goods to market as quickly as possible was to use passenger trains, but that was expensive and could only be justified by supply and demand when the market could bear high prices. Flowers from the Scilly Isles and the region around Penzance blossomed many weeks earlier than elsewhere in England, and are an example of conveyance by passenger train. In the late 1890s, about 400 tons per annum were being carried and by the late 1920s this had doubled. It was essential that flowers should be delivered in good condition to London and the northern cities in time for the early morning markets and the GWR contracted to do this without fail. The flowers were gathered in the Scillies in the early morning and packed in light, non-returnable wooden boxes, which were made up into packets of five. The thin planks of wood to manufacture these boxes were sent down from London to Penzance by goods train. The GWR quoted through rates from the Scillies, even though carriage by sea to Penzance (in about four hours) was performed by private steamers (see *GWR Docks & Marine*).

At the end of the C19th flowers for London were, as a rule, conveyed by the 4.50pm fast mail and passenger train from Penzance that reached Paddington at 4am the next morning. The flowers were conveyed in ordinary passenger train brake vans,

Cornish flower traffic being unloaded at Paddington passenger station overnight. Note the cartage vehicles on the left. *GWR*

an extra one being often attached for the purpose. In the height of the season there would frequently be extra loads of flowers that would be too much for the mail train. If over 10 tons of flowers were dispatched, one or more additional special trains had to be run ahead of the mail. In such cases, all profit was lost by the GW. Running with only 75-minute intervals between the first and last train over the greater part of the GW main line (through Bristol in those days) required careful working of the traffic, particularly in pre-1905 days when the Penzance-Plymouth section was still single line. All cattle, goods and mineral trains and even stopping passenger trains had to be kept clear of the flower and broccoli specials. Not all flowers that left Penzance found their way to Covent Garden in London; a large proportion went to Manchester and Birmingham: Manchester traffic was detached at Bristol, from where a train left at 1.5am, arriving Manchester at 5.50am. The Birmingham traffic was conveyed from Didcot by a train leaving at 3am and arriving at Birmingham at 5.15am.

The 'Up Jersey' leaves Weymouth at 6.35pm bound for Paddington in June 1938. The Y8 Fruit A vans were new in 1938 and are full of fruit and vegetables from the Channel Islands. The '43XX' carries the C-headcode. Notice the curious flat-bottomed rail in the sidings. The train will stop at Dorchester (6.50-7pm) and Maiden Newton (7.17-7.30) to attach wagons if required (Q in the STT), and will be refuged at Evershot (7.40*-8.10, where the asterisk indicates that it will also perform work). The Stop Board before Yetminster is reached at 8.20 and the train stops at Yeovil (Pen Mill) from 8.32 to 8.50 (Q again). Castle Cary is passed at 9.10, and the train stops at Witham from 9.30 to 9.40 (Q) before arriving at Westbury (10pm-10.40). Bedwyn is passed at 11.30 before stopping at Newbury (11.52pm-12.8am, CRQ). The train passes on to the original GW main line at Reading (12.40-12.42) and eventually gets to Paddington at 2.10am. *GWR*

The following is an abridged outline of the 'when required' running of Flower Specials during 1899:

Train No 1: depart Penzance 1.5pm; arrive Truro 5.5pm and depart 5.30pm; Burngullow 5.33-5.36pm; stops Lostwithiel to take on water; Plymouth (North Road) 7.1-7.6pm; Newton Abbot 8.5-8.10pm; Exeter 8.53-9.5pm; Taunton 10-10.8pm; Bristol (Temple Meads) 11.22-11.32pm; Swindon 12.42-12.50am; Didcot 1.30-1.45am; arrive Paddington Passenger station 3.15am.

Train No 2: depart Penzance 3pm; Truro 5.20-5.25pm; stops Lostwithiel to take on water; Plymouth (North Road) 7.23-7.40pm; Newton Abbot 8.55-9pm; Exeter 9.48-9.55pm; Taunton 10.48-10.53pm; Bristol (Temple Meads) 11.58-12.3am; Swindon 1.18-1.25am; Didcot 2.4-2.30am; arrive Paddington 3.50am.

Train No 3: depart Penzance 1.55pm; Truro 6.26-6.32pm; Burngullow 6.53-6.56 pm; stops Lostwithiel to take on water; Plymouth (North Road) 8.35-8.40pm; Newton Abbot 9.45-9.50pm; Exeter 10.38-10.45pm; Taunton 11.35-11.43pm; Bristol (Temple Meads) 12.48-12.58am; Swindon 2.5-2.15am; Didcot 2.55-3.10am; arrive Paddington 4.30am.

Moving ahead in years, a 4.25pm departure from Penzance is shown in the 1933 STT for a flowers and parcels train arriving at Paddington at 1.50am. This latter train would have featured Siphon G vehicles in its make-up.

Until the 1850s, goods traffic from Cornwall was chiefly mineral (and china and ball clay continued to feature strongly around St Austell and Fowey beyond nationalisation), but after the decline of the mining industry, produce of the county was nearly all agricultural that took advantage of the favourable climate. Even before the 1850s an appreciable volume of early broccoli from Penzance, Marazion and St Erth was sent by rail throughout the country. By 1874/5 over 5,000 tons were forwarded; in 1900/1, 15,000 tons; and, by 1932/3 over 20,000 tons. The broccoli heads were lightly packed in boxes of one cwt and (originally) conveyed in open wagons sheeted against the frost. Vacuum-fitted opens and cattle trucks were later employed, followed by the new Y8 Fruit A fully ventilated vans, 200 of which came into service in 1938. These fruit vans and similar special vehicles had shelves on which baskets of fruit could be stacked, which improved the density of loading in comparison with using only the floors of luggage vans.

Before World War 1, most broccoli found its way to the northern markets, very little going to London, so the broccoli specials ran as far as Didcot, or via Didcot to Birmingham and Crewe. There were four broccoli specials at the turn of 19th/20th centuries, with the following timings:

A broccoli special seen at Bodmin Road on 19 December 1934. The 'Hall' carries C-headlamps. Some wagons have tarpaulin sheet supporter bars raised but have sheets flat across the wagons. There's a tarpaulin over the first van, indicating that it lets rain in.
A G Atkins collection

A broccoli special leaves for London in April 1942. The cab side windows of No 4940 *Ludford Hall* have a metal slide to cut down glare from the firebox door during blackouts.
GWR

Broccoli traffic being unloaded at Paddington Goods depot on 1 April 1942.
D J Hyde collection

Train No 1: depart Penzance 1.5pm; Truro 5.18-5.28pm; Plymouth 8.40-8.50pm; Exeter 11.15-11.30pm; Swindon 4.20-4.35am; Didcot terminate at 5.30 am.

Train No 2: depart Penzance 3pm; Truro 7.13-7.25pm; Plymouth 10.50-11.5pm; Exeter 1.30-1.45am; Swindon 6.30-7.5am; Didcot terminate at 8.5am.

Train No.3: depart Penzance 1.55pm; Truro 6.44-6.55pm; Plymouth arr 9.40pm; Exeter 1.55-2.10am; Swindon 7-7.20am; Didcot 8.15-10am; Oxford 10.25-10.40am; Bordesley Jct 2-2.40pm; Birmingham 2.49-2.30pm; Market Drayton 5.25-5.35pm; Crewe terminate at 6.30pm.

Train No 4 departed Penzance at 5pm; Truro 8.22-8.32pm; Plymouth 11.20-11.30pm, but the timings beyond Plymouth are not certain.

If there were traffic for London it was worked on from Didcot by the first available train, but should Train No 1 have contained six or more trucks for Paddington it was extended to leave Didcot at 6am for Paddington, arriving at 8.5am. Any produce for South Wales was taken off at Bristol, and worked via the Severn Tunnel. The maximum loads of these specials were: Penzance to Plymouth 19 wagons and van; Plymouth to Exeter 29 wagons and van; Exeter to Bristol 35 wagons and van; and, Bristol to Didcot 33 wagons and van. Sometimes it was necessary in heavy seasons to run two trains to the north from Didcot and it would have been the stationmasters at Penzance, Marazion and St Erth who had to ensure that enough empty vehicles were available. Before the change of headlamp codes in 1903 (see Chapter 2), these special trains would have carried an 'S' at the chimney base and a white

diamond on a black ground over the middle of the locomotive buffer beam; subsequently they carried C-headcode lamps and many ran as partially-fitted express goods trains. There was at one time limited traffic in French broccoli through Weymouth from Nantes, St Nazaire and Brest, and the Walford Shipping line started a service from Roscoff, but this business was irregular, being affected by tariffs imposed on imported vegetables.

Special arrangements applied to potato traffic from the West Country, which by 1900 amounted to some 12,000 tons per annum. In the early days, potatoes were packed in hampers, later in sacks. Here again, the greater amount of traffic went north via Didcot, or via Bristol and the Severn Tunnel. In 1900, three 'conditional' (RR) potato specials were timetabled to depart from Penzance: the first, for Bristol, left at 2.30pm (No 1 special, terminating there at 4.10am); Nos 2 and 3 for Didcot departing at 5.0pm and 6.45pm, arriving/departing Bristol at 5.55/6.10am and 7.10/7.25am respectively, and arriving at Didcot at 8.50 and 10.35am. London traffic was worked forward from Didcot by the first available express train but, again like the broccoli specials, if it involved six or more wagons, the train was extended to Paddington. Northern traffic was similarly sent forward by conditional express goods trains to Manchester, Liverpool, Leeds, Sheffield, Stockport, Bradford and Halifax as well as to Glasgow.

Cornish vegetable traffic increased tremendously after World War 1 and the train organisation involved in its distribution became more complicated. This is illustrated particularly by the events of the 1933/4 season that, instead of extending over some three months, was compressed into little over a month owing to the weather. In April 1934 over 230 special trains were run by the GWR to all parts of the country, conveying over 16,000 tons of broccoli. On one day 12 trains, comprising over 580 wagons, were dispatched, and for the first time in the history of the Cornish

French strawberry traffic being unloaded from ship to shore at Plymouth Millbay docks (West Wharf) in 1937 into goods fruit vans and various Siphons. *GWR*

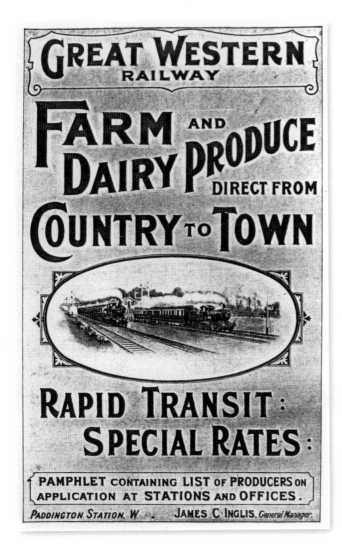

the principal market towns either on the next day or second day after dispatch. The 'Up Jersey' express C-headcode goods train left Weymouth for Paddington at 6.35pm each day. 'Perpot' was the telegraph code word meaning 'Special train of potatoes, vegetables and other perishable traffic leaving Weymouth at...'

Brest strawberry traffic into Plymouth was in full swing between May and July. In 1900, 1,800 tons of strawberries were imported through Plymouth; in 1923 it was 2,500 tons and in 1931 3,360 tons. These were all record years in their time. Often four steamers would be engaged in carrying the traffic, making perhaps 50 trips per season. The 2,500 tons imported in 1923 represented nearly 800,000 baskets, 67,000 boxes and 39,000 sieves of produce from Brittany passing through Millbay docks in the brief season; these included over 18,000 bags of peas out of the same ships. Unloading of the boats was by crane, using trays on which 80 crates (about one ton) were loaded. To transport the strawberries, 800 or more railway vehicles might be used and over 50 special trains run. The principal market for the fruit was Manchester.

The Worcester fruit season began in June. At least 200 fruit vans were specially marked for return to the Worcester district for loading at Pershore, Aldington Siding, Littleton & Badsey and Evesham. Two nicknamed fitted trains from Worcester for fruit and vegetable traffic in 1933 were: the 'Worcester Fruit' (6.45pm Worcester to Cardiff, calling at Toddington to pick up more vans *en route* and marked in the STT 'November to March inclusive'); and, the 'Sparagras' (8.35pm Worcester to Crewe calling at Kidderminster). Another train, the 8.40pm Worcester to Southall, ran when required during the fruit season, calling at Oxford and Slough serving the jam factories in those places. These were C-headlamp trains and the vans used would have been Diagrams Y1/2/3 supplemented by six-wheel Siphons in the early 1930s. The Y8/9/11 special vans built in the late 1930s for this sort of traffic were fully-ventilated, vacuum-braked, screw-coupled vans suitable

broccoli industry some 2,000 loads were dispatched to the markets within a fortnight.

Channel Islands crops were next in the calendar and they required additional cargo boat services to Weymouth and extra staff at the ports (see *GWR Docks & Marine*). Sometimes the cargo from two boats a day had to be loaded into pre-ordered railway wagons and dispatched in several special trains. As nearly the whole of the Guernsey tomato crop was grown under glass, the rate at which traffic arrived in Weymouth could be controlled to some extent, but that was not the case for outdoor-grown Jersey produce during August to October which was affected by the weather. In 1937, over 2½ million baskets of tomatoes were carried by the GW — equivalent to 16,378 tons. In 1947 over five million chips and trays of tomatoes were carried. To ease sorting at Weymouth, Guernsey produce bore coloured address labels, viz: green for Birmingham; red Manchester; white for all other English towns; yellow for Scottish towns; and, blue for Welsh towns. The various London markets were distinguished by coloured lines diagonally across the white labels, as follows: Covent Garden — red lines; Spitalfields — blue; Borough — green; and, Stratford — yellow.

Much of the Jersey potato crop went to northern markets via Westbury, and to Wales via Bristol. The produce reached nearly all

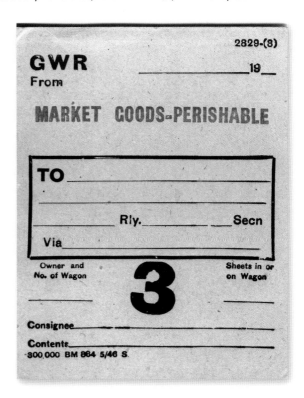

for running in express trains. The new vehicles were also intended for vegetables requiring ample ventilation. Cattle trucks were also converted to Y10 in 1938 to be suitable for fruit traffic (see *GWR Goods Wagons*).

During World War 2, when the Channel Islands were occupied by Germany, early potato crops from Cornwall and Pembrokeshire replaced the Jersey crop. Many special trains were run for these crops; those from Cornwall in particular met shortages in the Midlands and the north. Christian Barman in *Next Station* highlights the satisfaction it gave the staff of the GWR to see the special fruit services fully restored in the 1945 season and the flower expresses from Cornwall to run again for the first time in April 1946.

The railway provided appropriate facilities for loading vegetables and made improvements when there was demand; for example, in 1927 two additional sidings were laid down at Ponsandane and the loading bank extended for broccoli traffic. In 1928 as a result of an application from farmers and local residents for station accommodation to be provided between Hartlebury and Droitwich Spa to serve the villages of Elmley Lovett, Rushock, Elbridge, Cutnall Green, Hampton Lovett and Doverdale, the GW Directors authorised the construction a passenger halt at Hampton Lovett (later called Cutnall Green) together with a siding to take 12 wagons and the requisite wharfage, with an approach road and 20-ton cart weighbridge. Hitherto the district had been served for heavy traffic by Hartlebury and Droitwich Spa, GW; by Stoke Works and Bromsgrove, LMS; and, by the Birmingham & Worcester Canal. In 1932 an additional siding and loading bank were provided at Gwinear Road.

Train services were also improved as the years went by and as road competition crept in. For example, in 1932 the 2.30pm Penzance to Paddington (the 'Searchlight') was accelerated by starting later at 4.33pm but arriving in London at the same time as before (2.20am), with the schedule being quickened between Penzance and Tavistock Jct (Plymouth); after the latter point stops were made only at Taunton and Reading. This train conveyed traffic for Birmingham (via Taunton), Reading and London and might have been be hauled from Plymouth by a 'Castle' or even a 'King'.

No wagon with a wheelbase smaller than 15ft was permitted to run in trains travelling at speeds greater than 60mph, but this distinction had not been made in the GW telegraph codes. In the nationwide 1943 telegraph code unification, the long wheelbase GW Fruit C and Fruit D vans were recoded Pasfruit C and Pasfruit D. The shorter wheelbase GW Fruit and Fruit A vans retained the same code as before, but the Fruit B code for banana vans disappeared, being replaced by Banana.

CHAPTER TWENTY

BANANAS

AT the turn of the 19th/20th centuries, the banana was still a comparative rarity in Britain but the Colonial Office, wanting to develop Jamaica, offered a £40,000 annual subsidy for a mail/passenger steamship line to run a boat service between Britain and Jamaica, part of the arrangement being that 20,000 bunches of bananas would be brought back each trip. As explained in *GWR Docks & Marine*, the Elder-Dempster Line won the contract, and the SS *Port Morant* refrigerator ship (the first of a purpose-built fleet) sailed from Avonmouth in February 1901. She returned a month later with 14,000 boxes of oranges as well as the bananas: never before had such perishable fruit been carried such a long way. A weekly service in summer (fortnightly in winter) was begun in 1904 from Port Limon (Jamaica), and Avonmouth became the principal centre for the European banana trade. By 1939 Elders & Fyffes was handling over six million bunches a year. (A bunch is the long stalk containing from six to nine 'hands', each of which has about 15 'fingers' ie individual bananas.) Just before World War 2, the record unloading for the port was 77,679 bunches in an eight-hour day; on average, a van left the dockside, fully loaded, every minute.

The GW pioneered the railway conveyance of bananas (see *GWR Goods Wagons*). The first consignment was taken by two special fully-fitted express trains formed of Y1/2 fruit vans from Avonmouth. After unloading at Paddington (passenger) station, a half-mile long procession of 100 horse vans bearing labels 'Jamaica Bananas' in huge letters headed for Stratford, Spitalfields, the Borough, Covent Garden and other markets. For future traffic, special new vans (originally V8 in the wagon Diagram Book, later becoming Y6) were designed in 1905 that were both insulated and could be steam heated. They were the first GW vans to have adjustable shuttered louvres and were coded Fruit B (recoded Banana in the 1943 telegraph code unification).

The day before a banana boat was due at Avonmouth, Messrs Elders & Fyffes telephoned the GW yardmaster giving provisional details as to the number of vans required and the stations for which they were to be consigned. Depending on the precise stage of ripeness of the bananas, on the length of the journey to the wholesalers and on the likely weather during the rail journey, experts decided what temperature would be required for each consignment. To reach the consumer in good condition, bananas must be kept at a temperature of about 50°F; once chilled, they never ripen properly. The times at which the vans were collected into the railway yard allowed a sufficient margin of heating to be carried out *before* setting off, but if the weather were cold, the vans would be heated *en route* as well so that the temperature would not drop. The normal steam-heating capacity of the train engines employed at Avonmouth was 17 vans, but as a rule the dock pilot, or an engine sent down specially for the work, lent a hand. With an engine on each end, 34 vans could be dealt with at one time. When steaming was not needed *en route*, 60 vans was the maximum capacity of the train but this number was reduced to a limit of 34 vans if steam heating during the rail journey was necessary.

All banana trains were specials and shown with scheduled paths in the timetable. For example, in the 1933 STT, C-headcode banana trains left Avonmouth at the following times: 10.55am to Acton (due 2.55pm) (CR Reading); 12.15pm to Banbury or Old Oak Common as required; 1.30pm to Reading (due 4.10pm); 3pm to Reading (due 6.25pm) (for SR); 6.5pm to Paddington (due 10.55pm). The 9.20pm J-headcode goods from Avonmouth to Salisbury via Trowbridge and Westbury, arriving on the SR at 3.49am, was 'To carry E Head Lights when conveying Banana traffic' — fitted banana vans on the locomotive would provide the necessary vacuum component for this upgrade from J to E. LMS banana trains departed at similar intervals and are shown in the GW STT. In the later 1930s, there were more and more trains scheduled. Empties were returned by the 3.40pm ex-Paddington, calling at Swindon at 7pm to attach more vans *en route* to Avonmouth and departing 7.30pm. Very often a '43XX' locomotive would have hauled these trains. The *Railway Magazine* reported that in mid-August 1932, No 2914 *St Augustine* with the eight-wheel tender from the *Great Bear*, was seen on an express banana train from Avonmouth.

There were two regular unusual consignments from Avonmouth. The first was for the Channel Islands and travelled in containers packed with wood fibre; arrangements for passing this traffic forward were made direct with Weymouth Quay. The other unusual consignment was dispatched by train to Hull or Newcastle, there to be re-shipped for Scandinavia.

The C-headcode 6.50pm Bristol-Birkenhead goods (Train No 262, nicknamed the 'Farmer's Boy' and headed in the STT as the 'Birkenhead Goods') also carried banana traffic. It left Avonmouth Old yard and headed to Filton West Jct via Hallen Marsh Jct (Section 4 of the STT, page 230). Wagon destinations on leaving Bristol were, from the locomotive: Shrewsbury, Welshpool, Crewe, Wrexham, Birkenhead (vac fitted); then non-vac stock in reverse order. Moving to page 116 of Section 4, the train is shown passing Filton at 7.9pm and stopping at the Stop Board before Patchway Tunnel for the nominal one minute between 7.13 and 7.14. At Pilning it stood from 7.20-7.51 to let other trains pass and also 'for Severn Tunnel purposes' (* in the STT). With the pilot, the 'Farmer's Boy' entered the Tunnel at 7.55 and left at 8.7, to pass STJ at 8.11 pm. Section 12 of the STT, page 73 then gives the train as passing Maindee East Jct at 8.24 pm, Pontypool Road station at 8.43, Abergavenny at 8.56, and arriving at the Stop Board at Red Hill Jct at 9.30pm for a one-minute pause. Having descended the bank into Hereford (Barton Goods) the train stopped between 9.36-9.56, but the train called only 'to comply with incline instructions when not required to call for traffic or locomotive purposes'. Even so, priority was given to loads for northernmost destinations picked up *en route* at Hereford and also later on at Saltney (Chester). After leaving Hereford, Shelwick Jct was passed at 10.2, Leominster at 10.17, Woofferton at 10.26, Ludlow at 10.33, Craven Arms & Stokesay at 10.44 to arrive at the Church Stretton Stop Board at 11.2pm again for a one-minute pause. Coleham was passed at 11.23 to arrive at Shrewsbury (Coton Hill) at 11.28pm.

Connecting trains at Shrewsbury to take traffic to destination were the 3.45am Shrewsbury-Market Drayton and 8.30am Coleham-Welshpool. Departure from Coton Hill at 12.10am is found in Section 14, page 6, of the STT after which the train passes Gobowen at 12.45 (CR), Ruabon at 12.57, Wrexham at 1.6 to arrive at the Stop Boards before Wheatsheaf Jct at 1.9, and before Rossett at 1.20am. A stop was made at Saltney between 1.31 and 2.9, to drop wagons for connecting trains such as the 7.35pm Bristol-Manchester (the 'Lancashire Lad') which was almost a duplicate train to the 'Farmer's Boy', and the 6am Saltney-Manchester. On departure from Saltney, the 'Farmer's Boy' stopped at Chester Cutting between 2.18-2.30am (Chester Cutting was Chester No 6 Jct by means of which trains for the north could proceed without reversing which they had to do if they entered Chester General station). Thereafter Ledsham Jct was passed at 2.45, Hooton South at 2.50 and the train arrived at Birkenhead at 3.20am.

The train running in the opposite direction was the 7.45pm Manchester-Bristol (the 'Mon') described earlier in Chapter 17.

2-6-0 No 6399 on an Up C-code banana train at Reading in 1931. Note the 'County' 4-4-0 in the background on the right. A Brightman

An H-headcode goods train 'carrying through load to destination' passes Claverham (near Yatton in Somerset) on 19 May 1938 headed by No 4982 *Acton Hall*. The first four vehicles are banana vans. *SLS*

'43XX' No 6397 on a C-headcode banana train at Swindon on 22 November 1922. The two leading vans are Nos 95602 and 93405, both to diagram Y4. GWR

CHAPTER TWENTY-ONE

LIVESTOCK TRAINS & AGRICULTURAL TRAFFIC

CONVEYANCE of livestock by goods train on the GWR doubled between 1871 and 1910 in which year three million head of livestock were transported, of which sheep and lambs accounted for about 40%, cattle and pigs 20% each, horses and calves making up the rest. Animals could be conveyed by passenger or goods train, payment of the passenger rate guaranteeing faster transits, but that distinction became blurred after the introduction of the vacuum-fitted C-headcode goods trains early in the C20th. GW cattle trucks were coded Mex.

Traditionally, in Britain, cattle were slaughtered where the meat was going to be eaten, rather than be slaughtered locally and the carcasses be sent forward to market. Many home-reared cattle used to be taken by cattle train from the countryside to abattoirs in towns. For example in 1868/9, stations in Cornwall sent 7,000 head of cattle to Plymouth and 4,000 to Devonport to feed the local population and to victual Royal Navy and Merchant Navy shipping. In the C19th, and for part of the C20th, beef was imported 'on the hoof' from Ireland and America, and the practice of sending cattle to local towns for slaughter was continued, with regular trains of 'fat cattle' being timetabled from licensed ports on the GW (Birkenhead, Bristol, Cardiff and Fishguard) to cattle markets all over the country. (The reason for licensing is explained in the section on Birkenhead in *GWR Docks & Marine*.)

Railways were under legal obligation to water certain types of animal if they were longer than 24 hours on the journey. Animals differ in their needs: horses, asses and mules were not to be without water for more than 24 hours; cattle and pigs 27 hours; and, sheep and lambs 36 hours. 'Shamble' was the GW Telegraph code word for 'arrange to feed and water at ...'. Fodder was provided by the railway at reasonable charges approved by the Ministry of Agriculture and when animals were fed and watered (and cows milked) in transit, a note was made on the wagon labels where and at what time this had been done. In the STT, goods trains were often timetabled to stop for the locomotive to take on water; cattle trains were additionally timetabled to stop to feed and water the animals.

The cattle business was important at New Milford and later at Fishguard where Irish animals were unloaded. The 1899 STT stipulated that special cattle trains from Milford for Acton and beyond must contain more than 10 trucks of cattle but with a maximum load of 20, and that the trucks were 'to be fitted with screw couplings'. At Fishguard there were 65 pens capable of holding many hundred head of cattle at the same time. In the 1927 annual GW report on its goods activities, improvements in livestock accommodation at Wexford are listed. Between 1913 and 1937, numbers of cattle shipped from Ireland were never less than 90,000 per year and often near 200,000. Cattle were landed on a special gallery that ran along the entire length of the quay wall underneath the passenger stage, so that passengers saw nothing of the animals. After a 10-hour quarantine, they were despatched in special express C-headcode trains to the various large cattle markets such as at Norwich or Bristol, and thence to abattoirs. Special Train Control arrangements existed in order to ensure the most rapid journey times for the trains to their destinations. They ran at the standard point-to-point times for Class C trains. Hence from Fishguard to Cardiff, trains with more than 35 wagons were examined at Llandilo Junction where also locomotive water was required; but with fewer than 35 wagons, train examination took place at Carmarthen Jct and no water was required. Beyond Cardiff, Irish cattle had various destinations with different examination and watering points *en route*. From Cardiff to Acton via the Severn Tunnel there was examination at STJ and at Reading. Cattle going on to Stourbridge Jct from Cardiff via Hereford and Worcester required water and examination at Hereford. Those to Bordesley Jct via Gloucester from Cardiff required examination and water at Gloucester, and water only at Stratford-upon-Avon. If grease axlebox wagons were involved, the trains carried the E-headcode and were not to run more than 50 miles before examination. Fishguard engines and men worked the specials to Cardiff, then Canton provided suitable power and men on to destination.

Similar arrangements applied in reverse for empty cattle wagons being supplied to Fishguard where they were required by

There was no passenger station at Burbage between Savernake and Pewsey on the main line through Newbury to the west, but there was a goods wharf connected to the Kennet & Avon Canal. W5/8 cattle trucks stand ready for loading to market. Owing to the rising 1/132 gradient for Up trains, there were special instructions for shunting were a train passing on the main line. *LGRP*

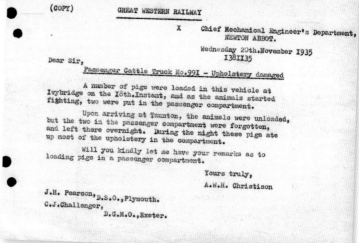

(COPY)

GREAT WESTERN RAILWAY

X   Chief Mechanical Engineer's Department,
NEWTON ABBOT.

Wednesday 20th.November 1935
138II35

Dear Sir,

Passenger Cattle Truck No.991 - Upholstery damaged

A number of pigs were loaded in this vehicle at Ivybridge on the I6th.Instant, and as the animals started fighting, two were put in the passenger compartment.

Upon arriving at Taunton, the animals were unloaded, but the two in the passenger compartment were forgotten, and left there overnight. During the night these pigs ate up most of the upholstery in the compartment.

Will you kindly let me have your remarks as to loading pigs in a passenger compartment.

Yours truly,
A.W.H. Christison

J.H. Pearson, D.S.O., Plymouth.
C.J. Challenger,
D.G.M.O., Exeter.

noon to meet the steamers. Trains of empties came from Wolverhampton, Bordesley, Bristol, Cardiff and so on, hauled by engines 'capable of maintaining vacuum timing, and wherever practicable 29XX and 43XX should be supplied'. Such C and D power-group locomotives could convey 60 empty Mexes; group B locos, only 48; and, group A engines only 40 (see Chapter 6). Stops for locomotive water and train examinations were arranged as follows. Trains from Wolverhampton and Bordesley Jct were to call at Stratford-upon-Avon, Gloucester and Port Talbot for water and were to be examined at the last two yards. Trains from Bristol stopped at Port Talbot for examination and water (they will have stopped at Pilning and STJ for Severn Tunnel purposes).

In 1909, the GW commenced conveyance of horses to and from Ireland by the Down Fishguard boat express departing Paddington weekdays at 4.31pm and by the corresponding Up boat express leaving Fishguard at 6am (**MX**) arriving Reading at 11.52am and Paddington at 12.40pm.

For the Taunton Bacon Co there was flat rate charging for pigs over a defined area in the West of England. Similar arrangements were made for other firms. If a weekend was involved, sometimes the pigs arrived in horseboxes by passenger service.

As watering of animals took time, the aim was to 'get the animals home' as quickly as possible. Between stations on the GW system this usually presented no difficulty. Even so, because the flow of livestock was often between stations in agricultural districts that generally were not so well served with goods trains as industrial areas, it was often necessary to use passenger trains at the commencement or conclusion of a journey in order to keep the transit time within reasonable limits. For this reason, many GW cattle wagons (telegraph code 'Mex') were vacuum-fitted. Vehicles for pedigree cattle (coded 'Beetle') and horseboxes (coded 'Paco') were invariably vac-fitted. Beetles could accommodate four animals. Enlarged Beetles had mangers, water tanks and a central compartment for stockmen, but later Beetles omitted the water tank as the herdsmen preferred to obtain water fresh from station taps. Since Beetles and Pacos often travelled over other companies' lines, many of these vehicles were dual-braked

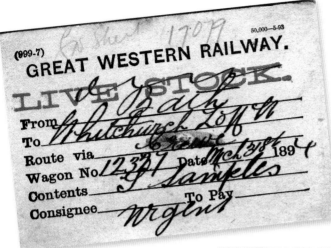

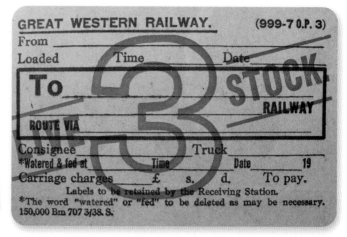

A rake of four W1 large cattle trucks with one W2 medium cattle truck in the middle, all with oilboxes but one-sided lever brakes, is headed by an Armstrong standard goods '388' class. The headcode of two lamps (one at the chimney and one in the middle of the buffer beam and called the F code) applied between 1903 and 1918 for an express cattle train. The animals, in fact, are horses. *LPC*

The cattle dock at Witney with its water tower that supplied cattle drinking troughs and hose hydrants. *LGRP*

(ie Westinghouse and vacuum-fitted) up to 1934. There were difficulties about cattle movements over weekends. On Fridays, some foreign lines preferred not to accept animals for transit on certain routes unless there was a connecting weekend service to the destination. At Acton, no traffic for the GN Section of the LNER via King's Cross, nor for the LMS (Midland Section), would be accepted on Fridays. In the 1933 STT, it was noted that livestock ex-Gloucester Saturday market for Romford, Bishops Stortford and Barnet (LNE) via Acton, would be forwarded by the 4.30pm Gloucester-Paddington parcels train (8.30am ex-Fishguard) to

come off at Acton. The enginemen had to be told and the information given to Controllers at Reading and Acton.

GW telegraph code words associated with animal movements were: 'Loot' — 'undermentioned wagons of live ... left here on train named. Work forward all speed'; 'Manx ' — 'wire immediately name of sender, number and kind of animals and floatage requirements'; 'Daunt' — 'following sender will load undermentioned wagons livestock at your station on ... for ... Arrange'; 'Dauntles' — 'ditto load at a different station'; 'Emigrant' — 'the following spare cattle wagons are on hand ... today'; 'Novac' — 'dispose of foreign cattle wagons not fitted with vacuum brake and foreign cattle wagons fitted with pipe only as follows'. For pigs off to bacon factories 'Railpig' meant 'make all necessary arrangements and rail to ... to arrive before ... on date named'; 'Roadpig' was the same for conveyance of pigs from the farm all the way to the factory by GW road motors.

When a stationmaster received an application for the movement of pedigree cattle, he would quote the best service available, taking into account the maximum length of wheelbase permissible on attached vehicles; of regulations governing feeding and watering, animal diseases, and so on; and that the addition of special vehicles was prohibited on some passenger trains. A suitable vehicle was ordered from a nearby depot to be sent ready for loading and the superintendents of divisions through which the traffic would pass were informed by telegram.

The Paddington cattle dock photographed on 18 May 1930. It was on the north side of the goods station, with an entrance from Harrow Road beside the Red Lion pub. Sometimes, when horses were carried in cattle wagons, a tarpaulin was placed over the roof and down the sides to prevent the animals spooking and pushing their heads between the bars. The two 1895-vintage Mexes are to diagram W1, now with NCU plates. *GWR*

An Up cattle train from Fishguard Harbour leaves the single-track section at Manorowen on 10 August 1946. No 5908 *Moreton Hall* carries the C-headcode. Note the travelling post office apparatus at the lineside. The 2¼-mile climb up from Goodwick, the major part of which rises at 1 in 50, was the only section of the old steeply-graded Rosebush Railway that was incorporated in the new cut-off line for Fishguard when opened on 30 August 1906 between Clarbeston Road and Letterston. *H G W Household Swindon STEAM*

For journeys on to other railways, lists of trains generally available for such vehicles were usually interchanged between the companies. According to the timetables for 1840, the GW was prepared to take forward horse and carriage traffic at 10 minutes

notice! When animal(s) had been loaded and the vehicle attached to a through train, the sending station advised the destination station by telegraph; or advised the transfer station if the vehicle had to be attached to a different train later in the journey. For example, if a Beetle or Paco was being sent from Chippenham to Kidderminster, Chippenham telegraphed Swindon or Didcot that a pedigree cattle van or horsebox was in such-and-such a train, giving its position on the train; Didcot advised Oxford, who passed the information to Worcester; and, Worcester to Kidderminster. (Similar telegraphing took place where saloons and other special carriage stock were sent through.) The GWR often carried valuable consignments of dairy cattle from Cornwall to destinations in the north by special train; the journey between Redruth and York, for example, was covered in little over 24 hours, including a stop *en route* for a couple of hours for milking, feeding and watering.

In addition to 'specials' there were some regular long-distance cattle trains in the working timetables, eg the 4pm St Phillip's Marsh (Bristol) to Reading, carrying E headlamps, stopping at Swindon for train examination and for the watering of the animals if necessary. Another relevant train in the 1933 STT, which carried mainly cattle and fodder (for Westbourne Park) was the 9.25pm (9.37pm **SO**) Aylesbury-Paddington (E-headcode with locomotive power group C). The train first called at Princes Risborough to detach wagons (i) for the 1.10am Old Oak Common-Bordesley Junction (F headcode); (ii) cattle traffic for stations between High Wycombe and Maidenhead for the 11.30pm Oxford-Taplow train. A feeding train at Princes Risborough was the 6.20pm auto ex-Thame which might have conveyed one or two cattle wagons for attachment to the train from Aylesbury. The next call was at Saunderton to pick up any station truck work or important goods only. Calls were then made at West Wycombe, High Wycombe and High Wycombe South to attach wagons for Old Oak Common, Acton, Paddington, Reading West Junction, Reading, South Wales and Bristol. A call was also made at High Wycombe North for cattle traffic only. The train then also called at Bourne End if required to detach cattle traffic for Marlow only. The next stop was at Maidenhead to detach Bristol and South Wales wagons for the 1.25am ex-Old Oak Common-Stoke Gifford (H-headlamps). Other connecting trains at Maidenhead were 3.10am Acton-Reading (F-code) and 3.30am Old Oak Common-Leamington (J-headcode). A feeding train at Maidenhead was the 8.17pm ex-Loudwater. Wagons for Old Oak Common were detached at West Drayton for the 10.40pm ex-Reading West Jct. Feeding trains at West Drayton were the 5.55pm ex-Staines and 7.55pm ex-Uxbridge. Destinations of connecting trains at Acton were: 4.15am to Victoria & Albert Docks; 5.15am St Pancras and Tilbury Line; 6am Temple Mills (LNER); 3.45am Smithfield; 6.30am Poplar; 4.10am Old Oak Common; 5.5 or 7.25am to South Lambeth. The Aylesbury-Paddington train conveyed the following station trucks in 1933: ST31 Aylesbury-Paddington from Aylesbury to Paddington; ST32 Aylesbury-Reading from Aylesbury-High Wycombe; ST414

Loudwater-Paddington from Maidenhead-Paddington; ST528 Oxford-Paddington from Princes Risborough to Paddington; and, ST720 Staines-Paddington from West Drayton to Paddington. A train associated with the 9.25pm Aylesbury goods was the K-headlamped 'hay and straw' train that left Old Oak Common at 2.25am and arrived at Portobello Jct at 2.30am. This train took on the goods that was conveyed from Aylesbury.

Special arrangements were made, according to the 1927 WTT, for cattle traffic on Sundays originating on the Berks & Hants line. Telegrams would be sent to Reading Control, not later than 4pm on the Saturday, from any stations intending to dispatch cattle. When fewer than six trucks were ordered for loading, vac-fitted Mex B vehicles were used and were sent down the line from Reading West Jct on the 6.50pm ex-Didcot. Should six or more trucks have been required to be loaded with cattle, a special train was run to Lavington from Reading West using ordinary (non-fitted) Mex. It left at 2.15pm on Sundays, calling at Hungerford, Savernake (LL), Pewsey and arriving at Lavington at 4.55pm (CR at Aldermaston, Newbury, Burbage Siding and Patney & Chirton). When only five or fewer cattle trucks were involved, the loaded return vehicles were attached to the 4.40pm milk train ex-Trowbridge to Reading; any traffic from Lavington was sent via Patney per the 2.50pm ex-Yeovil. From Reading, the traffic was forwarded on the 5pm goods ex-Swindon. Should six or more trucks have been required, the return loaded special left Lavington at 5.10pm, and arrived back at Reading General at 9.20pm calling at the same stations (and those CR stations) as before. If the train were big enough, it was extended to Acton; otherwise it would be worked back to Reading West Junction to connect with the 5pm goods ex-Swindon as for five wagons or fewer. Local stationmasters had to make the necessary arrangements for opening signal cabins on Sundays.

Cattle Markets and Horse Fairs

Cattle markets and horse sales were held periodically in market towns all over the GW system and the company provided cattle wagons as necessary to take animals to market and to bring them away. Often animals arrived and departed by ordinary goods train.

For example, on Mondays, Tuesdays and Wednesdays the 3.50pm Oswestry-Machynlleth K-headcode train conveyed cattle ex-Welshpool, Newtown and Oswestry markets. Special regulations sometimes applied. For example, cattle for Southampton market (Wednesdays) from stations on the Didcot, Newbury & Southampton line were to be loaded in vac-fitted vehicles. Although markets at different places were regular, they were not daily events, so most market cattle trains were shown in the STTs as 'running when required' (**RR**). Thus a C-headcode horsebox train ran from Newtown to Shrewsbury on fair days only.

At the close of business from Exeter Cattle Market sidings on Fridays there were usually three trains. Loading, charging, invoicing and getting the money was quite a job for the Cattle Inspector, especially in bad weather. This task was repeated all over the system. To give an idea of the work that might be entailed, 272 trucks of sheep were loaded between noon and 9pm at the Craven Arms sheep sales in August 1927 which was a record for a single day. Eight special trains were required.

Before a market began, it was important that sufficient cattle wagons would be available for loading at the close of business. For the horse sales at Hereford, stations in the area telegraphed the Divisional Superintendent at Gloucester early on the previous day to identify what horse boxes would be available on the day of the sale which could be picked up by these particular passenger trains heading to Hereford: the 7.15am and 9.45am trains ex-Gloucester; and, the 9.40am ex-Monmouth. When sending off animals after the sales, up to eight boxes could be sent on the 4.10pm Hereford-Gloucester train to go forward from Gloucester on the 6pm and 7.5pm trains. Cattle sales at Chepstow were held on alternate Tuesdays (as were those at Ross). A special train left STJ with empty vehicles ordered by Chepstow. The locomotive carried out shunting in the yard there until loading of cattle was completed, and then returned with the loaded wagons. Chepstow telegraphed STJ about the amount of traffic conveyed, the time of departure and the traffic consigned for that station. Word of these arrangements had also to be sent to the Controller at Newport.

The Cirencester and Tetbury branches met the main line at Kemble, both junctions facing Swindon. The market at Tetbury was held on the second Wednesday of each month. Cirencester held a market on the first and third Mondays of each month for which the 9.50am E-headcode from Gloucester T sidings to Cirencester Town took empty Mexes — with assistance if necessary from a banking engine at Brimscombe (10.30-10.35) — on the Up journey, to arrive at Kemble at 11.5am. It departed Kemble at 11.26 on the single-line branch (worked by electric train staff and block telegraph) to arrive at Cirencester at 11.36. The return train carrying a K-headcode left Cirencester at 4.25pm (Kemble 4.35) and returned to Gloucester loaded with cattle for onward destinations. To avoid any delay at Kemble an extra brake van would be coupled next to the locomotive, which permitted a quick run round for the return journey. Any cattle from Cirencester for the Up direction were picked up at Kemble by the 9.25am Bordesley Jct-Swindon H-headcode goods that would later arrive at Swindon at 4.50pm. According to the 1933 STT this train, when required, picked up 'flock traffic' at Brimscombe (3.5-3.45) for Exeter, Weymouth and Southampton (via Salisbury), and connected with the 8.10pm J-headcode from Swindon to Newton Abbot that ran via Chippenham, Trowbridge and Westbury. Cirencester had to telegraph Kemble, and Kemble Swindon, with all particulars regarding the amount of traffic dispatched. If the amount of Up cattle traffic was sufficiently heavy to justify a special train, Cirencester ordered a locomotive, brake van and guard to leave Swindon at 5.15pm under the G-headcode and then take the train from Kemble.

Between Totnes and Ivybridge on the main line in Devon, activity in the goods yard at Brent is photographed some time after 1903 (the locomotive chimney headlamp is no longer fixed by 'spigot and socket'). After horse sales and cattle markets, animals were taken off by train (horses and ponies in this case in cattle wagons). *D J Hyde collection*

SATURDAY, JULY 4th—Continued.

Train No. G.W. 8   Up Train.

To Reading.

To load at Dock "A."

EMPTY TRAIN.

	Light Engine.	
	arr. a.m.	dep. a.m.
Shrewsbury	—	5 30
Gobowen	6 0	—
Gobowen	—	6 25
Coton Hill	7 0	8 8
Abbey Foregate (S.U. Sidings)	8 15	—

Inspector RALPHS to provide Guard, Mr. DRUCE Engine.

STOCK SPECIAL.

	arr. p.m.	dep. p.m.		arr. a.m.	dep. a.m.
Abbey Foregate	—	10 0	Leamington	12 40	—
Wellington	10 25	—	Banbury	1 30	—
Oxley Sidings	11 5	11 17	Oxford	2 0	—
Wolverhampton	—	11 25	Didcot	2 20	2 40
Birmingham	M 12 0 L	—	Reading	3 10	—

Formation (on leaving Abbey Foregate):—

Engine.
Brake.

Uffington	...	siphon (Adams)	...	...	...	...	14 Sheep
Shrivenham	...	paco (Nickisson)	...	...	...	...	Horse
Challow	...	paco (Henderson)	...	...	...	...	Mare and Foal
Faringdon	...	Scorpion road van (Adams)	...	...	...	Sheep *
Sutton Scotney	...	brake van (Phillips)	...	...	...	...	8 Sheep
Hampstead Norris	...	paco (Cooper)	...	...	...	...	Mare and Foal
Hampstead Norris	...	beetle (Cooper)	...	...	...	...	2 Bulls
Kingsworthy	...	brake van (Nicholl)	...	...	...	Sheep
Haslemere	...	snake (Barlow)	...	...	...	...	4 crates Pigs
Haslemere	...	beetle A (Barlow)	...	...	...	4 Cattle
Haslemere	...	beetle A (Barlow)	...	...	...	4 Cattle
Bookham	...	siphon (Hayward)	...	...	...	3 crates Pigs
Ewell	...	paco (Curtis)	...	...	...	...	1 Cow
Egham	...	mex B (Schroder)	...	...	...	Cattle, 8 Sheep, Pig in crate
Ascot	...	van (Mccombie)	...	...	...	...	Pig in crate
Bracknell	...	paco (Downshire)	...	...	...	3 Horses
Virginia Water	...	beetle (Stern)	...	...	...	Cattle
Virginia Water	...	paco (Stern)	...	...	...	Horses
Virginia Water	...	mex (Stern)	...	...	...	Horses
Virginia Water	...	paco (Muller)	...	...	...	Horses
Virginia Water	...	paco (Muller)	...	...	...	Horses

Brake Third.

* Form next Engine.

Part of the special instructions issued for return trains at the 1914 Royal Show at Shrewsbury. Note that the Mex B going to Mr Schroder at Egham has cattle, eight sheep and a pig in a crate, all in the one vehicle. *GWR*

The 1.23pm passenger train from Kemble to Tetbury was a 'mixed' train which took empty cattle wagons to the market (1.30 at Rodmarton Platform; 1.33-1.36 at Culkerton; arrive Tetbury 1.42pm). In mixed passenger trains, goods vehicles and those conveying livestock were coupled to the rear. The maximum number of vehicles in a mixed train was not to exceed 30, and speed was not to exceed 25mph. Stockmen, grooms, or other persons travelling in charge of livestock were not charged as fare-paying passengers, but when a separate coach was provided for their accommodation, regulations stated that it was to be formed next to the locomotive and be provided with a continuous brake. After market, mixed trains left Tetbury at 3.10pm and 4.40pm with livestock and, after paying attention to the Stop Board outside Kemble, connected with (i) the Down 3.30pm ex-Swindon B-headcode passenger train for Gloucester and beyond due Kemble at 3.57; and, (ii) with the Up goods train that had left Bordesley Jct at 9.25 that morning for the south (see Cirencester above). Cattle wagons ordered by Tetbury for its market were to be stabled the previous day at Kemble, Culkerton, or Tetbury, whichever had siding accommodation and was most convenient. When it was expected that there would be more than 15 wagons of cattle to be conveyed, a loco, brake van and guard were ordered to leave Swindon at 2pm for Kemble to await a special cattle train

run from Tetbury at 6pm, to which it then coupled and returned to Swindon. Kemble had to telegraph both Swindon and Gloucester Control with particulars of loading.

Wednesday was market day in Bridgwater. Leslie King told the author that in the 1930s Mr Goldstein would send one or two truckloads of crated fowls to Smithfield. The GWR collected the goods from the market and, as the goods shed closed at 6pm, the crated fowls were loaded at the passenger station. Staff would search the crates for eggs before the wagon was sheeted down!

By the Animals (Transit & General) Order of 1895 made by the Board of Trade, trucks in which shorn sheep were being carried had to be covered and enclosed (without obstruction to ventilation) so as to protect the sheep from the weather. This applied between 1 November and 30 April. It was not applicable to sheep shorn more than 60 days prior to travel. Cows with calves had similar cossetting during March and April. Immediately after World War 2 there was a backlog of wagons awaiting repair and the railway could not always supply sufficient cattle trucks. To alleviate the problem, the Ministry of Agriculture in 1946 exempted the GW for a limited period from the provisions of the 1927 Transit of Animals Order whereby sheep were supposed to be carried in roofed vehicles having ventilation at floor level and which could be inspected at floor level. Instead, sheep could now be carried in open wagons having five planks or more, providing that the journey was no more than 100 miles long and did not last longer than 12 hours.

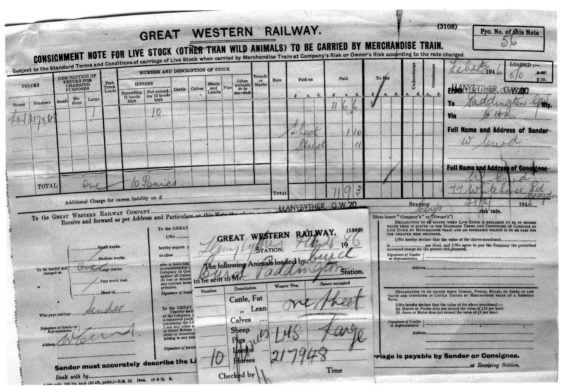

A consignment note for 10 horses to be conveyed to Paddington from Llanybyther (between Carmarthen and Lampeter) on 28 February 1946.

An Up horse special post-1918 C-headcode train photographed near Challow conveying Irish animals from Fishguard headed by rebuilt 'Badminton' class 4-4-0 No 4114 *Shelburne* (formerly No 3306, built in 1898 and cut up in 1927). A Paco horsebox is immediately behind the locomotive, followed by about 10 Mex cattle wagons. *LGRP.*

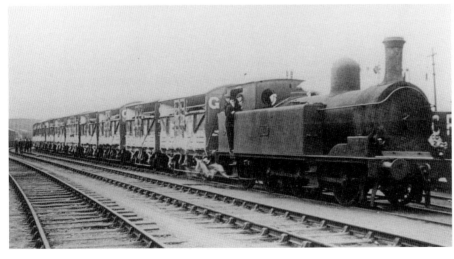

Ex-Cardiff Railway 0-6-2T No 28 (GW No 159), built by Kitson's in 1887, heads a rake of cattle wagons at Bute docks just after the Grouping. Note the mast of a ship on the extreme right. Lime wash disinfectant is very obvious. The headlamp over the right buffer (left facing the locomotive) is higher than the one on the left. Together they supposedly give the B headcode for an express passenger train, but not in this case. A Cardiff CD2 diamond-shaped target is on the right. *A G Atkins collection*

The first batch of yearling mountain sheep swarm up the ramp of a wayside station for loading in North Wales from the passenger platform while the driver and fireman of a 'Dean Goods' looks on. The actual location is unknown. *Farmer's Weekly archive/Museum of English Rural Life, University of Reading*

A W1 large Mex photographed at Bodmin. Built on Lot 185 in 1898, No 68050 has screw couplings, but is un-piped. *D J Hyde collection*

A '43XX' hauls a C-headcode train consisting mostly of cattle trucks interspersed with a few vans. *A G Atkins collection*

Agricultural Shows

A large part of passenger-rated livestock traffic concerned agricultural shows. Shows involved a large variety of farming goods and exhibits (dead stock) as well as livestock all concentrated in a short period of time, and the railway had to introduce abnormal working arrangements. Up to World War 2 at least, hardly any long distance traffic of this sort would have come by road all the way. The distance by road between the receiving goods yard and the show ground established the time in which road vehicles could depart, unload and return to the railway sidings and this, in turn, determined how many vehicles the GW Road Transport Department had to provide. The distance by road between the railhead and the show ground also determined the intervals at which special cattle trains could be accepted or dispatched. The maximum load of such special trains was governed by the unloading facilities at the show station, at which it was frequently necessary to build temporary cattle docks. In practice it was found a maximum of 25 vehicles was the limit, as over that number shunting difficulties arose in attaching or detaching. Times for special trains arriving for a show were worked out by timing back from the show reception sidings to ensure that incoming trains could be accepted.

Because cattle sold at the show, as well as agricultural machinery, would be departing to different destinations, it was difficult to fix return train schedules precisely. The effort involved was significant, even when detailed remarshalling was avoided,

since literally hundreds of vehicles had to be transferred from, and to, various trains stabled anywhere within an area of 20 miles of the showground. Even so, train times and routes were decided in broad terms on the opening day of the show by the train clerks of the different railway companies involved. By way of illustration, for the Royal Show at Tredegar Park near Newport in 1927, 88 special times were prepared for the forward and return trains into the temporary depot built adjacent to the locomotive sheds at Ebbw Jct. One train every hour was accepted from 4.45am on the Saturday 2 July to 7.30pm Sunday, and from 6.50am to 3.25pm Monday. The total number of vehicles received with livestock was 916 and the last load left the station for the show ground at 5pm on the Monday. Each rail vehicle used was cleaned inside and out, and thoroughly disinfected as soon as possible after arrival — nearly 1,000 had to be treated. After the show, 39 trains containing

Below: Pedigree livestock being unloaded at Canton sidings, Cardiff, for the Royal Welsh Show in August 1929. The Beetle special cattle vans with doors open (intended for pedigree cattle) are No 943 built in 1898 (Diagram W4 not having a groom's compartment) and No 990 dating from 1909 (W7 with central compartment). Beetles were 'brown vehicles' by this time but remained in the wagon index. Three Paco horseboxes are seen to the left near the Albert Street gate to the yard, with Turner's stone works beyond. One of the men near No 990 carries a watering can. There is a bull being led down the temporary ramp towards GW road cattle float No 1374 ('Speed 5 mph' on side); this had a winch at the end to be used for reluctant beasts when necessary. The author grew up at the other (Cowbridge Road) end of Albert Street. *GWR*

The cattle dock at Reading, *circa* 1920, with attendants' hut. Daily cleansing and scraping was mandatory under the Diseases of Animals Acts, so water hydrants, lighting and tools for the job (dung forks etc) as seen here were standard equipment. After the Animals (Transit and General) Order of 1927, a new disinfectant called 'white cyllin' was distributed from Swindon to replace the lime wash previously used. *GWR/D J Hyde collection*

FOOT AND MOUTH DISEASE.

The following is the up-to-date position as regards Foot and Mouth Disease :—

INFECTED AREA No. 1.

In the County of WILTS.

Stations affected :—

Southern Railway.

Dinton	Semley	Tisbury

OTHER THAN THOSE IN THIS CIRCULAR THE ONLY INSTRUCTIONS NOW IN OPERATION ARE CONTAINED IN L.S.D. 2341, 2348, 2555, 2561, 2564, 2565, 2570, 2578, 2579, 2582, 2584, 2585, 2586, 2591, 2592 and 2593.

Therefore only numbers 2341, 2348, 2561, 2564, 2565, 2570, 2578, 2579, 2582, 2584, 2585, 2586, 2591, 2592, 2593 and 2594 should appear in the summary Circular L.S.D. 2503.

A. MAYNARD,
Chief Goods Manager

The railway companies also helped to lay temporary roads in showgrounds: at Cardiff in 1938, the GWR supplied 20,000 sleepers for this purpose and a similar number was jointly supplied by the GWR and SR for the Centenary Royal Show at Windsor in 1939. Over 2,100 wagon loads of material for show stands and exhibits were received at Cardiff and nearly 1,700 tons of equipment was transferred to Windsor. These sorts of activities were typical at other agricultural shows on GW territory (Shropshire & West Midland, Bath & West, Royal Cornwall, Three Counties Shows and so on). In 1923 the GW and LMS worked closely together in making arrangements for the Bath & West Show held in Swansea that year. Some 256 vehicles of livestock were conveyed by the GWR and handed over to the LMS at Swansea South Dock Junction for transfer to Swansea Bay station on the line to Llandilo, which was close to the entrance of the showground at Singleton Park; 263 vehicles in 15 special trains were returned from the show ground. Containers featured increasingly in show work through the 1930s and nearly 200 were employed at Windsor in 1939. The Royal Show at Taunton in July 1875 speeded up the laying of the third rail between Bristol and Taunton so to avoid transfer of goods between gauges.

in all 920 vehicles with livestock were dispatched. At the Reading Royal Show in 1926, sidings as far away as Didcot and Rodbourne (Swindon) were used for storage of empty trains including 58 Pacos in which showjumpers had travelled.

The programme of return livestock special trains from Shrewsbury after the 1914 Royal Show indicates the sort of arrangements made on these occasions. Siphons (milk vans), Pythons (covered carriage trucks) and Snakes (passenger brake vans) were used for animals such as poultry in cages and baskets. In all there were 20 specials and one more 'to run if required'; 414 vehicles were used, the longest train having 30, the shortest six; 12 vehicles carried wheeled traffic (animals in road lorries on rail wagons) and 30 vehicles carried pigs in crates.

As well as the animals at agricultural shows, many tons of material and exhibits were dealt with by ordinary goods train (over 4,000 tons in the case of the 1927 Newport Royal Show).

Foot & Mouth Disease

Railways were very much involved with the efforts made by the Government to control animal diseases such as foot and mouth disease, swine fever, sheep scab and TB. Sometimes railway journeys could only be undertaken when authorised by the issue of a licence that had to accompany the animals throughout the movement. As soon as the railway was alerted by the Ministry of Agriculture about outbreaks of disease, all GW stations (both goods and passenger) were informed immediately by the Chief Goods Manager's Office at Paddington. The names of the railway

An Agreement made the twenty-six
day of April. One thousand nine hundred and thirty four
B E T W E E N   THE GREAT WESTERN RAILWAY COMPANY (hereinafter
called "the Company") by RANDOLPH GEORGE POLE their Divisional
Superintendent at Bristol Temple Meads Station of the one part
and JOHN FLAY 9, Quarbarton, Curzon Street, Calne (hereinafter
called "the Contractor") of the other part WHEREBY IT IS
AGREED AND DECLARED between and by the parties hereto as
follows :-

1.   THE Contractor shall as and when required thoroughly
cleanse and disinfect Cattle Wagons and the Washing Roads on
each side of the cleaning platform and the said cleaning
platform and the cattle pens at the Company's Station at Calne
and so as to satisfy the regulations of the Company as to such
cleansing and disinfection and to the entire satisfaction
of the Company.

2.   THE Company will provide material and appliances necessary
for the purpose of cleansing and disinfecting such cattle
wagons and Washing Roads and cleaning platform and cattle pens.

3.   THE Company will pay to the Contractor for the services
aforesaid

   1. The sum of seven pence halfpenny per wagon in respect
   of every Cattle wagon so cleansed and disinfected as
   aforesaid.

   2. The sum of Three shillings and nine pence in respect
   of the cleaning and disinfecting of the said cattle pens.

   3. And in addition shall allow the Contractor to have for
   his own use any manure deposited upon the said cleaning
   platform cattle wagons and cattle pens and this shall
   be considered of the value of One shilling per week.

4.   THE Contractor shall be responsible for and will indemnify
and save harmless the Company from and against all actions

stations situated within the infected area were listed in alphabetical order, and a circular prepared. Sets of addressed envelopes (one for each GW station, District and Divisional office) were kept in readiness, and these, together with the draft circular, were turned over to a firm of printers under contract with the company. Within a few hours they were ready at Paddington station for despatch to all parts of the system by train. Draft circulars handed to the printers as late as 7pm were despatched from Paddington the same evening to arrive certainly by early morning at out-stations. The railway issued to every member of the staff concerned with livestock a blue pocket folder of instructions relating to movement into, out of, and within an infected area, together with a brief note regarding licences and the marking of animals. 'Outfoot' was a GW Telegraph code word saying that animals must not be accepted for dispatch, and received animals must not be unloaded until authorised. 'Nofoot' cancelled the foregoing telegram. 'Racoon' was 'Do you hold licence for cattle for...'

Other features of railway operations affected by these regulations related to the cleansing and disinfecting of cattle wagons and livestock loading pens. Under an Order issued by the Ministry of Agriculture, every cattle wagon had to be scraped, swept, scrubbed and disinfected after each loaded journey and again before being used for the conveyance of livestock. The livestock loading pens at each station had to be treated in the same way every 24 hours. Originally cattle wagons and loading pens were limewashed, as confirmed by photographs of cattle wagons and cattle docks. By 1927 this was not considered by the authorities to be an effective method of disinfection, and white cyllin was supplied to stations to be diluted with water to the required strength.

Under normal conditions when animals were transported by rail, there was a presumption that they were healthy. If there were any doubt about the fitness or otherwise of livestock to withstand rail transit, railway staff could insist on a Veterinary Surgeon's Certificate being obtained, but this power rarely had to be invoked. However, in a letter from the Bristol District Goods Managers Office in October 1944, we read:

'The present use of horse flesh as food for human consumption has resulted in a considerable increase in the traffic in old and worn-out beasts consigned to knackers for slaughter, and a number of instances have arisen where animals have died, or collapsed in transit and had to be slaughtered, or observed to be in a distressed condition *en route* by representatives of the RSPCA or other animal bodies, legal proceedings resulting in some cases ... [Since] it is very difficult for railway staff to judge accurately the condition of animals tendered for conveyance ... please issue instructions to all staff that they must not accept any old, worn-out or unfit horses or cattle consigned to knackers for slaughter unless the sender produces a Veterinary Surgeon's Certificate.'

Farm Removals

Closely allied to the special arrangements for pedigree animals at shows was the removal of live- and dead-stock of whole farms. There was much publicity about GW farm removals in the 1930s, but this sort of thing had been going on for many years previously. An early instance was the removal of a farm from near Newquay in Cornwall to the Sherborne estate in Gloucestershire in 1883. St Columb Road was the nearest station to the point of departure, but as the line was still broad-gauge there, it was decided to charter a special train from Grampound Road where it was mixed gauge to Swindon at a cost of £100.

An example of a farm removal from 1934 was the special train run from Kidwelly in Carmarthenshire to Newport Pagnell (LMS) conveying a farmer and his household, together with the furniture, livestock, implements and other effects. The train comprised a brake coach conveying 10 passengers and luggage, two containers with furniture, six wagons of livestock and five wagons (Scorpion or Hydra type) containing farm implements. It left Kidwelly at 7.15pm and arrived at Newport Pagnell at 6.30 the following morning.

In 1939, a complete herd of about 40 pedigree Jersey cattle was transported from Sevenoaks to Cirencester. The special train left Sevenoaks at 11am and, travelling via Kensington (Addison Road) and Swindon, arrived at Cirencester Town at 3pm. The train

An elevator is loaded by a Ransomes mobile crane on to a Scorpion carriage truck at Llantarnam (on the Newport-Pontypool Road line) as part of a farm removal to West Grinstead on 30 September 1947. *GWR*

was made up of about 14 vehicles, including a passenger coach for the dairy staff and their families, furniture containers and trucks of farm implements. The GW had three special live-stock road vehicles waiting at the station and the removal to Waterton Farm, Ampney Crucis, about three miles away, was completed in two journeys. As with Household Removals using containers, a reduction of 33% in the ordinary single fare was available to the farmer and his employees.

The following letter from Lennard Bros, The Manor Farm, Bucklebury, near Newbury was published in the *GWR Magazine* of 1934 and paid tribute to the handling of a farm removal:

'We cannot allow time to pass without commenting on the extraordinary arrangements you made towards our removal, consisting of household effects, farm implements, livestock, and poultry from St Clears to Thatcham near Newbury. Please convey our sincere thanks to your staff at both ends, St Clears especially, for the excellent and efficient manner the goods

were dealt with ... You will be pleased to know that there was absolutely no breakage or damage of any kind, in spite of the fact that there were some very fragile articles. As regards the livestock and poultry, they arrived in good condition, and without any accident whatsoever. This being our first experience of removal by rail, we shall have every confidence in recommending our friends to the Great Western Railway Company'.

The GWR also performed 'factory removals', with the same scope as farm removals, whereby the whole equipment of factories was transferred from one place to another. A notable example was featured in an article in the March 1939 *GWR Magazine*, page 117. The Yeovil factory of Petters the engine manufacturers was to be taken over by the Westland Aircraft Works, and all Petters' equipment and machinery was moved by train to a new factory at Loughborough. Over 840 wagons and 250 containers were employed to relocate 4,090 tons of machinery and equipment; 85 wagons of scrap were also moved. In addition,

The arrival at Crudgington of a farm removal from Bletchington in September 1936. A photograph of the train's departure is shown under D-headcodes in Chapter 17. The removal concerned 130 head of cattle, all the farm equipment and the contents of four households. Scorpion carriage trucks dating from 1914 (P15 in the Carriage index) carry a variety of wheeled vehicles whilst newer container traffic is on 1933-built Conflats. *GWR*

'Dean Goods' No 2382 (built in 1890) heads a farm removal train at Llanwrdra, just south of Llandovery on the Central Wales line, on 2 October 1934. The locomotive carries C-headlamps. *GWR*

some 52 staff were relocated by 'household removals' trains.

CHAPTER TWENTY-TWO

REFRIGERATED TRAFFIC

AS explained in Chapter 21, it was common in Britain for animals to be slaughtered where the meat was going to be eaten, so there were many trains from country areas, and from ports where animals were imported, which conveyed live cattle, sheep and pigs to town abattoirs. As the years went by, a growing number of imported animals were slaughtered at the ports, and the carcasses were chilled before sending on to market. Meat vans that were merely ventilated were adequate to keep such meat fresh when moved in fast trains. In the case of carcasses being taken to Smithfield market in London from Birkenhead, the total time involved was less than 22 hours, of which 12 were in chilling at the dockside after slaughter and about seven in the train journey. At Fishguard, in addition to sending live Irish cattle off to market by train, there was a slaughterhouse from which carcasses were dispatched.

The first refrigerator ships were introduced in the 1880s and thereafter more and more frozen meat, particularly from Australia and New Zealand, had to be handled. Frozen meat required refrigerator meat vans rather than ventilated-only vans. Hence the different types of GW Mica vans and, later, different types of refrigerated containers. When first introduced, temperatures were kept low with water ice packed in compartments inside the Mica vans; in later years, Drikold solid CO_2 refrigerant was used (see *GWR Goods Wagons*). Fully-fitted 30-40-van meat trains, hauled by passenger locomotives, were running from Birkenhead to London by the late 1880s. The 86 miles to Oxley was run non-stop, followed by 136 miles also non-stop to Acton. These specials carried an 'S' at the chimney base and a white diamond on a black ground over the middle of the locomotive buffer beam (see Chapter 2); subsequently they were C-headcode. Between the

A stopping goods passes through Trawsfynydd on the GW Bala-Blaenau Festiniog line in the early years of the C20th. There is a white-painted refrigerated Mica meat van immediately behind the saddle tank heading the train. The headcode of two buffer beam lamps to the right facing the locomotive is unusual. *STEAM Swindon*

No 4905 *Barton Hall* heads a C-headcode express meat train in the early 1930s. The vans are not the usual Micas but rather Diagram X6 insulated vans converted in 1918 from V17 goods vans built in 1916 for overseas use. *GWR*

wars, meat trains departed Birkenhead at 1.40, 2.55 and 3.55pm for Acton arriving before midnight to be taken on to Smithfield. These trains normally were limited to 40 vans, but if more than 40 they were allowed to arrive at Acton some 18 minutes later.

The GW goods depot underneath Smithfield dealt with over 100 tons of meat a day, as well as a great deal of merchandise traffic for the City. There were four regular meat trains to Smithfield from Old Oak Common/Acton on Monday to Thursday nights in the 1927 STT (all F-headcode), the first at 11.25pm; then at 12.20am; 12.40am; and, finally, 1.40am (1.35am from Acton). There was a special extra train at 11pm (**FSX**). Trains ran to Aldersgate on the underground and reversed into sidings outside the depot leased from the Metropolitan Railway. In addition, mixed goods and meat trains ran at night from Acton to Smithfield (taking about half to three-quarters of an hour). Regular goods trains (not concerned with meat traffic) also ran at roughly hourly intervals from Acton to Smithfield and return. The maximum load for all Smithfield trains was 25 wagons and one special brake van (AA7 in the wagon diagram index). Trains were to be at least 33% and up to 50% piped to the engine during normal hours, but between 12.30am and 4.40am any available vacuum stock up to 33% could be connected to the locomotive. Guards had to have in their vans short drawbars in case there were coupling fractures, sprags to place under wheels, and sticks to be placed between the spokes — all safety measures to prevent trains that might have been stationary for some time on inclines on the underground lines, from running back. Locomotives were the special condensing tank engines, fitted with an automatic clip-up apparatus for the ATC shoe that lifted up when over electrified lines. Originally Wolverhampton 0-6-0T engines and 'Metro' tanks were used, which were superseded from 1930 by condensing '57XXs', Nos 9700-9710.

Meat trains carrying frozen carcases also ran from the Victoria Dock in London to Cardiff, using the ex-SWR X3 Mica A vans (Plate 581 GWR Goods Wagons).

A large tonnage of meat and poultry was imported from Eire each Christmas and extra sailings would be put on from Cork and Rosslare to Fishguard which required a number of special trains. For example, at Christmas 1927, the peak in such traffic was reached over Saturday night 17 December and three special trains conveying pork and poultry passenger-rated traffic left for London on the Sunday. The last steamer from Ireland did not arrive until 8.10pm on Sunday but a special train of 39 wagons of meat for Smithfield left at 12.55pm, arriving there 12 hours later. The load of such specials was not to exceed 40 Class 3 traffic (400 tons

LOADING SCHEDULE OF TRAINS FROM SMITHFIELD.

Time.	To	To convey traffic for following trains. Wagons to be formed from Engine in the order in which the Main Line trains are shewn.	If not fully loaded to be made up with traffic for the following trains, formed in the order in which the trains are shewn.
a.m. 12.41	Old Oak Common and Acton.	1.30 a.m. Paddington to Didcot ... 2. 0 a.m. Paddington to Aylesbury 2.10 a.m. Ladbroke to Southall 2.15 a.m. Paddington to Southall 3.10 a.m. Acton to Reading 5. 5 a.m. (MX), 4.55 a.m. (MO) Old Oak Common to Bordesley. 3.30 a.m. Old Oak Common to Leamington.	
a.m. 1. 6	Acton ... MX RE.		To run only when required for traffic which cannot be accommodated on 12.41 a.m Smithfield.
a.m. 4.11	Acton and Southall*	Empty Stock ... ... Empty Meat Vans ... ... Brake Vans ... ... Cripple Wagons ... ... * To be extended to Southall when conveying Meat Vans.	
a.m. 4.41	Old Oak Common and Acton.	Empty Stock ... ... Empty Meat Vans	7.45 a.m. Acton to Stoke Gifford.
a.m. 11.23	Old Oak Common and Acton.	Empty Meat Vans ... ... Brake Vans ... ... Cripple Wagons	Any loaded traffic for trains serving Old Oak Common or Acton.
p.m. 3.26 SX p.m. 3.35 SO	Old Oak Common and Acton.	7.40 p.m. Acton to Cardiff ... 8. 5 p.m. Paddington to Bristol ... 10.30 p.m. Paddington to Cardiff ... 9. 8 p.m. Park Royal to Stourbridge Junction.	Any loaded traffic for trains serving Old Oak Common and Acton.
p.m. 5. 0	Old Oak Common SO	Any traffic available for subsequent Main Line trains from Old Oak Common.	
p.m. 7.17	Acton	8. 5 p.m. Paddington to Bristol ... 9.27 p.m. Acton to Cardiff ...	10.30 p.m. Paddington to Cardiff. 12. 5 a.m. Paddington to Worcester.
p.m. 7.57	Hanwell Bridge Sdgs.	9.27 p.m. Acton to Cardiff ... Vacuum Stock only.	
p.m. 8.29	Old Oak Common	9.10 p.m. Paddington to Oxley Sdgs. 10.10 p.m. Paddington to Laira ...	10.50 p.m. Paddington to Weymouth.
p.m. 9. 3	Acton and Park Royal (RR Sats.)	11.35 p.m. Paddington to Newton Abbot. 1. 0 a.m. Acton to Bristol ... 10.30 p.m. Paddington to Cardiff ... 11.5 p.m. Paddington to Oxley Sdgs.	
p.m. 9.30	Old Oak Common and Park Royal.	10.50 p.m. Paddington to Weymouth 1.30 a.m. Park Royal to Worcester 2.10 a.m. Crimea to Bordesley ... 11. 5 p.m. Paddington to Oxley 1.10 a.m. Old Oak Common to Bordesley. 2. 5 a.m. Park Royal to Severn Tunnel Junction.	
p.m. 10.36	Acton ... SX	11.35 p.m. Paddington to Newton Abbot. 12. 5 a.m. Paddington to Worcester 12.55 a.m. Paddington to Gloucester 1. 0 a.m. Acton to Bristol ... 1.30 a.m. Paddington to Didcot ...	
p.m. 11. 3	Old Oak Common RR SO.	12.10 a.m. Paddington to Fishguard 2. 0 a.m. Paddington to Aylesbury	

gross). Specials ran to Cardiff without intermediate examinations or stopping for water, and thence to Acton. Point-to-point and passing times from Fishguard in the 1933 STT were one hour nine

The lift between the GW underground goods depot at Smithfield and the meat market above. Two porters carry a carcass as the lift rises. *GWR/D J Hyde collection*

minutes — Carmarthen Junction; two hours 18 minutes — Port Talbot; arrive Cardiff three hours 10 minutes for examination and locomotive water; depart three hours 25 minutes, arrive STJ three hours 58 minutes, departing at four hours 13 minutes; pass Badminton five hours three minutes; arrive Reading Station six hours 32 minutes, departing six hours 42 minutes; arrive Acton seven hours 27 minutes.

There was also pork, beef, mutton and rabbit traffic from the West of England to Smithfield. In the 1886 STT the 5.30pm narrow gauge Exeter-Paddington-Smithfield express goods, conveying perishable and important traffic only, arrived at Paddington at 1.45am (5.5am **SO**). The running of this train was telegraphed ahead in those days and every effort was made to keep the road clear for it. An empty meat van was attached 'next the Break Van' for meat from intermediate stations (Cullompton 5.54pm; Tiverton Junction 6.9pm; Taunton 6.50pm; Bridgwater 7.28pm; Bristol 8.40pm; Swindon 10.31pm). A van containing traffic for stations north of Crewe was also formed next to the engine to be detached at Didcot.

The C-headcode 4.5pm Exeter to Old Oak Common ('Flying Pig') was accelerated in 1926 to cater for the ever-growing meat traffic from the West of England to Smithfield. With a power group D engine and up to 40 meat vans, it served directly, or by connexions, Cullompton, Uffculme, Tiverton and Tiverton Jct, South Molton, Dulverton, Taunton, Chard, Ilminster, Martock, Weymouth, Bridport, Frome, Chippenham and Trowbridge. The train was due into Old Oak at 11.25pm giving transfer to Smithfield just after midnight, six hours earlier than the meat had formerly reached London.

An excellent example of GWR canvassing for new traffic in the late 1930s, demonstrating the advantages of refrigeration, concerns Devon rabbits from stations on the Barnstaple branch being sent to London. It was pointed out to the traders that they could rely upon the traffic arriving in better condition than if sent in the normal way (ie not chilled), and in consequence higher prices might be realised for their produce. Furthermore, provided the traffic was handed to the GW in good condition, the risk of its being condemned as unfit for sale would be eliminated. A Mica B van was used as the Barnstaple station truck, No 34, which picked up traffic for London from stations on the branch. This travelled on the 2.55pm ex-Barnstaple to Taunton (K-headcode) and then was worked forward on the 5.25pm partially-fitted C-headcode goods from Newton Abbot (the 'Hackney') that left Taunton at 9.40pm and was due Paddington at 3.25am. A hundredweight of ice was used daily (twice as much on Saturdays). On some occasions there was sufficient traffic to justify through refrigerated Micas or FX containers to Smithfield from certain stations on the branch.

Despite the emphasis on meat traffic to Smithfield, the one entry in the 1939 Telegraph Code Book in the 'Collection' category was 'Bittong' — 'Arrange special collection today on account of Woodley and Co of Cardiff, and despatch by first train in refrigerator cars consigned to Woodley & Co at the places named, the following Consignment of meat'.

During World War 2 convoys of large numbers of merchant ships arrived sporadically at western ports. Consequently there had to be strict control of the movement of insulated rolling stock for the arrival of meat boats.

After World War 2, fruit, meat, frozen rabbits, sausages, bulbs, flowers and fish were being carried mostly with dry ice as a refrigerant, while cream, soft fruit, butter, beer and milk (by passenger train) were carried very successfully mostly with water ice. Two thousand tons of ice-cream was carried in containers during 1946.

A return meat train from Smithfield passing Paddington Goods depot on the underground lines, with the GWR Chief Goods Manager's Office visible at top right. The first four vehicles are Minks, followed by a Mica, followed by many white-painted AF insulated containers. The condensing pannier carries the F-headcode.
D J Hyde collection

A '28XX' heads a post-1936 H-headcode goods train through Sonning Cutting. There are four Mica meat vans immediately behind the engine.
A G Atkins collection

CHAPTER TWENTY-THREE

FISH

MILFORD HAVEN was the principal port for fish on the GWR. Shortly after its opening in 1888, 10,000 tons/year were being landed which grew rapidly to 40,000 tons/year just before World War 1; 51,000 tons in 1931; and, 60,000 tons/year after World War 2. Milford Haven had over 100 steam trawlers landing their catches. In 1911, the GW conveyed 100,000 tons of coal for bunkering these ships. That represented about 200 10-ton wagons per week, or about 20 tons per vessel per week. Fish from Milford Haven was sent as far north as Glasgow, west as far as Penzance and east as far as Paris. Before the change of headlamp codes in 1903, fish specials carried an 'S' at the chimney base and a white diamond on a black ground over the middle of the locomotive buffer beam; subsequently they were became C-headcode trains.

Between the wars, the first timetabled C-headlamp fish train left Milford Haven at 3.15pm for Carmarthen (arrive 4.35) after which it merged at Llandilo with a fish train from Swansea South Dock and took the LMS Central Wales line to serve the North of England and Scotland. At 3.50pm another train departed with fish for South Wales, Bristol and the West of England (and also Birmingham and the Midlands, taken off at Gloucester). It ran along the old SWR main line through Cockett, with its steep gradients in both directions. At 5.10pm a train ran direct to Paddington (arriving at 1.30am), calling at Swindon and Reading.

This train took the Swansea Avoiding lines rather than the Cockett route. Towns off the various GW main lines were served from these fish trains by connecting trains (eg Stroud and Kemble fish were sent on from Gloucester by the Up mail). The locomotive for the 5.10 Paddington train left Neyland engine shed at 3.55pm, and

St Ives in the early 1900s with the viaduct in the middle centre, beyond which is the engine shed. The curved station platform is at bottom and middle right, with signal cabin above bay at end of platform; the goods shed is out of picture to the right of signal cabin. The end of branch is at bottom left. Fish vehicles in are, from left to right, open No 42532 (ex-four-wheel carriage truck No 980 built on old series lot 608 in 1891), elliptical-roof six-wheel Siphon No 987 or 697 (?) to O1 (O2) diagram, arc-roof four-wheel Siphon (number indecipherable), ex-broad-gauge four-wheel open fish wagon No 42617 (?) to diagram S7, arc-roof six-wheel Siphon and a passenger brake van. *STEAM Swindon*

Main photograph: 2-6-0 No 5347, with C-headlamps, heads a fully-fitted fish train on 19 October 1921. The train comprises six Bloater fish vans, a Tadpole A bogie open fish wagon (no guard's cabin) and a passenger brake van. The formation is Bloater A No 2127 (Diagram S8, both Westinghouse and vacuum brake), Bloaters Nos 2231 and 2219 (S9, vac-fitted only), then an S8 and two S9 vehicles. The bogie open with large GW lettering is No 2008 built on the underframe of the old Royal Saloon. The brake van has 6ft 4in Dean bogies and is probably an early Diagram K2 vehicle. The locomotive was new in 1918 and was not one of the 65 '53XXs' given extra weight on the pony truck for curved West country lines and renumbered into the '83XX' series. *GWR/D J Hyde collection*

GWR notice about mackerel and other fish. *STEAM Swindon*

A Down fish empties, C-headcode, pictured near Reading in 1933. 'Saint' No 2980 *Coeur de Lion* was built as a 4-4-2 in 1905 and rebuilt to 4-6-0 in 1912. Notice the burnished smokebox fittings and buffers as well as the long signal arms. *M W Earley*

took the branch at Johnston (4.5) to arrive at the exchange sidings with the private Milford Dock Co at 4.20pm. Similar arrangements applied to the other fish specials. Telegraph codes in the 1939 Telegraph Code Book relating specifically to Milford Haven fish traffic were 'Newt' meaning '3.15pm Fish Train Milford Haven to Carmarthen left at … '; 'Ovum' — '3.50pm Fish Train Milford Haven to Gloucester left at … '; 'Starling' — '5.10pm Fish Train Milford Haven to Severn Tunnel Junction (London fish) left at … '.

These post-World War 1 Milford trains were made up of vac-fitted vans from the S-index of Wagon Diagrams including large Bloater fish vans, with a passenger brake van (K in the Carriage Diagram index) at the rear. In fact, the GW built no *vans* especially for fish until 1909 when the V13 (later S2) 16ft over headstocks design was introduced for the new partially-fitted C-headcode express goods trains. The larger Bloater fish vans appeared a few years later. Prior to that, fish loaded in barrels or boxes was conveyed from GW fishing ports in various broad- and narrow-gauge open wagons. These four- or six-wheel, or bogie, vac-fitted wagons were the Tadpoles, some of which had guard's boxes to avoid attaching a separate brake van. All fish vehicles were grey with wagon numbers until 1913 when they became brown and were renumbered (but the vehicles remained in the Wagon Diagram Index). Just at nationalisation a new type of fish van (coded 'Insixfish') was developed, based on the 1936 GW insulated van designed for Palethorpe's sausage traffic (see *GWR Goods Wagons*).

In addition to Milford, there were also fishing fleets at Swansea, Cardiff and in the West Country. The fishing industry in the West Country was at its height at the turn of the 19th/20th centuries, but declined later when pilchard shoals failed to return to local waters (see *GWR Docks & Marine*). In 1947, the weekly loading of fish required 250 vans at Milford Haven, 120 at Swansea and 12 at Penzance (for Newlyn). In the West Country, fish vans from St Ives met the main line at St Erth; from Looe at Liskeard; from Kingsbridge at Brent; and, from Brixham at Churston.

Empties for West Wales left Paddington at 4am on a pilot train to Ladbroke Grove arriving at 4.12am; more empties left Paddington at 6.5am and 8.40am for Old Oak Common, both calling at Ladbroke Grove, from which full trains of empties left at 12.50pm and 2pm bound for Neyland and Milford Haven. There were, of course, fish empties for the West Country as well, Section 3 of the 1927 STT showing the 2.45pm Swindon-Laira fish empties (MX, RR) leaving Chippenham at 3.25pm and leaving Taunton (64 miles further on) at 5.20pm; the train was 'To be kept clear of excursions'.

Other telegraph code words relating to fish traffic were: 'Fish' — 'fish expected to leave here today about following time. Will wire particulars on departure of train'; 'Lobster' — 'following packages of London fish today approximate weight … tons'; and, 'Magpie' — 'fish particulars today approximately … tons trawl … herrings … mackerel … '.

Fish came on to the GW from other railways and was carried forward by GW train to destination. Fish that came over the North London line, for example, was taken on by the 9.55pm from Acton that ran when required to Maidenhead, Reading and Didcot (CR) arriving at Swindon at 1.23am. Fish from Grimsby via Banbury was taken to Birmingham by a C-headcode train that departed Banbury at 2am; called at Leamington, 2.30; Moor Street, 3.18; Snow Hill, 4.20; terminating at Hockley at 4.30am. The 1933 STT states that 'wherever practicable the Fish Train will run in advance of the booked times'. In reverse, fish empties back to the LNER via Banbury departed Swindon at 3.20pm for Stainforth (north of Doncaster).

Below: A C-headlamps fish empties for Neyland leaving Ladbroke Grove West London Jct behind 'Saint' No 2943 *Hampton Court* (built in 1912). There are 16 Bloaters, a passenger brake van, and two shorter two-door fish vans (S6 diagram) that are marshalled directly behind the locomotive. Kensal Green gas works is visible in the distance. *Commercial postcard*

CHAPTER TWENTY-FOUR

DANGEROUS GOODS

MANY substances carried over the railway system by goods train were of a dangerous nature and much thought was given to devising suitable arrangements for their safe conveyance. Dangerous types of merchandise were:

- explosives;
- inflammable liquids;
- corrosive and poisonous substances;
- compressed and liquefied gases; and,
- a miscellaneous group comprising substances liable to spontaneous combustion.

The explosives category covered not only ammunition, but also blasting materials for the mining and quarrying industries, rockets and flares for ships, and fireworks. Petrol made up the bulk of the second group, but other inflammable liquids, such as industrial alcohol, benzole and naptha were also carried. Corrosive and poisonous substances included acids, caustic alkalis and so on. Tank wagons (rectangular and cylindrical) — mostly private owner, but with some railway-owned vehicles for company use — were used to carry many of these liquids in bulk, but cans, drums and glass carboys were also frequently employed. A drum was defined as a cylindrical vessel with flat ends of equal diameter; a can was an iron or steel vessel tapered at one end; and, a carboy was a globular glass bottle of not more than 12 gallons capacity packed in a hamper of iron strips or wickerwork with a minimum ½in thickness of straw packing. Compressed and liquefied gases were used in welding processes and liquefied chlorine was used as a bleaching agent in the paper making industry. Loose shunting of wagons containing dangerous substances was forbidden. Vans containing explosives were to be placed as far away from the engine and also from wagons conveying inflammable liquids and other dangerous goods.

In contrast to most other goods traffic, railway companies were *not* Common Carriers of dangerous goods and, if railway companies elected to carry them, they made their own regulations, bye-laws and conditions for movement by train under the authority of, for example, the Explosives Act of 1875 and the Railways Act of 1921. The London underground did not permit conveyance of dangerous goods at all. As explained in Volume 1 of *GW Goods Services*, there was the *Dangerous Goods Classification*, a bulky document, separate and quite distinct from the *General Goods Classification*. Senders of dangerous goods were required to complete a special consignment note appropriate to the particular substance to be carried and these documents were printed on distinctive coloured papers. Special wagon labels were also used to distinguish the traffic from other merchandise. The company chemist at Swindon was the authority when there were queries and uncertainties about whether something was dangerous or not.

The *Red Pamphlet* of instructions relating to the conveyance of explosives and other dangerous goods, explained that safety cartridges, percussion caps and safety fuses for blasting could, with appropriate precautions, be carried by passenger train or in goods guards vans (as could railway fog signals), but usually explosives were carried in specially constructed gunpowder vans (Z in the Wagon Diagram Index and coded Cone). The GW had about 60 of these in peacetime, each of which could be loaded with not more than 10,000lb weight at any one time. Gunpowder vans were never permitted through the Severn Tunnel. Gunpowder vans were constructed to protect the contents from contact with fire, either from sparks from the engine or thrown up from the track, and even from friction with metallic substances in the van itself, or during loading or unloading operations. To prevent danger, the men engaged in these operations had to wear special rubber boots ('magazine boots') over their ordinary boots, and one pair was part of the normal equipment of each gunpowder van (see *GWR Goods Wagons*). Most often loading and unloading was done by the senders and consignees, and not by railwaymen. In wartime, owing to the limited number of gunpowder vans available, some clauses in the *Red Pamphlet* (and also in the *Green Pamphlet* that dealt specifically with conveyance of Government military traffic) were

The yard of Fishguard & Goodwick station pictured with gunpowder van No 16996 built in 1903 on the siding to right. An O2/10 seven-plank open wagon with top swing doors stands behind. Open wagons with wooden end stanchions and tip ends labelled 'GW' are visible on the left. 'Llewellyn Chemist & Druggist' can be seen on the back of the building behind signal post on left. *D J Hyde collection*

suspended thus allowing other wagons such as covered or sealed vans or sheet opens having oil boxes to be used for the job.

Packages containing small quantities of dangerous goods had to be labelled in a distinctive manner, and labels for poisonous and corrosive chemicals indicated that they should not be loaded in the same wagon as foodstuffs. Wagons containing any sort of explosives or dangerous goods, or traffic of an inflammable nature such as oily rags, oily waste etc were not permitted to be placed inside any railway shed or warehouse, and had to be separated from other vehicles in the yard. Railway company bye-laws prohibited the conveyance of more than five wagons of explosives coupled together and they were always marshalled at the rear on any one train unless accompanied by a Secretary of State's warrant indemnifying the railway company. Then up to 60 wagons of dangerous substances could be marshalled in one train, as happened often during wartime when the number of gunpowder vans was insufficient. No fire was permitted in the guard's van whatever the weather, and examination for hot boxes at stops had special significance. As discussed in Chapter 17, grease axleboxes in ammunition trains caused problems in World War 1 and led to a number of C-headcode express goods trains being downgraded to E-headcode. After the war this led to the introduction of the Accelerated-E classification of train.

Special regulations applied when tank wagons containing dangerous substances ran in goods trains. The first RCH specifications for tank wagons appeared in 1905. Originally, all dangerous traffic in tank wagons had to travel in slow trains, but in 1913 the RCH said that if certain conditions were satisfied, tank wagons could be taken in faster trains at speeds up to 35mph with 40 miles between examinations. The principal requirement was that the tank wagons had to have oil axleboxes and have been 'run in' for 100 miles in slow trains first (the need for running-in was cancelled in 1937). Conformity with this ruling was indicated by a star two-feet across on the right hand corner of the tank, with a dated plate on the underframe. On white or yellow tanks, the star was painted black, but was white for tanks painted other colours. The star system developed to distinguish between degrees of inflammability and the rules varied over the years. Originally no tank wagons whatsoever were permitted to run in C-headcode trains. Private-owner starred wagons, GW and Allsopps beer tank cars, could run in accelerated-E, normal E and F trains. All other tank wagons, loaded or empty, ran in H-, J- and K-headcode goods trains. The 1933 STT states that the F-headcode 4.25pm Hereford-Gloucester goods (arriving at Gloucester T Sidings at 7.15pm) must carry J-lamps when conveying unstarred tank wagons. By the late 1930s GW or private owner vehicles with *one star* painted on each side of tank could be conveyed by trains carrying D-, E, or F-headlamps. GW or private owner vehicles marked with *two stars*, that additionally were both vac-fitted and six-wheeled and were carrying highly inflammable liquids (so-called Class A

liquids, having a flash temperature lower than 150°F) could be run in part-vac fitted trains with C- headlamps — except those timed faster than 40mph. Tanks were to be marshalled towards the end of the vacuum portion of train and inside the last vacuum-coupled vehicle. The same rule applied to GW and private owner vehicles marked with *three stars*, that additionally were both vac-fitted and six-wheeled and were carrying non-inflammable liquids. Tank wagons containing inflammable liquids were permitted to run in mixed trains: they had to be marshalled inside the rear goods brake van and in all cases with one ordinary goods wagon between the tank wagon and vehicles containing passengers.

Tank wagons containing Class A liquids were required to have steel underframes and were not to have bottom outlets to the tank. Originally they were painted a light stone colour with a bright red band six inches wide running horizontally round the centre of the tank. The light stone colour was changed to aluminium-coloured paint in June 1939, still with the red band. However the livery was conspicuous to enemy aircraft in World War 2, so a dark lead colour was used until after the war. It was a general rule that tank wagons were not to be coupled next to a vehicle carrying inflammable material such as hay or straw.

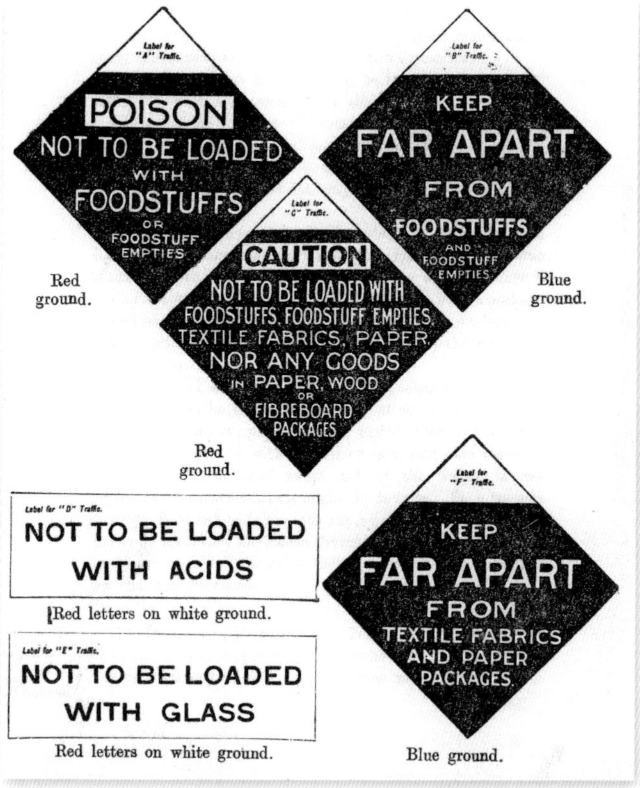

Label for "A" Traffic.
POISON
NOT TO BE LOADED WITH FOODSTUFFS OR FOODSTUFF EMPTIES
Red ground.
Label for "B" Traffic.
KEEP FAR APART FROM FOODSTUFFS AND FOODSTUFF EMPTIES
Blue ground.
Label for "C" Traffic.
CAUTION
NOT TO BE LOADED WITH FOODSTUFFS, FOODSTUFF EMPTIES, TEXTILE FABRICS, PAPER, NOR ANY GOODS IN PAPER, WOOD OR FIBREBOARD PACKAGES
Red ground.
Label for "D" Traffic.
NOT TO BE LOADED WITH ACIDS
Red letters on white ground.
Label for "E" Traffic.
NOT TO BE LOADED WITH GLASS
Red letters on white ground.
Label for "F" Traffic.
KEEP FAR APART FROM TEXTILE FABRICS AND PAPER PACKAGES
Blue ground.

(6536.)

GREAT WESTERN RAILWAY.

PETROLEUM SPIRIT.

INFLAMMABLE.

CAUTION.

Great care must be taken in bringing any light near to the contents of this vessel as they give off an inflammable vapour at a temperature of less than 73° Fahrenheit's thermometer.

500—EST.891—12-45.)

GREAT WESTERN RAILWAY.

(3112 C) REFERENCE

NOTICE OF ARRIVAL OF INFLAMMABLE LIQUIDS AND SUBSTANCES, CLASS A, AND RETURNED EMPTY VESSELS AND TANK WAGONS WHICH HAVE CONTAINED SUCH LIQUIDS OR SUBSTANCES (each and all of which are hereinafter referred to as Inflammable Traffics) CARRIED BY MERCHANDISE TRAIN.

GOODS DEPARTMENT.

Mr.
Messrs.. ....Station, ...194....

The undermentioned Inflammable Traffics consigned to you under special conditions have arrived.

Please order their immediate removal. If they have not been removed at the expiration of the following times after delivery of this notice they will remain here at your sole risk and subject, in addition to the charge for carriage, to a further charge of 5s. per ton per hour (minimum 5s. per consignment), until they are removed from the Company's premises :—

Inflammable Liquids and Substances, Class A (except Bisulphide of Carbon)........ 4 working hours.
Tank Wagons, loaded or empty........ 6 working hours.
Returned Empty Vessels (except those which have contained Bisulphide of Carbon)........ 1 clear day.
Bisulphide of Carbon and Returned Empty Vessels which have contained Bisulphide of Carbon........ 4 working hours.

If the Inflammable Traffics have not been removed at the expiration of the following times after delivery of this notice they may be forthwith at the option of the Company either (a) returned to Sender, (b) sold by the Company, or (c) destroyed or otherwise disposed of :—

Inflammable Liquids and Substances, Class A (except Bisulphide of Carbon)........ 12 working hours.
Tank Wagons, loaded or empty........ 14 working hours.
Returned Empty Vessels (except those which have contained Bisulphide of Carbon)........ 2 clear days.
Bisulphide of Carbon and Returned Empty Vessels which have contained Bisulphide of Carbon........ 12 working hours.

Application for the Inflammable Traffics must be made not before..........a.m. and not later than..........p.m., Mondays to Fridays, and..........p.m. on Saturdays.
This notice shall not be evidence of the condition or of the correctness of the nature, quantity or weight of the Inflammable Traffics herein referred to.

For The Great Western Railway Company.

Signature..

No. and Description	Weight				Rate	Carriage			Paid on			Cartage			Total to Pay		
	T.	c.	q.	lbs.		£	s.	d.	£	s.	d.	£	s.	d.	£	s.	d.

Invoice No.......................... When you apply for the above please produce this Notice. Wagon No..........................

GENERAL CONDITIONS.

1. Each package must bear a label securely attached showing in legible and durable characters :—
(a) The full names and addresses of the Sender and Consignee,
(b) The Station or place of destination,
(c) The name of the contents in the terms defined in the Classification,
(d) The words "Highly Inflammable" (in the case of Bisulphide of Carbon "Bisulphide of Carbon—Highly Inflammable") printed in bold letters, except in the case of full truck loads of empty vessels (other than traffic for shipment) to one destination for delivery to one consignee, and
(e) Any other particulars required by the Classification.

2. The Sender must give the following information on the front of this Agreement in the spaces provided for that purpose—
(a) The full names and addresses of the Sender and Consignee,
(b) The Station or place of destination,
(c) The name of the contents in the terms defined in the Classification,
(d) The actual weight of the Inflammable Traffics (inclusive of packing), and
(e) The number of packages forming the consignment.

The Company shall, if so required, sign a document, prepared by the Sender, acknowledging the receipt of the Inflammable Traffics, but no such document shall be evidence of the condition or of the correctness of the declared nature, quantity or weight of the Inflammable Traffics at the time they are received by them.

3. Every truck and every Tank Wagon loaded in a siding not belonging to the Company shall (except as otherwise agreed in writing generally, or in respect of a particular consignment) be labelled by the Trader with two labels, which shall be securely affixed, one on each side thereof, and such labels must be of type and pattern approved by the Company and show thereon :—
(a) The name of the Sender,
(b) The name of the Consignee (except where the truck is loaded with Inflammable Traffics for more than one Consignee),
(c) The Station or place of destination, and where such Station or place is served by more than one Company, the name of the delivering Company,
(d) The actual weight, or where this is not practicable, the approximate weight of the Inflammable Traffics (inclusive of packing),
(e) The name of the owner and number of the truck or Tank Wagon,
(f) The name of the contents in the terms defined in the Classification, and
(g) Any other particulars required by the Classification.

Every truck and every Tank Wagon loaded in a siding not belonging to the Company must also bear on each side in bold letters the words "Highly Inflammable," by separate label or other equally efficient means except in the case of full truck loads of empty vessels (other than traffic for shipment) to one destination for delivery to one consignee, in which case the word "Inflammable" must be used.

4. In the case of a consignment carried at Company's Risk the Company shall, subject to these Conditions, be liable for—
(i) Any loss or misdelivery of or damage to Inflammable Traffics occasioned during transit as defined by these Conditions, unless the Company shall prove that such loss, misdelivery or damage has arisen from :—
(a) Act of God,
(b) Act of War or of the King's enemies,
(c) Arrest or restraint of Princes or Rulers, or seizure under legal process,
(d) Orders or restrictions imposed by the Government or any Department thereof,
(e) Act or omission of the Trader, his servant or agent,
(f) Inherent liability to wastage in bulk or weight, latent defect or inherent defect, vice or natural deterioration of the Inflammable Traffics, or
(g) Casualty (including fire or explosion).
Provided that where loss, misdelivery or damage arises, and the Company have failed to prove that they used all reasonable foresight and care in the carriage of the Inflammable Traffics, the Company shall not be relieved from liability for such loss, misdelivery or damage.
(ii) Loss proved by the Trader to have been caused by delay to or detention of or unreasonable deviation in the carriage of the Inflammable Traffics, unless the Company prove that such delay or detention or unreasonable deviation has arisen without negligence on the part of the Company or their servants.

5. In the case of a consignment carried at Owner's Risk, the Company shall not be liable for loss, damage, deviation, misdelivery, delay or detention of or to a consignment or any part thereof, except upon proof that the same arose from the wilful misconduct of the Company or their servants.

Provided that nothing in this Condition shall exempt the Company from any liability they might otherwise incur in the following cases :—
(a) Non-delivery of the whole of a consignment or of any separate package forming part of a consignment, unless such non-delivery is due to accidents to trains or to fire
(b) Pilferage, provided the pilferage is pointed out to a servant of the Company on or before delivery.
(c) Misdelivery where Inflammable Traffics are not tendered to or placed at the disposal of the Consignee within 28 days after receipt of the consignment by the Company to whom the same was handed by the Sender.
Provided, however, that the Company shall not be liable in the said cases of non-delivery, pilferage or misdelivery upon proof by them that the same has not been caused by the negligence or misconduct of the Company or their servants.

6. Every consignment of Inflammable Traffics, which the Company undertake to carry partly by land and partly by water, or wholly by water, shall as regards the carriage by water be subject to the Company's

100 pads, 50 lvs. 8/48. (8). S.

SEE BACK FOR FURTHER GENERAL CONDITIONS.

Carboys are a forgotten type of container for corrosive liquids. Here they are packed closely together in an undiagrammed three-plank open wagon No 34920 built with grease axleboxes under old series lot 289 dating from 1882. *GWR/D J Hyde collection*

A rake of Petrol tanks seen at Aldermaston on 10 June 1943. The World War 2 aviation fuel storage and distribution depot was connected by pipeline to Avonmouth and Walton-on-Thames. The various different types and sizes of tank wagon were all painted lead-grey during the war.
The nearest has its handbrake on, being at the end of the rake. The large six-pointed star is clear.
The wagon bears the legend: 'For Repairs Advise Petroleum Board. Shell-Mex-House. London WC2'. *GWR*

A J-headcode freight hauled by Collett 0 6 0 No 2265 with ROD tender passes Claverham near Yatton in Somerset and heads towards Bristol on 10 May 1938. As instructed in the Rule Book for loose-coupled H, J and K trains, the tank wagons are separated from the locomotive by a wagon. Certain types of tank wagon could travel in trains where there were vacuum vehicles coupled to the locomotive and, in such cases, the tank wagons were marshalled inside the last coupled vehicle of the vacuum portion. *SLS*

A view from the guard's van of a World War 2 tank wagon train as it departs from Aldermaston on 10 June 1943. *D J Hyde collection*

Oil empties pass through Reading on 14 September 1943 hauled by 'USA' 2-8-0 No 2318. *D J Hyde collection*

A through goods (H-code) in 1930 headed by a '28XX'. There are no intermediate wagons between the locomotive and the leading four tank wagons, presumably because the contents were not dangerous. *Railway Magazine*

A World War 2 train of tank wagons headed by '2884' class No 3854 carrying K-headlamps. There is one wagon between the locomotive and the tank wagons. *STEAM Swindon*

CHAPTER TWENTY-FIVE

THE LOADING GAUGE: EXCEPTIONAL LOADS

THE shape and size of the largest load that in ordinary working could travel safely over most of the railway (with the exception of a few branch lines, sidings and sheds noted in company circulars) was determined by the standard loading gauge, at least one of which was erected at all stations or points of loading to test height of loads before passing into traffic. Of course, there had to be additional clearance of several inches between the dimensions defined by the loading gauge and the actual dimensions of arches, bridges, tunnels and other structures under and through which trains passed in order to allow for lateral and vertical oscillation. Consequently the loading gauge was *not*, as sometimes averred, the lowest arch that trains could pass under: instead it defined the outline of the largest permissible loads. The dimensions of structures that trains passed under was defined by a complementary 'Minimum Structure Gauge' used by the civil engineers when designing new bridges and so on. The minimum structure gauge also determined how close to the track signal posts could be sited: clearly there was a danger that, when a signal was 'off', a long signal arm in conjunction with a short signal post might pass out of the minimum structure gauge or even encroach into the confines of the loading gauge. The GW minimum structure gauge illustrated for 1908 gives the distances from the rail for lower-quadrant semaphore signals at different heights having different length arms.

Different railway companies had different loading gauges, as set out in the RCH *Pink Pamphlet*. Owing to Brunel's broad gauge, the GW was blessed with a generous gauge over much of its system (even so, it seems that the B&E loading gauge was slightly different from the GW). The Bristol-Paddington broad-gauge load gauge was 15ft 6in high by 11ft 6in wide; the contemporary GWR standard-gauge load gauge was 13ft 2in high by 9ft wide. One of the loading gauges illustrated was introduced in January 1908 to incorporate minor alterations made to accommodate the 70ft long Dreadnought coaches. At 13ft 6in high by 9ft 8in wide it was wider than that of any other railway in Great Britain. The width of 9ft 8in was only available, however,

between five feet and 9ft 10in above rail level; below five feet it corresponded with the earlier standard gauge and, as before, further diminished below platform level. The top arc springing from the height of nine feet reduced the gauge, so that the width was nine feet again at a height of 11ft and the curve continued to reduce so that the maximum 13ft 6in height extended only for nine inches on both sides of the centre line. No clearance dimensions were given for the loading gauge between rail level and 3ft 6in above since no *normal* load could exceed the width of the wagon; also a clear space of six inches above rail level was kept beneath the bottom of all loads to allow ballast to be deposited before spreading, and for clearance of ATC ramps.

From 1933, all exceptions from the standard GW loading gauge found on inherited lines were listed in GW maximum load gauge circulars. The GW standard load gauge was in force on the following joint lines and joint stations: GW/GC Northolt Jct-Ashendon Jct and the Aylesbury branch; GW/LMS Brynmawr and Western valleys; Chester-Birkenhead; Chester-Walton Jct (Warrington); Hooton to Helsby and West Kirby; Common Line (Lansdown Jct) Cheltenham and Tramway Jct, Gloucester; Shrewsbury-Hereford. (The maximum width of loads in normal traffic between Saltney and Chester station and through Chester yard was, however, limited to nine feet.) The GW gauge was also the standard in force for GW/SR lines at Weymouth-Portland (including Castleton Tramway); Easton & Church Hope Railway (including Admiralty Extension Railway); and, joint stations at Chard, Plymouth North Road and Yeovil Town. For the GW/Metropolitan Railway, the GW loading gauge applied only between Hammersmith, Uxbridge Road and Westbourne Park. GW circulars emphasised that on lines over which the GW had running powers and/or where trains were worked by arrangement, loads and vehicles should not exceed the foreign company's loading gauge.

The dimensions of the loading gauge were decided by the Chief (Civil) Engineer whose department had to ensure that the clearances indicated did actually exist over the system.

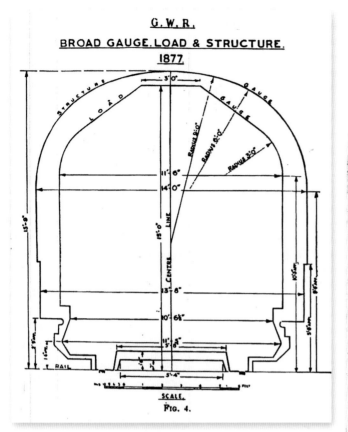

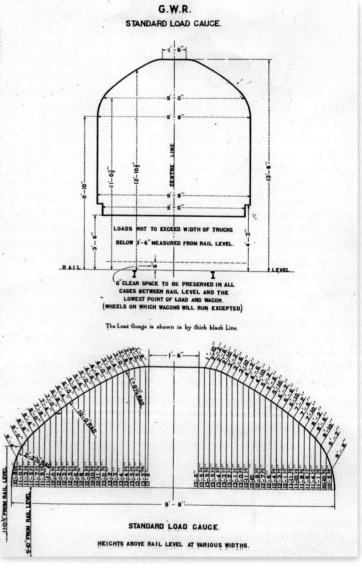

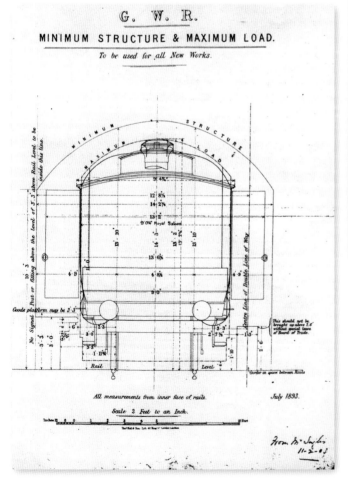

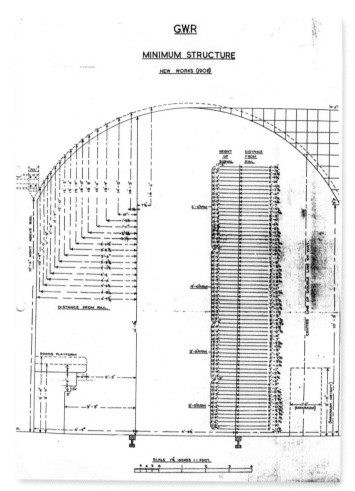

It influenced the designs for locomotives and rolling stock that had, of course, to conform to the gauge and it regulated the goods loads that could enter traffic as ordinary, as opposed to exceptional, loads. Loading gauges were always hung over a straight length of track, since on curves the possible effects of track super-elevation and overhang of long wagons or loads would place the cross-section of the loaded wagon off centre and into the six-foot way. In fact, *length* was an important dimension *not* covered by the gauge. Clearly long loads (girders, baulks of timber etc), even within gauge, required more clearance than normal when passing over curved track and the situation was aggravated the wider the load. For that reason the load gauge applied to loads not exceeding 40ft long. With loads of greater length the permissible width had to be reduced as follows: loads of 40ft but not exceeding 50ft in length had not to be more than nine feet wide, and loads exceeding 50ft but not more than 60ft in length had not to exceed five feet in width, while loads beyond 60ft in length, even though within the gauge profile in cross-section became *exceptional* loads and could only be carried by special authority in order to ensure that the clearances were guaranteed. It should be remarked that while GW 70ft coaches conformed to these restrictions, the GW had to take into account variability in lateral movement that might arise with long loads coming on to the GW system on the wagons of other companies that had different spacing of wheels and bogies.

What about those loads that were not excessively long, but which were outside the loading gauge in width and/or height? They formed the majority of *Exceptional Loads* that were defined as 'consignments subject to special arrangements when of unusual length, height, width or weight, or of exceptional bulk in proportion to weight' in respect of which railway companies were *not* Common Carriers by statute. Special wagons had usually to be provided for such loads. Typical exceptional loads would be boilers, vats and tanks, ships' propellers, long girders, large electrical plant and railway equipment for overseas. Typical GW special wagons were the Pollens, Totems, Crocodiles, Beavers, Macaws and so on which either could carry heavy weights, or long loads, or both. The Pollens were multiple-wagon sets like bogies with buffing gear that could be separated if necessary to carry long loads chained to each wagon. They had turntables at the point of attachment that permitted long loads to swivel on curves. Such wagons were only to travel in trains carrying the E-headcode or an inferior headcode. The wagons were sketched in various editions of the GW 'special wagon book' (that eventually included World War 2 military wagons such as Parrot, Warwell, Warflat, USAflat etc) and are discussed and illustrated fully in *GWR Goods Wagons*. The earliest C19[th] editions of *Diagrams of Special Wagons* concentrated on boiler wagons, ships' anchors and so on, and methods of loading, but after the Grouping, editions began to include Micas, fruit vans, banana vans, ale wagons and so on. In one or two cases, where special wagons from absorbed companies were not given a wagon diagram index number, the drawings and dimensions in special wagon books are the only source of information of what the wagons looked like, eg Loriot G (ex-TVR) and Loriot H (ex-RR).

Before World War 1 it was the practice to move heavy naval guns between the ordnance factories and dockyards by coastal shipping. To provide an alternative system, in 1909 the GW carried out successful trials at Devonport Dockyard with a 58-ton 12in breech-loading gun loaded on Pollen wagons. The breech rested in a deep recess and the 'chase' on a raised saddle.

When an exceptional load was offered to the railway, the practice was to refer the enquiry to the Chief Goods Manager (CGM), who consulted Swindon in order to select the most suitable wagon(s), and then the CGM asked the Chief (Civil) Engineer whether, loaded as proposed, it could travel between defined points. Enquiries were sent out to the Divisional Engineers to see if the proposed route (or alternative routes) was acceptable. On receipt of Divisional Engineers' certificates that the load could travel, the Chief Engineer issued his own certificate to the CGM giving authority for the load to travel, subject to conditions as appropriate. The CGM's office coordinated all these activities, including charges to be levied. Refusals to carry were made only after exhaustive attempts to accommodate the traffic had been made. Blueprints of the load and wagon diagrams were carefully examined, and in difficult cases templates were constructed and tested over the proposed route. Even so, sometimes there was just no possibility of undertaking the transit. Over one important section of line, the Severn Tunnel, exceptional loads were never permitted to pass through under any circumstance.

The great majority of exceptional loads exceeded the gauge in width, and loads wider than 10 feet were worked by special trains in all cases. When stopped, it was permissible for such loads to be passed by passenger trains or other out-of-gauge loads on adjacent

Loads that became loose on a journey could become out-of-gauge. In the early 1920s, this lorry-mounted anti-aircraft gun was loaded on a G18 Loriot D No 42142 at South Lambeth and was dispatched with others in a train to Watchet for Territorial Army manoeuvres. The barrel was supposed to remain horizontal, first by a locking pin in the elevating apparatus, and secondly by the lashing around the muzzle, securing it to a metal clutch mounted on the lorry floor. When loaded, the gun was sheeted, and it was assumed that these safeguards were in place. During the journey the rope lashings loosened and the barrel angled upwards, so much so that the gun rammed Milley overbridge at Twyford breaking the back of the lorry. To supply evidence for the resulting enquiry, a similar gun was loaded on to G1 Loriot D No 42042 and fixed down in the proper way as the first should have been. *GWR*

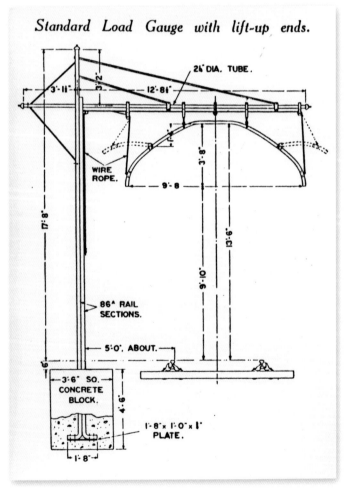

A motor launch, loaded on C15 Crocodile E No 41948 built in 1909, passes under a GW load gauge in 1913. The warning notice — 'Caution to drivers and firemen of tunnel engines. Look out for load gauges when shunting on these roads' — was put up as a result of accidents to footplatemen when leaning out of cabs on new locomotives that were bigger and higher than before. A modified gauge, with lift-up ends, was introduced shortly afterwards. Note that the motor launch is within gauge. *GWR/D J Hyde collection*

straight tracks, but they were not to be passed on curves and were to be shunted clear. In any event the timings of such specials were aimed always to avoid crossing passenger trains *en route* as far as possible, and they often travelled on Sundays. In the 1939 GW Telegraph Code Book, 'Ram' meant 'not to pass, nor be passed by passenger stock on adjacent lines' and 'Nopa' meant 'not to pass, nor be passed by other out-of-gauge load'.

When exceptional loads were required urgently somewhere, other trains were rescheduled to speed up the transit. For example in 1931 a ship at Falmouth was waiting urgently for a propeller shaft that had to come from Dumbarton. An LMS special wagon arrived at Crewe at 8pm on a Saturday evening for handing over to the GWR and, by running certain trains on the Sunday which normally would have run on the Saturday night or Monday morning, the consignment reached Falmouth by 8am on the Monday.

Sunday possession of the running lines also took place for other types of special (but not 'out-of-gauge') loads. For example, a large amount of round timber (logs) — about 25-30,000 tons annually between the wars — was forwarded from the Central Wales (Cambrian) district of the GWR. Many of the sites were inaccessible by road so that the timber could not be taken to station yards for loading. Instead, the logs were loaded alongside the running line, fences being removed and telegraph wires diverted temporarily. Over 100 tons of oak, elm, ash, beech, sycamore, larch, fir or spruce might be loaded in a single day, using railway breakdown steam cranes. A timber loading gang was employed in each Goods District. Those men were paid by the ton, and were not on the establishment. A District Timber Inspector oversaw arrangements and measured the timber for calculation of weights in the absence of nearby weighbridges. Fifty cubic feet of elm, fir, pine and other similar 'light' timbers were reckoned at one ton. Heavy timbers such as oak, ash, beech etc were reckoned at 40cu ft per ton. There were RCH travelling inspectors who sometimes checked the calculations of the railway company's inspector. Wagons carrying trees were marshalled towards the rear of a train, with the butts of the trees leading when the train moved off.

The loading gauge at Abingdon pictured in 1964 with ends lifted. The construction is somewhat more decorative than the drawing on the opposite page. *D J Hyde collection*

Lorot D No 42140, built in 1907 to Diagram G18, is loaded with a casting having manifolds at Dudley GW yard (West Midlands). The casting was made by Cochrane & Co of the Woodside Iron Works in Dudley *circa* 1920. *Commercial postcard*

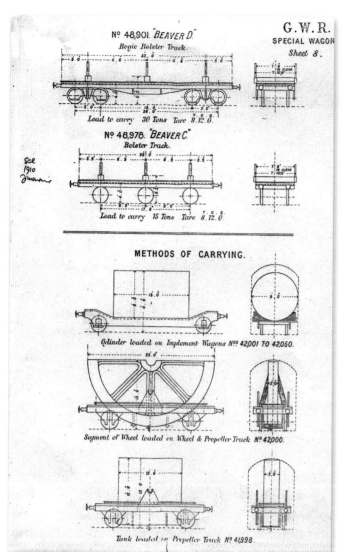

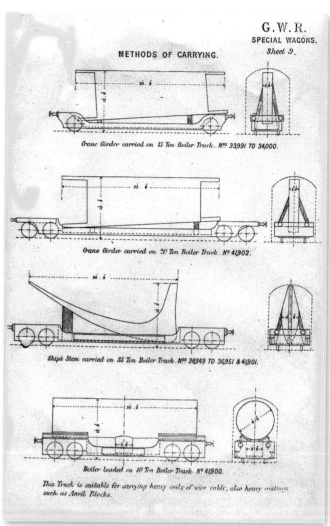

Some pages from the 1893 edition of the *GW Special Wagon Book.*

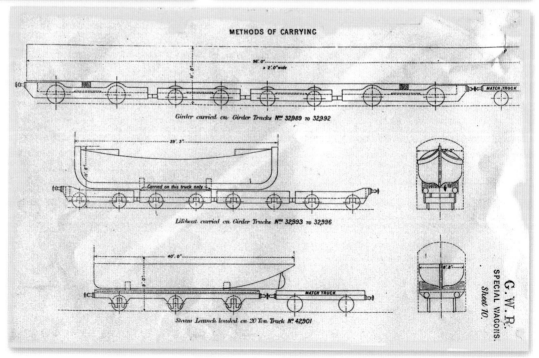

up so as to be in the space where the gauge was widest at 9ft 8in, ie between five feet and 9ft 10in above rail level. Sometimes exceptionally wide coaches manufactured in England for overseas railways were carried on special bogies belonging to the manufacturers which enabled the bodies to be lifted up to 18in during the journey and thus manoeuvred past obstacles. Loading below the five-foot level was limited chiefly by platforms, but also by other fixtures such as Post Office nets. Loading higher than 9ft 10in was difficult owing to the shoulders of the gauge and the springing of the arches of bridges and tunnels. In these circumstances, high loads might then be put slantwise on wagons, supported by a stout framework of timber baulks, with the load inclined towards the six-foot way. In one case the lowest portion of an inclined flywheel had to pass through the bed of a bogie Crocodile (the floorboards having been removed) to project into the forbidden six-inch region just above rail-level. When the clearance was that minimal, trains were instructed to pass certain structures at walking pace only.

If loads were large in extent, but relatively frail and delicate even when stiffened with timber, it was necessary to stipulate special train working and braking only from the locomotive to avoid damage. This occurred before World War 1 with two girders for East Street footbridge in Newport which were 108ft long, 11ft high but only 16in wide which had been floated up the Thames from the contractor's yard at Millwall to Brentford Dock and loaded on to Pollens by 40-ton crane. Other long loads were ships' masts: one steel mast carried on the GWR in 1906 was 138ft long, three-feet maximum diameter and 14-tons weight. Seven bolster wagons were required, the mast being secured on the second and fifth vehicles only, intermediate wagon bolsters being greased to ease lateral swing. That particular mast travelled from Birkenhead to Plymouth Millbay Docks, the same train carrying three other masts between 74 and 78ft long. On sharp curves in docks lines, travelling cranes on adjoining lines were used to ease the loads round and prevent them locking.

Other wide loads were boilers and large cylinders. Crocodile-type well wagons often enabled them to be loaded within gauge

Owing to track curvature, in order for long loads run in trains as ordinary traffic on main lines, there were width restrictions on within-gauge loads when longer than 40ft. Loads over 60ft in length became exceptional loads that could only be carried by special authority. This picture of a girder on a sharply-curved siding at Lysaght's factory in Bristol exaggerates the effect. Turntables on the articulated six-wheel Pollen B set (Nos 48981/2 of 1902) permit the load to swivel. The chained load acts as the only connexion between the paired trolleys. Note the large 'GW' on the wagons even as late as October 1937. *GWR*

Occasionally, when only a short journey was involved, a wide article may have been loaded off-centre all on one side, such as in the case of a 15ft diameter ventilating fan which projected 8ft 2in to one side. Counterbalance weights had, of course, to be fixed in the wagons. Since it extended beyond the six-foot way and over the adjoining line, it had to travel on double track. Flat wide loads were usually loaded one above the other on a wagon and packed

Below: Baulks of timber (about 90ft long) sit on the bolsters of two Macaw B wagons, the nearer of which is J14 No 84508 of 1914 and the other is J4 No 84100 of 1908. Both wagons are 45ft long over headstocks (48ft over buffers). There is one set of chains per wagon binding the baulks to the vehicles (at the third bolster from the nearest and furthest ends of the two Macaws), and another set around the timber (unattached to the wagons) over the gap between the two wagons. Although it can't be seen from this three-quarter view, the two wagons are buffered up, but uncoupled. *GWR/D J Hyde collection*

Part of a large shear legs for a private firm dealing with consignments of heavy machinery, this was photographed in 1911 at King's Dock, Swansea, loaded on to one of the two recently-built (1908/09) C15 Crocodile E vehicles, either No 41948 or 41949; there are Loriot runners at each end. The Crocodile E wagons were 62ft over headstocks. *GWR*

Three exceptional loads in 1911 consisted of 86ft 9in lengths of bar iron; they are shown here on 45ft over headstocks J4 Macaw B wagons at Swansea. *D J Hyde collection*

as regards to height. Care was, however, required that the extreme width was not increased inadvertently by forgetting the size of chains and shackles securing the load. Some steel cylinders were heavy as well as large: in 1933, a 14ft 4in diameter paper-making drum weighing 63 tons had been brought *by road* on a 16-wheel lorry from Bury (Lancs) to Keynsham (Bristol). After arrival, it was loaded on to a C27 Crocodile H by two 36-ton steam cranes in Keynsham yard in order to run it into the private siding of E S & A Robinson's factory.

With the increasing use of aluminium as a constructional material, the railway had to deal with bulky, but light, exceptional loads. At the other extreme, loads that were within gauge may have been exceptional owing to their weight — heavy castings for example. To relieve wagon axle loadings, ingenious methods such as counterbalancing the load with systems of levers and weights overhanging adjacent match trucks were sometimes utilised by the railway companies.

The frequency of exceptional load traffic is illustrated by the fact that in 1926 over 1200 special loads were carried by the GWR. In 1937 Richard Thomas & Co's Ebbw Vale steel works were modernised and over a million tons of goods were brought in, with nearly 200 trains conveying out-of-gauge loads of machinery, girders and so on. The activities of one weekend in July 1937 demonstrate the variety of exceptional loads carried across the whole GW system. In addition to a number of special consignments carried by ordinary goods trains, nine special trains were run as follows:

- A girder, 80ft in length, Banbury Jct to Ebbw Vale (ex-Middlesbrough);
- A tube, 9ft 10in wide, Bilston to Ebbw Vale;
- Four 65-ton castings, Newport Docks to Ebbw Vale (imported from USA);
- Four tanks, 10ft 3in wide, Oldbury to Chester (for Holywell);
- A boiler, 10ft 7½in wide, Oldbury to Wednesbury;
- Four new coaches, exceptional width at platform level, Gloucester to Lillie Bridge (for London's underground);
- Two new coaches, 66ft 3in long, Handsworth to Basingstoke (for Southern Railway); and,
- Two diesel railcars, extreme width 11ft 10in, Handsworth to Newport Docks (for shipment).

The last-mentioned diesel railcars were part of an order built by the Birmingham Carriage & Wagon Co Ltd for the Central Argentine Railway. Considerable difficulty was experienced in arranging transit owing to the exceptional dimensions of 76ft 6in length by 12ft 11in height by 11ft 1¼in with a weight of 28 tons; these dimensions were much in excess of those of GW standard passenger stock so that the vehicles could not travel on their own wheels. The cars were loaded on temporary bogies provided by the manufacturers that were fitted with a special traversing gear that could give a lateral movement of up to nine inches to either side as required. The permanent bogies of the railcars were carried separately (front bogies with the motor being loaded on Rectank wagons; the rear bogies on Loriots). The Chief Engineer's

On 23 April 1943, a Pickford's traction engine brought this 75ft-long/6ft-wide girder, weighing 33 tons 10cwt, from the works of T Braithwaite & Co in West Bromwich to Great Bridge goods yard for transfer to rail. The 40-ton capacity Macaw J wagon (Diagram J 26) was built in 1939, and the L22 match truck had been converted from an open wagon in 1935. Timber baulks on the road trailer made the height of the girder about the same as the Macaw J so, with the bolsters removed on that side of the wagon, the gantry crane could slew the load from one vehicle to the other. *GWR*

Below: Examples of terminology for exceptional loads, taken from the 1939 GW Telegraph code book, illustrating the complexity of these movements.

55

Subject.	Interpretation.	Code.
Exceptional Loads	Must not pass, nor be passed by any train on opposite or adjacent running lines between the following points.	Rampa
,,	Travel Main Line only.	Gwin
,,	Use may be made of Main or Relief Lines.	Usmar
,,	Use may be made of Main or Reliefs and Loops and Refuges specified.	Morla
,,	The following routing must be observed.	Gobi
,,	Travel slowly at :—	Tral
,,	Does my certificate of date named hold good.	Cotan
,,	Certificate of date named holds good.	Capra
,,	Can you suggest alternative routing or amended loading.	Sulto
,,	The following alternative is suggested.	Trill
,,	Advise me by wire the place or places where insufficient clearance exists.	Insul
,,	Insufficient clearances exist at the following :—	Nocle
,,	Advise me by wire maximum acceptable dimensions at place named.	Pontex
,,	The following are the maximum acceptable dimensions at place named.	Mito

D

56

Subject.	Interpretation.	Code.
Exceptional Loads	Excess width to be maintained to the 6 ft. side throughout.	Amar
,,	Not to go alongside Goods Wharves, Loading Banks or Cattle Pens.	Nodoc
,,	Traffic loaded and waiting.	Aflow
,,	Not to pass under load gauges.	Nog
,,	Care to be exercised in loops and sidings.	Scoop
,,	Platform edges to be kept clear.	Plej
,,	Can you accept the following load subject to conditions to be stipulated later?	Prep
,,	All adjoining lines to be blocked when using crossovers.	Blox
,,	Loaded centrally, equally ended and suitably checked.	Cenend
,,	Loaded centrally within gauge except extreme width secured.	Excol
,,	Loaded out of centre to six-foot side (specify distance in inches).	Sidon
,,	Scissors crossovers not to be used ; other crossovers and junctions, including those to and from Goods Loops and Refuge Sidings, to be used with caution and at slow speed. Care to be exercised in marshalling yards.	Sisco

GREAT WESTERN RAILWAY.

J.1550/1.

IMMEDIATE.

ENGINEER'S OFFICE,

January 17th 1913

DEAR SIR,

LOADS OF EXCEPTIONAL DIMENSIONS OR WEIGHTS

Cases: Bristol to Liverpool.

I shall be glad to know by return whether a load, as described hereunder, can travel safely, so far as your Division is concerned, from **Bristol** to **Saltney Junction** via **Didcot.**

Yours truly

For W. W. Grierson

J. M. Taylor Esq.,

Description of Article Cases

__23__ ft. __1__ in. in length, __10__ ft. __2__ in. in width or diameter............ ft. .... in. in height, and weighing .... tons

Method of Loading centrally flat on Macaws B with the extreme width when secured not exceeding 10ft 2ins and between 4ft 7ins and 9ft 6ins above rails.

Gauge exceeded in width only.

DIVISIONAL ENGINEER'S OFFICE

Paddington

17th January 1913

DEAR SIR,

From an Engineering point of view, so far as this Division is concerned, I see no objection to the load in question travelling between the points named subject to the following:—

Yours truly,

For J. M. Taylor

W. W. GRIERSON, Esq.

5.—ENQUIRY FORM.

An enquiry form and reply regarding the conveyance of long cases (that would be out-of-gauge in width only) between Bristol and Saltney via Didcot.

Centrally-flat cases pictured on Macaw B of 1914 are out-of-gauge in width only. *GWR*

Below: An ex-Vale of Rheidol engine, GW No 1212, is pictured loaded on a C10 Crocodile at Swindon yard in December 1932 when the locomotive had been put on the sales list. The capacity of the wagon was 15 tons, but the locomotive weighed 21 tons, which accounts for the slight bowing of the frame of the well wagon. No 33989 was built in 1898. *R S Carpenter*

Some loads that would be out of gauge when loaded one way, could be made within gauge when loaded in another, and then could run in ordinary traffic. It also depended on the wagon used, as shown in this picture of a group of girders for a bridge at Llwyncelyn (Trehafod) ordered by Rhondda Urban District Council in 1932. A short girder, on the left, when loaded vertically in the 33ft well of a Crocodile F wagon is within gauge, but the longer girder on the right has to be packed up on a slant on the 45ft over headstocks Macaw B bogie bolster wagon. Its length still requires Loriot runners. The height of the load was reduced from 13ft 9in originally to 11ft 6in. *GWR*

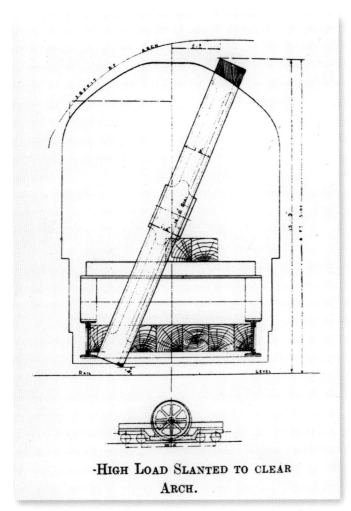

-HIGH LOAD SLANTED TO CLEAR ARCH.

A load that did not fit under the loading gauge for a single track, was able to travel successfully on double track when there were only arches over both lines for the journey. GWR

certificate made provision for the diesel cars to leave Handsworth centrally on the temporary bogies, but in order to pass through Snow Hill station a traverse of six inches had to be made towards the platform side, after which the car had to be slewed over six inches to the six-foot way to negotiate Snow Hill tunnel. Subsequently eight further traversing movements were made before reaching Chepstow. As it was known that the cars would foul practically all ground signal discs along the route, a Signal Engineer's fitter and mate travelled with the train and during the course of the journey removed over 100 discs, replacing each one immediately after the cars had passed. Great care was necessary in preparing the timetable, for the cars were prohibited from passing other trains on the opposite running line. At least 15 minutes had to be allowed for each traversing movement and allowances made for delay in removing and replacing signal discs. Moreover, the Engineer had stipulated that the conveyance from Chepstow to Newport Docks had to be performed only during the hours of daylight, and the speed between the various stops was not to exceed 15mph. The train left Handsworth at 1am and arrived at Alexandra Docks at 6pm, a time of 17 hours for the 80-mile journey.

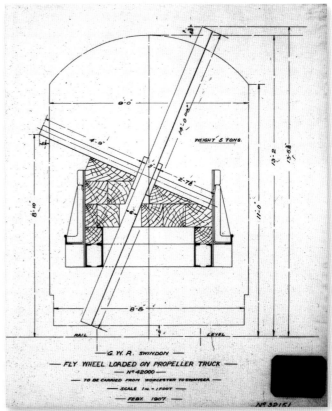

Swindon blueprint for method of loading a flywheel and axle on Morel propeller truck No 42000 for a journey in 1907 from Worcester to Swansea. Notice that the cross section of the underframe of this wagon rated at 25-tons shows double channel sections, and bulb-section raves around the floor. *GWR*

These pictures show how a 34-ton flywheel was removed from a factory at Dowlais (Merthyr) and loaded on to a bogie well wagon for transit in March 1934. In the first, it looks as if the building that contained the flywheel was demolished in order to get it out ('T Hilton Sweet & Co. The Old Clog Shop' is seen behind a rail-mounted crane). In the second, baulks of timber enable the flywheel to be moved to the Crocodile H wagon No 41900 where it was positioned on the skew by crane so as to make the width come within gauge. Plate 89 in *GWR Goods Wagons* shows the load finally ready for departure. This 45-ton capacity Crocodile H was built in 1915 as a replacement for a wagon to same design and running number, dating originally from 1889, and rebuilt in 1904 but sold to the War Office in 1914. GWR

Above and opposite page bottom: Lineside structures often caused problems of clearances for out-of-gauge loads. Sometimes such items could be moved out of the way as the train passed, or dismantled and later replaced (as with ground signals). At other times that was not so easy, and the presence of permanent structures often determined whether an out-of-gauge load could be accepted. Here, a large double-helical (herringbone) gear wheel weighing 31 tons, loaded on to a 45-ton Crocodile H bogie well wagon, was already out-of-gauge and had to pass a bascule bridge where clearances were rather fine. Manufactured by the Power Plant Co Ltd of West Drayton, the gears were on their way to Brentford on 23 February 1935. *GWR*

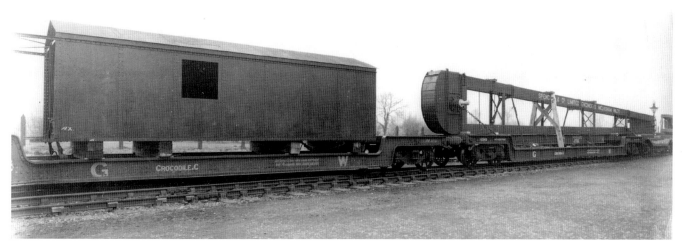

A coal conveyor for Port Talbot leaving Spencer's sidings at Melksham in 1925. The belt and framework is loaded on C15 Crocodile E No 41949 of 1909, and the weather protection for the structure is carried on a Crocodile C. Further information about its installation and use at Port Talbot will be found in *GWR Docks & Marine* on page 173. *GWR*

Another load from Spencer's of Melksham, this time loaded on the 70ft long Macaw C No 84996, wagon Diagram J15. *GWR*

This is not what it appears to be! 'The World's Mammoth Cylinder' weighing 63½ tons, for paper-making machinery, and built by associated firms Charles Warmsley & Co Ltd and Bentley & Jackson Ltd, both of Bury in Lancashire, has travelled *by road* to Bristol. On 14 May 1933 it is being loaded at Keynsham on to Crocodile H No 41974 (built in 1915) by GWR Ransome & Rapier 36-ton steam cranes, Nos 2 and 3, *for the last few hundred yards of the journey* into E S & A Robinson's private siding. Note at far left the L10 Balance Weight Tender No 2A built in 1909 when the 36-ton cranes were introduced. Also on the left is a loading gauge with one 'wing' up and the other down. The big bogie match trucks that accompanied the cranes (L11 in the wagon diagram index) are out of the picture. This Crocodile H was originally to Diagram C23 but, along with No 41973, was strengthened and fitted with additional cross members in 1931 to increase its capacity to 65 tons when it was assigned Diagram C27. In the photograph the painted figures have not been altered, but the tare is shown correctly increased by one ton to 23 tons 12cwt.
GWR/D J Hyde collection

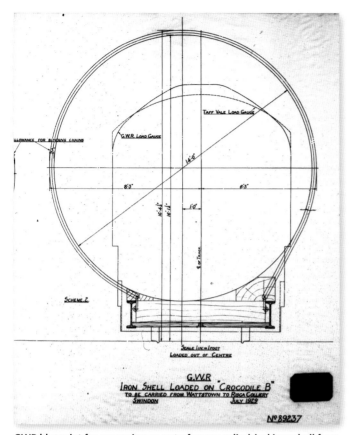

GWR blueprint for conveying an out-of-gauge cylindrical iron shell from Wattstown in the Rhondda Fach to Risca Colliery in the Western Valleys above Newport in July 1929. Note the differences in the GW and Taff Vale loading gauges, and that the cylinder is to be loaded off centre on a Crocodile B wagon. *GWR*

Girder work from Horsehay & Co (at the town of the same name near Dawley between Buildwas and Wellington in Shropshire) stands on four- and six-wheel Pollen sets. The container flat wagons used as match trucks date this picture to 1947 as they had just been built to Diagram H10. *GWR/D J Hyde collection*

A casing for what was then the largest generator in Europe (42 tons, 24ft 1in long, 11ft 4in high and 12ft 6in wide) nears the end of a 284-mile journey from the Metropolitan-Vickers works at Trafford Park, Manchester, to the new Battersea power station adjacent to the GW South Lambeth goods depot in London. The casing was nearly 3ft out of gauge in width but, when loaded on a 42-ton ex-LNWR bogie trolley wagon No 218851, was 2in under gauge in height. The operation to move this exceptional load took place over two weekends in August and September 1934 and ran over parts of all the 'big four' lines. It came on to the GW at Crewe. Preparatory work and co-operation between the railway companies involved a test run with a framework of identical dimensions mounted on a coach (resulting in a detour via Kidderminster, Worcester, Evesham, and Stratford-upon-Avon before rejoining the Birkenhead-London line at Hatton, since it would not go through the tunnel at Wolverhampton on the originally-proposed route). On the journey, there was wrong-line working at five locations; all Down lines alongside the route were kept clear of traffic; 100 platforms were kept clear as the load overhung by 18in; track was slewed by a foot near Addison Road and near Chelsea on the West London line; and, signals were dismantled and re-erected immediately after the train passed. Speed throughout varied from a maximum of 20mph to an absolute crawl. On the journey from Old Oak Common on the second weekend, the wagon was placed between two GW brake vans (AA3 No 56368 of 1898 based at Paddington and AA13 No 17847 of 1917 based at Old Oak Common). The locomotive was a '97XX' condensing pannier. The photograph was taken on 2 September 1934 as the train slowly approached South Lambeth under the bridge carrying the LSWR mainline above . The time was about 7.30am, the train having departed Old Oak at 5am. *GWR*

A 12,500kVA transformer manufactured by the Hackbridge Electric Construction Co Ltd seen loaded centrally on Crocodile G no 36950. The 35-ton well trolley wagon was in Diagram C16 by the time this picture was taken, but had started life in 1886 as a very early design (later coded Crocodile C) that was rebuilt in 1906 and again in 1909. As explained in *GWR Goods Wagons*, the rebuilds were all to do with the connexions between the end platforms under which the bogies sat and the well of the wagon. *GWR*

The 24-wheel, 89ft 6in long, 120-ton capacity Crocodile L was introduced in July 1930 to carry transformers and generators that were being installed around the country as part of a national scheme of electricity distribution. This was the largest vehicle built by the GWR. No 41977 is seen on arrival at Thornhill in Yorkshire on 17 July 1930 having borne a 63-ton transformer from Hayes, Middlesex. Instead of the side girders shown here, Crocodile-like well girders with cross beams could be substituted to carry other types of exceptional load (see *GWR Goods Wagons*). *GWR/D J Hyde collection*

Above and below: Rotary kilns, 77ft in length and 9ft in diameter, are prepared for transit from South Lambeth yard to South Wales on 20 August 1939. The kilns had been brought by road by E W Rudd Ltd of Poplar using Scammel haulage equipment. The first picture shows a kiln being lowered on to a bogie well wagon by means of the Babcock & Wilcox electric overhead gantry crane that, depending on the gearing, could lift 10 or 35 tons. Only one sling is used and the positioning is clever as the nearer end is lower than the farther, so the kiln comes down on to the timber baulks on the wagon one end at a time, permitting adjustment as necessary. World War 2 broke out a fortnight after this picture was taken, and in the right foreground are stacked steel components of Anderson air-raid shelters to be distributed to houses and erected in back gardens. In the second picture two of the kilns are seen loaded on C8 Crocodile J wagons, Nos 41906 and 41955, both dating from 1916, using G4 Loriot well wagon No 31312 dating from 1880 as a runner at this end, and a four-wheel C10 Crocodile in between the two bogie Crocodile J vehicles. At the destination, the kilns were put into a siding alongside the site and rolled off the wagons to be placed on prepared foundations.
F J Standerwick/GWR

The Fairfield Engineering Co of Glasgow took over the site of National Shipyard No 1 at Chepstow after World War 1 to build cranes and other structures (see *GWR Docks & Marine*). Many bridge girders and other erections, some of which were exceptional out-of-gauge loads, were delivered by the GW often to Newport Docks for shipment overseas. The picture, dating to 21 April 1936, shows an order for buoys that are chained to various bogie Crocodiles ready for dispatch. Notice that the wagons no longer have the number painted on the buffer beam. The wagon on the right is Crocodile B No 41923, Diagram C11, dating from 1905. The yard was to the south of the mainline on the Welsh bank of the River Wye. *D J Hyde collection*

The train of buoys photographed *en route* for Newport Docks. The locomotive is the last 'Aberdare' to be built (No 2620 of 1903), now with an ROD tender (the running numbers, including those of former 'Krugers', ran to 2680, but were not given to the engines in order of construction). The enclosed Toad on the locomotive is a 'Construction Pt Way' brake van fitted with a plough. *GWR/D J Hyde collection*

Behind the open-sided work sheds shown in the adjacent photograph was Fairfield's open-air construction yard with two travelling gantry cranes running on the same side rails. On 20 July 1938 a girder is being loaded on to the 70ft-long J15 Macaw C No 84996, built in 1912. A similar girder lies on the ground behind awaiting loading. If of comparable length and to be carried in the same train, it is likely that the other J15 bogie bolster wagon (No 84995 dating from 1914 — there were only two) was in the vicinity. *GWR/D J Hyde collection*

A special load of suction pipes photographed in July 1911 passing through Gloucester station on its way to Newport Docks. The train started from the works of the maker, the Lilleshall Co Ltd of Oakengates, Salop (on the Wolverhampton-Wellington line). On the right, beams hold up the structure between the four-wheel articulated Pollen D pair Nos 32991/2, Diagram A5. This arrangement enabled the bottom of the load to be closer to the rail than if carried by a bogie Crocodile, for example. However, as seen on the left, it was possible to carry other components of the suction system on a C12 Crocodile F wagon (with holes along the solebar). *GWR*

BIBLIOGRAPHY

Ahrons, A L; *Locomotive and Train Working in the latter part of the Nineteenth Century*; volume 4 Heffer, 1953

Atkins, A G and Hyde, D J; *GWR Goods Services*; volume 1 Wild Swan, 2000

Atkins, Tony; *GWR Goods Services*; volume 2A Wild Swan, 2007

Atkins, Tony; *GWR Goods Services*; volume 2B Wild Swan, 2009

Atkins, A G, Beard, W and Tourret, R; *GWR Goods Wagons*; originally published in two volumes by David & Charles, 1975/6; combined edition by Tourret Publishing, 1986; then much enlarged and revised by Tourret, 1998; reprinted again by Oxford Publishing Co,2013

Barman, C; *Next Station*; George Allen & Unwin, 1947 (reprinted as *The Great Western Railway's Last Look Forward; D*avid & Charles, 1972)

Brewer, F W; 'Modern Locomotive Practice on the Great Western Railway' (a series of articles) in *Railway Magazine* 1928-1931

Chapman,W G; *Track Topics. A book of railway engineering for boys of all ages*; GWR, 1935

Cooke, R A; *Track layout Diagrams of the GWR*; privately published

Fraser, D, Green, D and Scott, B; *The Great Western Railway in the 1930s*; volume 2 Kingfisher, 1985

Fraser, D and Green, D; *The Great Western Railway in the 1930s*; volume 2 Kingfisher, 1987

Gibson, J C; *Great Western Locomotive Design*; David & Charles, 1984

Grant, G; 'Reminiscences of a Retired Great Western Railway Superintendent' in *Railway Magazine*, 1930

Holcroft, H; *An Outline of Great Western Locomotive Practice 1857-1947*; Ian Allan Ltd, 1957 (reprinted 1971)

Inglis, C; *Applied Mechanics for Engineers*; Cambridge University Press, 1951

Nock, O S; *The Great Western Railway — An Appreciation*; Heffer, 1951

Nock, O S; *Tales of the Great Western Railway*; David & Charles, 1984

Page, J; *Rails in the Valleys*; David & Charles, 1989

Pratt, E A; *British Railways and the Great War*; Selwyn & Blount, 1921

Railway Correspondence & Travel Society; *The Locomotives of the Great Western Railway: Part 8 Modern Passenger Classes*; RCTS, 1953

Russell; J H; *A Pictorial Record of Great Western Engines: Volume 1 Gooch, Armstrong and Dean Locomotives*; Oxford Publishing Co, 1975

Russell; J H; *A Pictorial Record of Great Western Engines: Volume 2 Churchward, Collett and Hawksworth Locomotives*; Oxford Publishing Co, 1975

Russell; J H; *A Pictorial Record of Great Western Engines: Volume 3 Absorbed Engines*; Oxford Publishing Co, 1978

Street, J W; *I Drove the Cheltenham Flyer*; Nicholson & Watson, 1951

The last goods train on the Calne branch photographed leaving Black Dog Halt. The guard was Monty Fell who, under changed BR rules, did not have to provide side lamps on his Toad. *D Lovelock*

Cocket Tunnel
Llanelly
side

Details of the construction of pre-1903 head and tail lamps are clear in this picture taken on the Llanelly side of Cockett Tunnel (west of Swansea and the highest point the SWR). Outside-framed 0-6-0ST No 1599, built at Swindon in 1879, carries a lamp at the top of the bunker having a white diamond painted on the side (see Chapter 2). There is a socket for the spigot of a lamp above the centre of the buffer beam, but none at the buffers. The locomotive has a five-link coupling with a shackle and pin at the hook. The wooden-underframe open verandah brake van No 17770 was the first of a series with an extended cabin and dates from 1874 (see Chapter 30 of *GWR Goods Wagons*). The vehicle retains its original wooden brake blocks.Unlike the other lamps, the side lamp has no handle and is not held by spigots, rather by side-irons as later adopted for headlamps. The rear lamp is a yet different pattern from the others. There is both inside-keyed and outside-keyed track. *K Robertson collection*

Timber felled near the line (top right of picture) being loaded into four-wheel open wagons from various pre-Grouping companies, including Great Central (first and sixth wagons), Midland (fourth, seventh and 10th) and SECR (ninth), all of which seem to have grease axleboxes and rudimentary brakes acting on one wheel only. The second wagon is an undiagrammed GW four-planker dating from 1891 (now with oil axleboxes), and the fifth wagon is an Open A to Diagram O3 as built with oil boxes. The large 25in 'GW' lettering was introduced in 1904. The inside-framed 0-6-0ST is Wolverhampton-built locomotive No 769, dating from 1873 and condemned in 1930. Note the boards on the back of the bunker to increase coal capacity.

K Robertson collection

Straight-footplate '28XX' No 2805, built in 1905, recorded at the eastern end of Salisbury SR station on a J-headcode freight in the early 1930s. The GW passenger terminus is the building in the background. Stephenson Clarke & Associates (SC) 20-ton wooden coal wagons. The GW engine will be changed here for an SR locomotive and the train will continue to Eastleigh. Traffic for Basingstoke would have gone via Reading (the branch to Basingstoke was the 'Hants' part of the 'Berks & Hants' GW line through Hungerford).

K Robertson Collecton

'57XX' 0-6-0PT No 7730 stands outside Salisbury GWR signal box. The engine was delivered from the North British Locomotive Co in December 1929. The pannier is attached to M1 shunter's truck No 41818 dating from 1899 using the truck's Instanter coupling. Marcroft Wagons Ltd repair shop is at the top right; the sign says that the firm has sidings at Radstock, Cardiff, and Port Talbot. *K Robertson collection*

Mogul No 4360, built in 1914, pictured at the eastern end of Salisbury SR station. The GW passenger terminus is the building in the background. A tarpaulined GW wagon with Dean-Churchward brake is visible immediately behind engine followed by Stephenson Clarke & Associates (SC) 20-ton steel coal wagons. One headlamp at the chimney and one in the middle of the buffer beam indicates an F-headcode goods train. The lamps are painted red, so predate 1936; the SC wagons date from the late 1920s.

K Robertson Collecton

An accident at Cardigan at the end of the C19th resulted in this pile-up. Iron Mink No 58462 dates from 1895 and looks almost new. The photograph gives great detail of the undersides of the van and the smashed wooden-underframe open wagon. Another iron Mink stands at the left of the picture. The through drawgear of the open has been pulled out of its headstock yet the three-link coupling is still attached to the hook of the Mink. One of its buffer rods has been bent through 180° leaving the head of the buffer facing away from the men on the edge of the platform. *K Robertson collection/GWS*